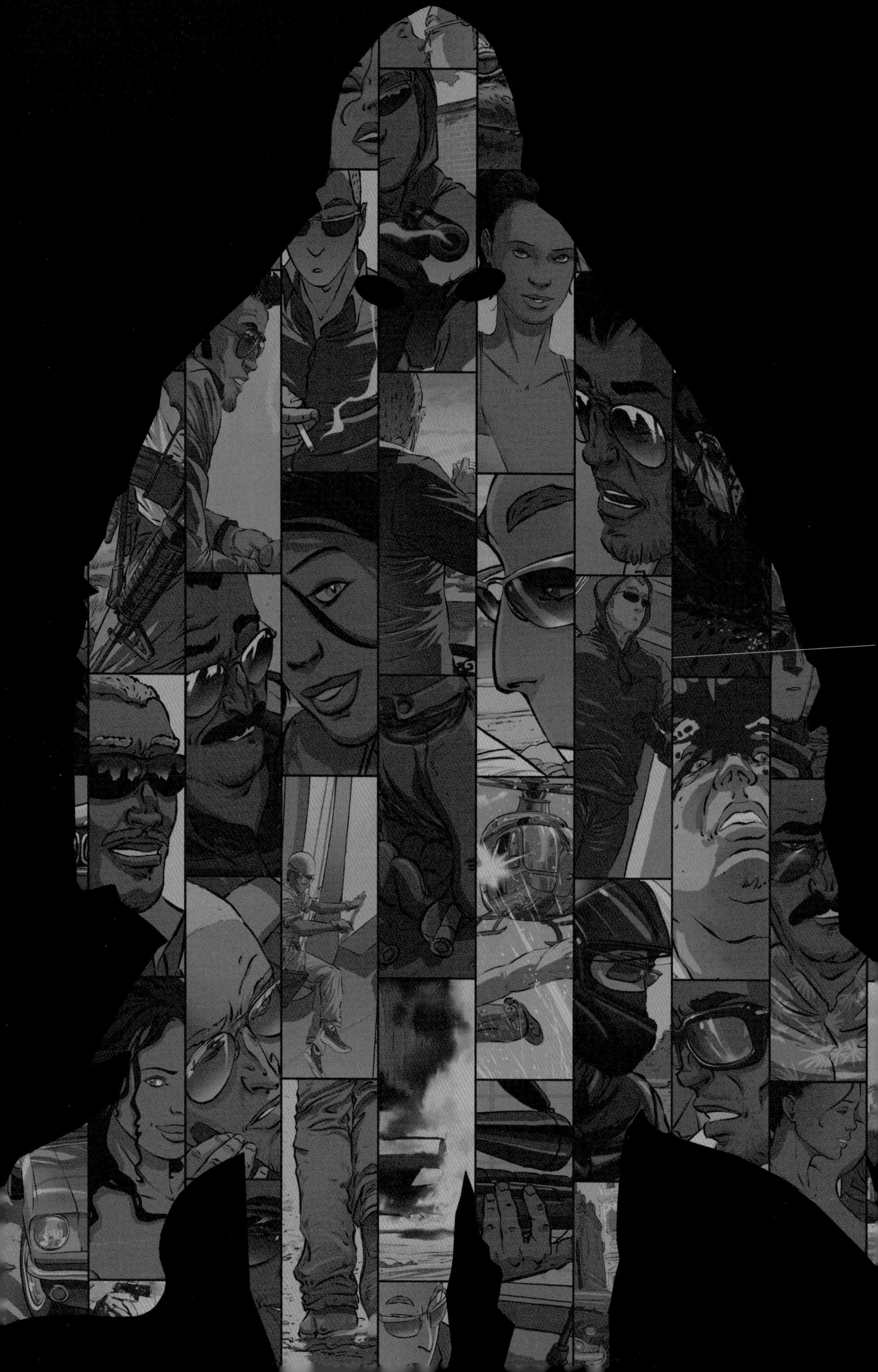

JACAMON & MATZ

THE KILLER™

UNFAIR COMPETITION

WRITTEN BY **MATZ**

ILLUSTRATED BY **LUC JACAMON**

LETTERED BY **MARSHALL DILLON**

DESIGN BY **SCOTT NEWMAN**

EDITED BY **REBECCA TAYLOR**

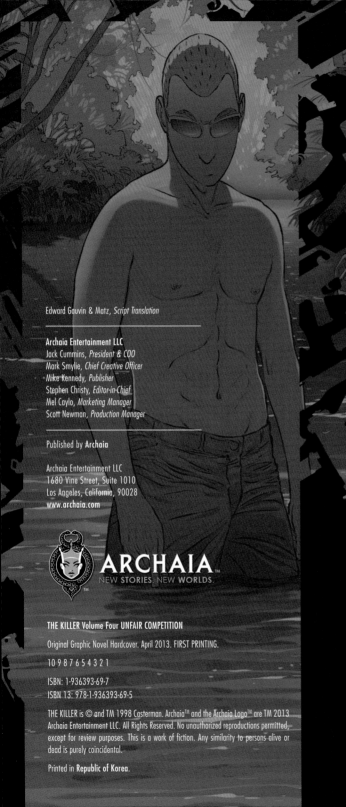

Edward Gauvin & Matz, *Script Translation*

Archaia Entertainment LLC
Jack Cummins, *President & COO*
Mark Smylie, *Chief Creative Officer*
Mike Kennedy, *Publisher*
Stephen Christy, *Editor-in-Chief*
Mel Caylo, *Marketing Manager*
Scott Newman, *Production Manager*

Published by **Archaia**

Archaia Entertainment LLC
1680 Vine Street, Suite 1010
Los Angeles, California, 90028
www.archaia.com

ARCHAIA™
NEW STORIES. NEW WORLDS.

THE KILLER Volume Four UNFAIR COMPETITION

Original Graphic Novel Hardcover. April 2013. FIRST PRINTING.

10 9 8 7 6 5 4 3 2 1

ISBN: 1-936393-69-7
ISBN 13: 978-1-936393-69-5

Printed in **Republic of Korea**.

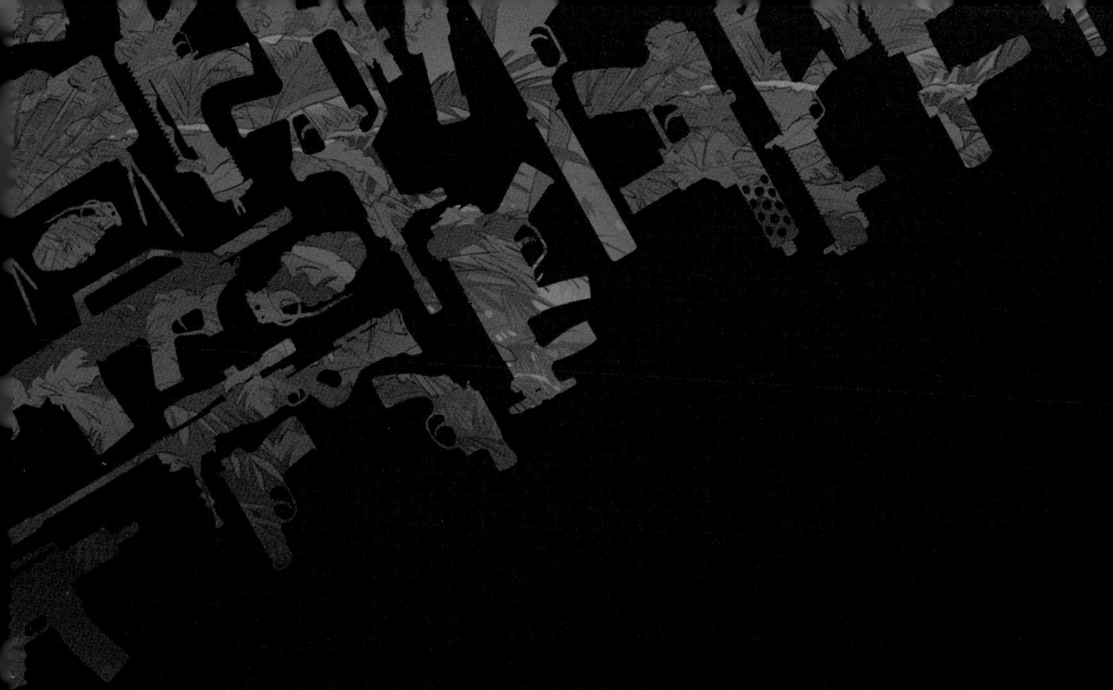

TABLE OF CONTENTS

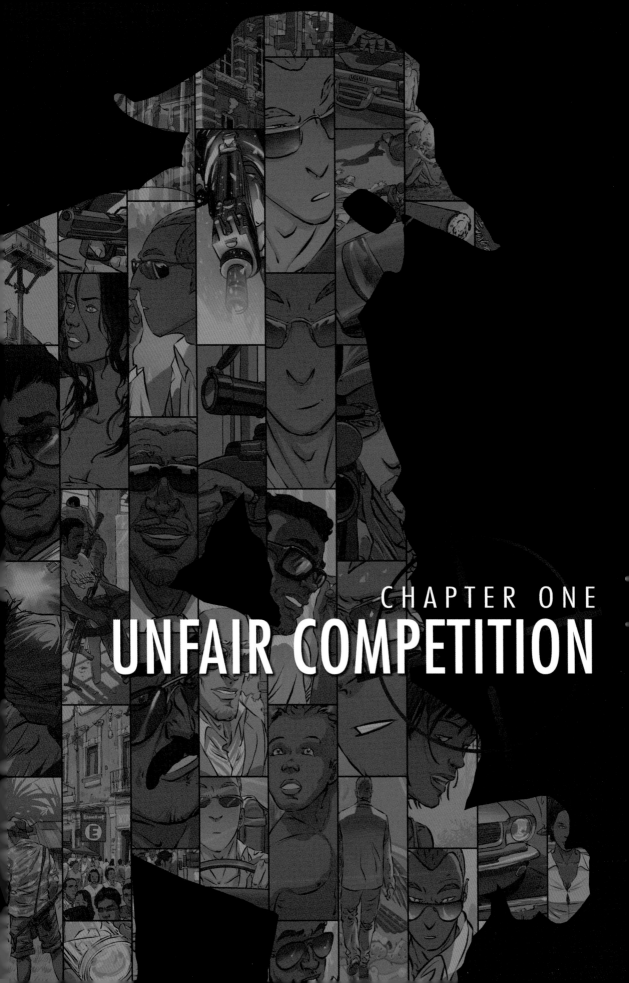

CHAPTER ONE
UNFAIR COMPETITION

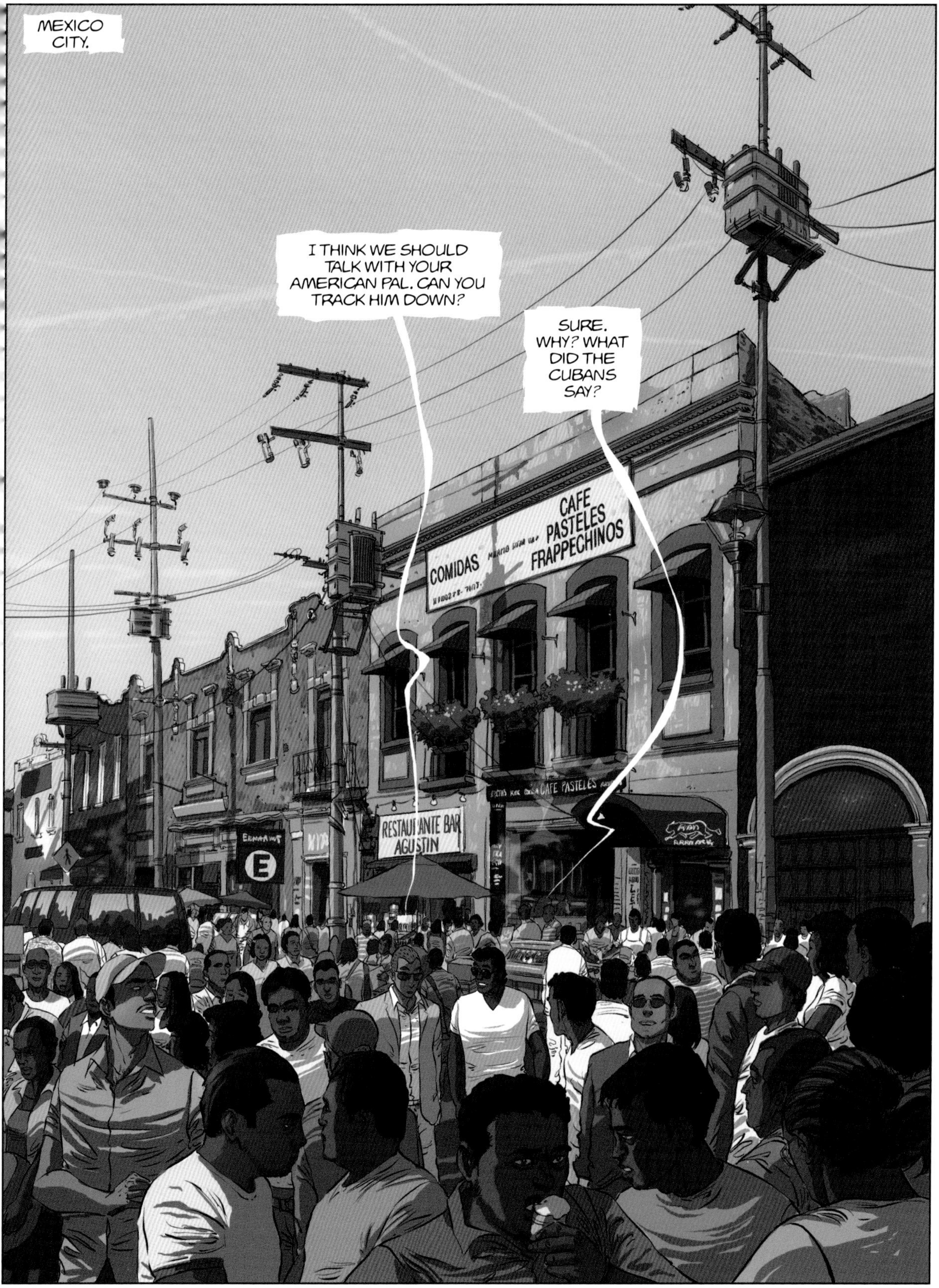
MEXICO CITY.
I THINK WE SHOULD TALK WITH YOUR AMERICAN PAL. CAN YOU TRACK HIM DOWN?
SURE. WHY? WHAT DID THE CUBANS SAY?
COMIDAS
CAFE
PASTELES
FRAPPECHINOS
CAFE PASTELES
AGUSTIN
E

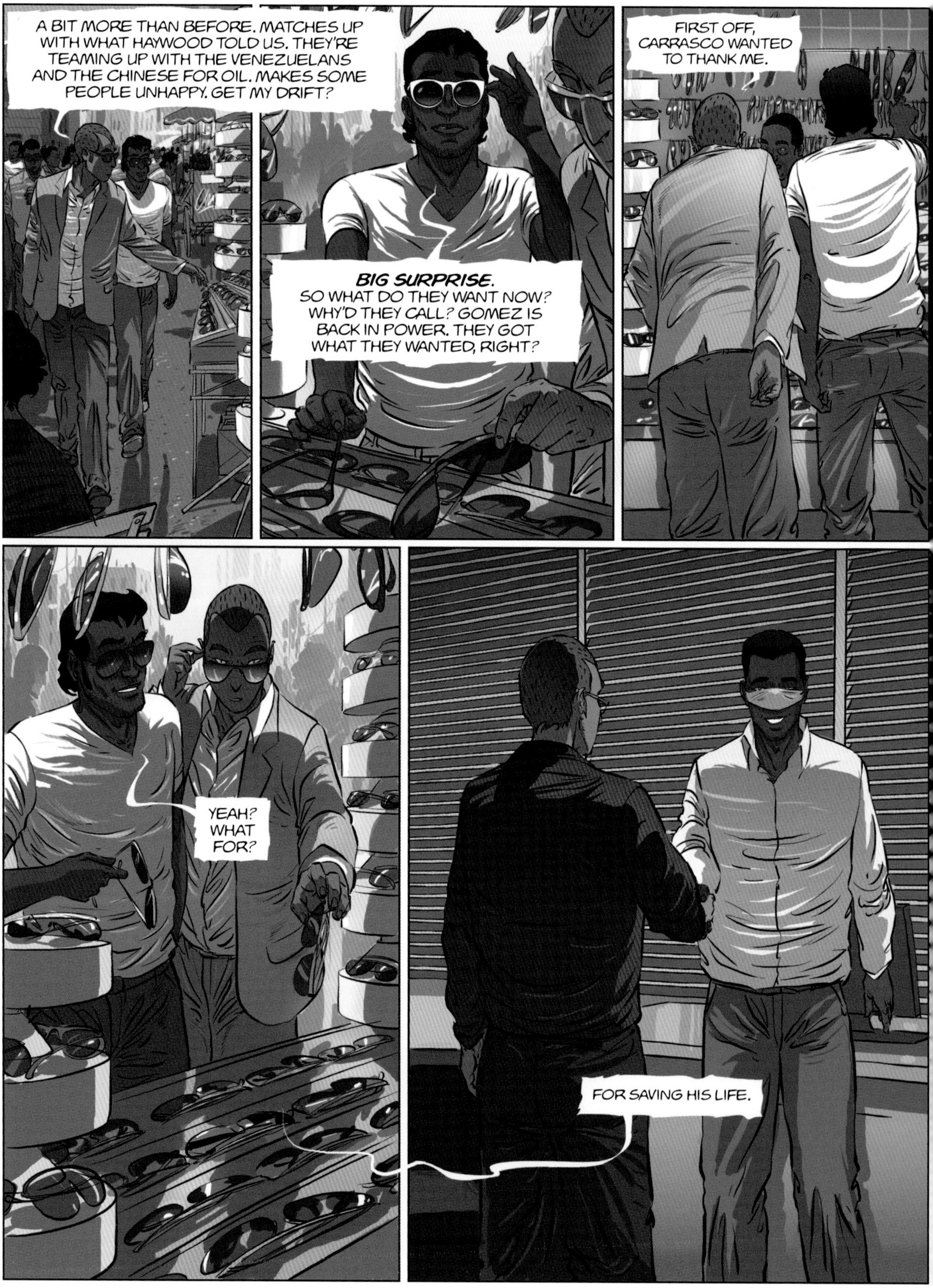
A BIT MORE THAN BEFORE. MATCHES UP WITH WHAT HAYWOOD TOLD US. THEY'RE TEAMING UP WITH THE VENEZUELANS AND THE CHINESE FOR OIL. MAKES SOME PEOPLE UNHAPPY. GET MY DRIFT?
BIG SURPRISE. SO WHAT DO THEY WANT NOW? WHY'D THEY CALL? GOMEZ IS BACK IN POWER. THEY GOT WHAT THEY WANTED, RIGHT?
FIRST OFF, CARRASCO WANTED TO THANK ME.
YEAH? WHAT FOR?
FOR SAVING HIS LIFE.

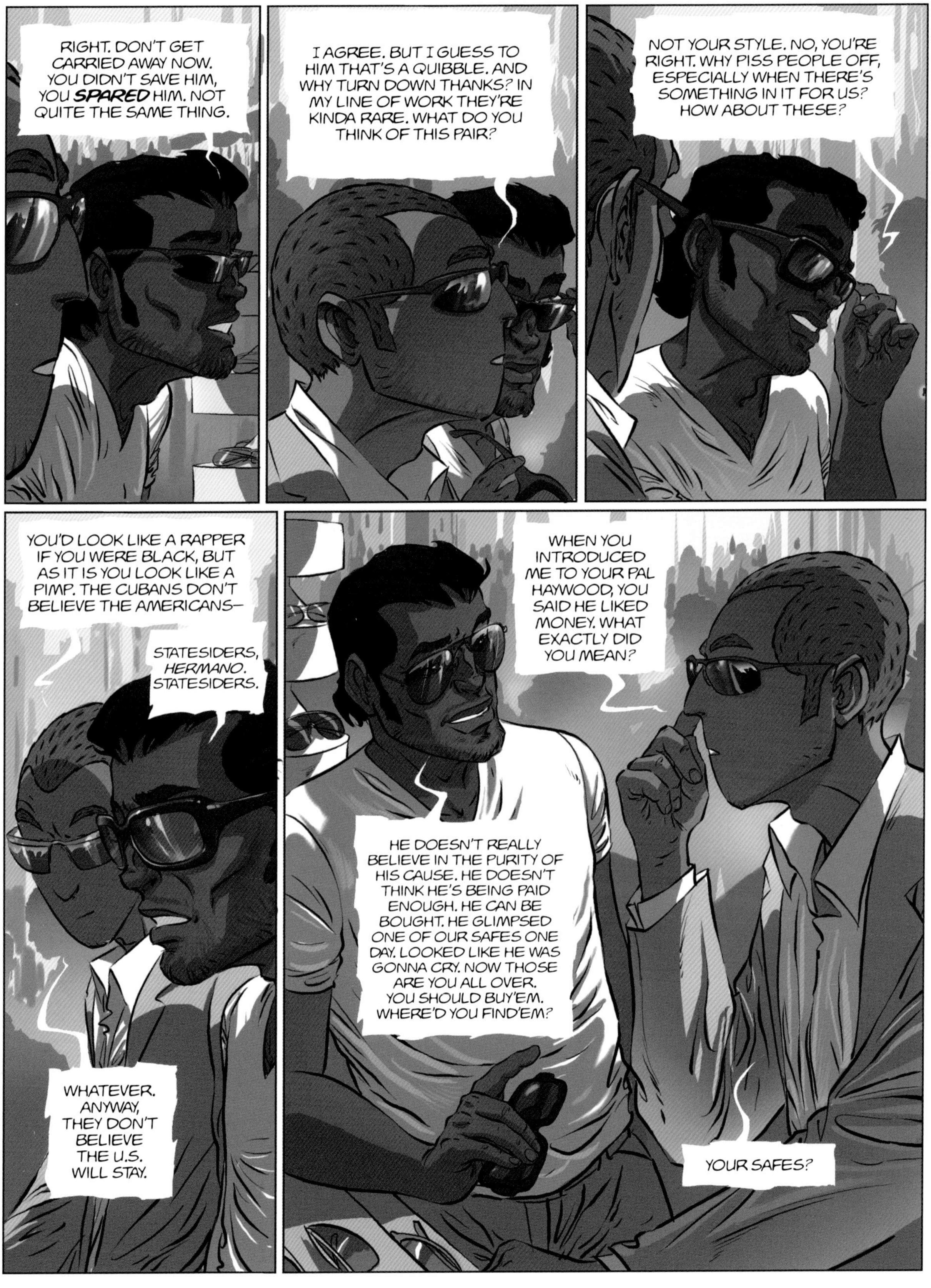
RIGHT. DON'T GET CARRIED AWAY NOW. YOU DIDN'T SAVE HIM, YOU SPARED HIM. NOT QUITE THE SAME THING.
I AGREE. BUT I GUESS TO HIM THAT'S A QUIBBLE. AND WHY TURN DOWN THANKS? IN MY LINE OF WORK THEY'RE KINDA RARE. WHAT DO YOU THINK OF THIS PAIR?
NOT YOUR STYLE. NO, YOU'RE RIGHT. WHY PISS PEOPLE OFF, ESPECIALLY WHEN THERE'S SOMETHING IN IT FOR US? HOW ABOUT THESE?
YOU'D LOOK LIKE A RAPPER IF YOU WERE BLACK, BUT AS IT IS YOU LOOK LIKE A PIMP. THE CUBANS DON'T BELIEVE THE AMERICANS—
STATESIDERS, HERMANO. STATESIDERS.
WHATEVER. ANYWAY, THEY DON'T BELIEVE THE U.S. WILL STAY.
WHEN YOU INTRODUCED ME TO YOUR PAL HAYWOOD, YOU SAID HE LIKED MONEY. WHAT EXACTLY DID YOU MEAN?
HE DOESN'T REALLY BELIEVE IN THE PURITY OF HIS CAUSE. HE DOESN'T THINK HE'S BEING PAID ENOUGH. HE CAN BE BOUGHT. HE GLIMPSED ONE OF OUR SAFES ONE DAY. LOOKED LIKE HE WAS GONNA CRY. NOW THOSE ARE YOU ALL OVER. YOU SHOULD BUY'EM. WHERE'D YOU FIND'EM?
YOUR SAFES?

ONE OF THOSE COLOMBIAN SAFE HOUSES WHERE WE STACK CASH WAITING TO BE LAUNDERED. I'LL SHOW YOU SOMEDAY.

THOSE MOUNTAINS OF CASH NEVER GIVE ANYONE IDEAS?

THERE'RE ARMED GUARDS IN AND AROUND THE SHACKS, BUT ON THE RICHTER SCALE OF STUPID THINGS TO DO, I'D SAY GOING AFTER PADRINO'S MONEY CLOCKS IN AROUND 15.

THAT THE MONEY YOU'RE GOING TO FINANCE GOOD DEEDS AND ELECTIONS WITH?

MAYBE. EASIER TO LAUNDER BY PASSING IT TO SOCCER PLAYERS. LIKE THE RUSSIANS.

PROBABLY. NARCS AREN'T KNOWN FOR THEIR PHILANTHROPY.

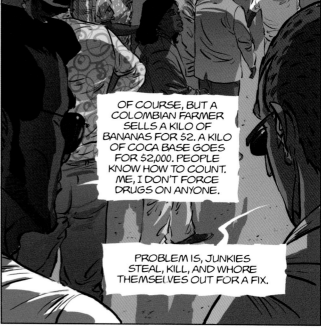

OF COURSE, BUT A COLOMBIAN FARMER SELLS A KILO OF BANANAS FOR $2. A KILO OF COCA BASE GOES FOR $2,000. PEOPLE KNOW HOW TO COUNT. ME, I DON'T FORCE DRUGS ON ANYONE.

PROBLEM IS, JUNKIES STEAL, KILL, AND WHORE THEMSELVES OUT FOR A FIX.

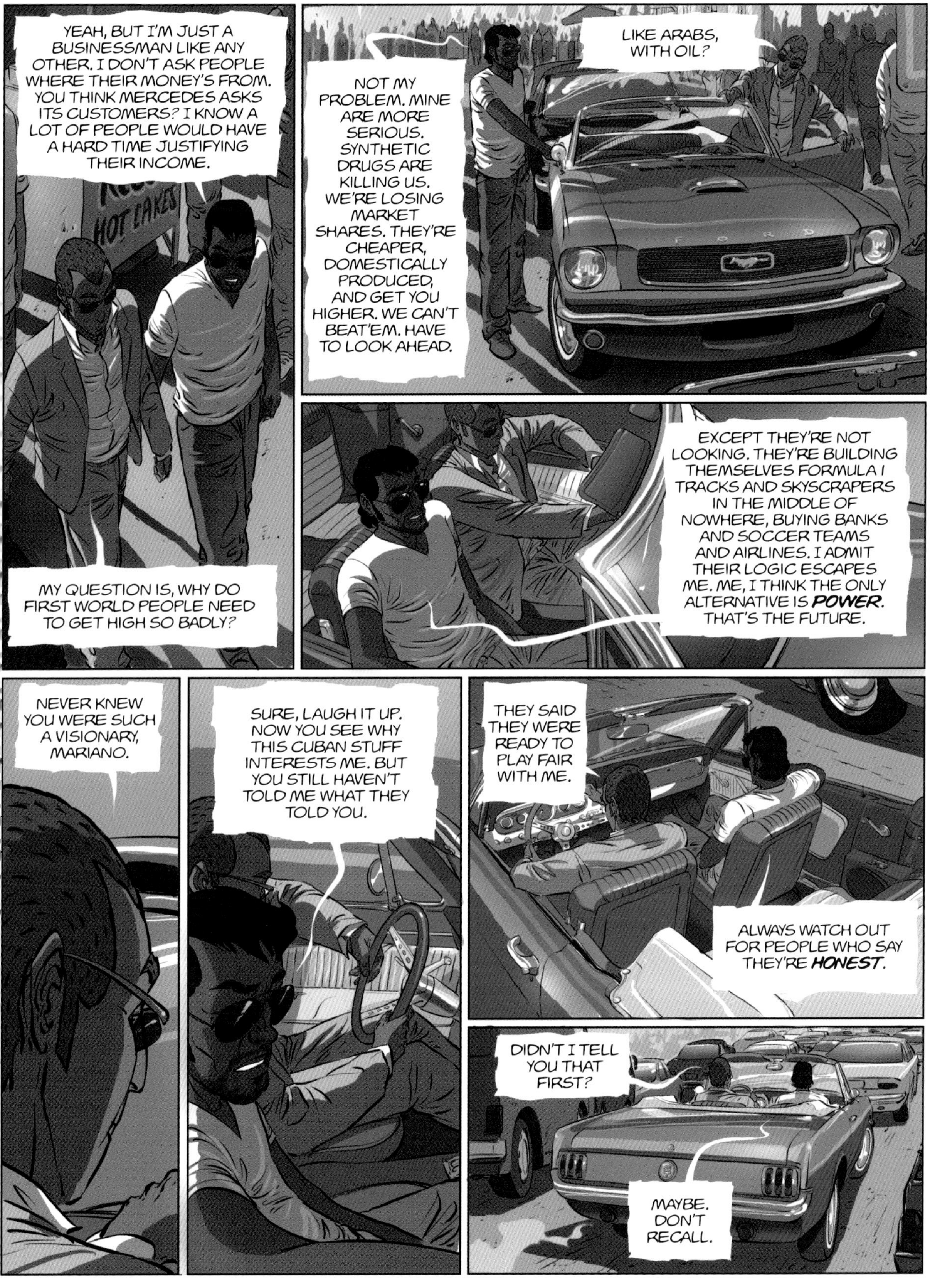
YEAH, BUT I'M JUST A BUSINESSMAN LIKE ANY OTHER. I DON'T ASK PEOPLE WHERE THEIR MONEY'S FROM. YOU THINK MERCEDES ASKS ITS CUSTOMERS? I KNOW A LOT OF PEOPLE WOULD HAVE A HARD TIME JUSTIFYING THEIR INCOME.
HOT CAKES
MY QUESTION IS, WHY DO FIRST WORLD PEOPLE NEED TO GET HIGH SO BADLY?
LIKE ARABS, WITH OIL?
NOT MY PROBLEM. MINE ARE MORE SERIOUS. SYNTHETIC DRUGS ARE KILLING US. WE'RE LOSING MARKET SHARES. THEY'RE CHEAPER, DOMESTICALLY PRODUCED, AND GET YOU HIGHER. WE CAN'T BEAT'EM. HAVE TO LOOK AHEAD.
EXCEPT THEY'RE NOT LOOKING. THEY'RE BUILDING THEMSELVES FORMULA I TRACKS AND SKYSCRAPERS IN THE MIDDLE OF NOWHERE, BUYING BANKS AND SOCCER TEAMS AND AIRLINES. I ADMIT THEIR LOGIC ESCAPES ME. ME, I THINK THE ONLY ALTERNATIVE IS **POWER**. THAT'S THE FUTURE.
NEVER KNEW YOU WERE SUCH A VISIONARY, MARIANO.
SURE, LAUGH IT UP. NOW YOU SEE WHY THIS CUBAN STUFF INTERESTS ME. BUT YOU STILL HAVEN'T TOLD ME WHAT THEY TOLD YOU.
THEY SAID THEY WERE READY TO PLAY FAIR WITH ME.
ALWAYS WATCH OUT FOR PEOPLE WHO SAY THEY'RE **HONEST**.
DIDN'T I TELL YOU THAT FIRST?
MAYBE. DON'T RECALL.

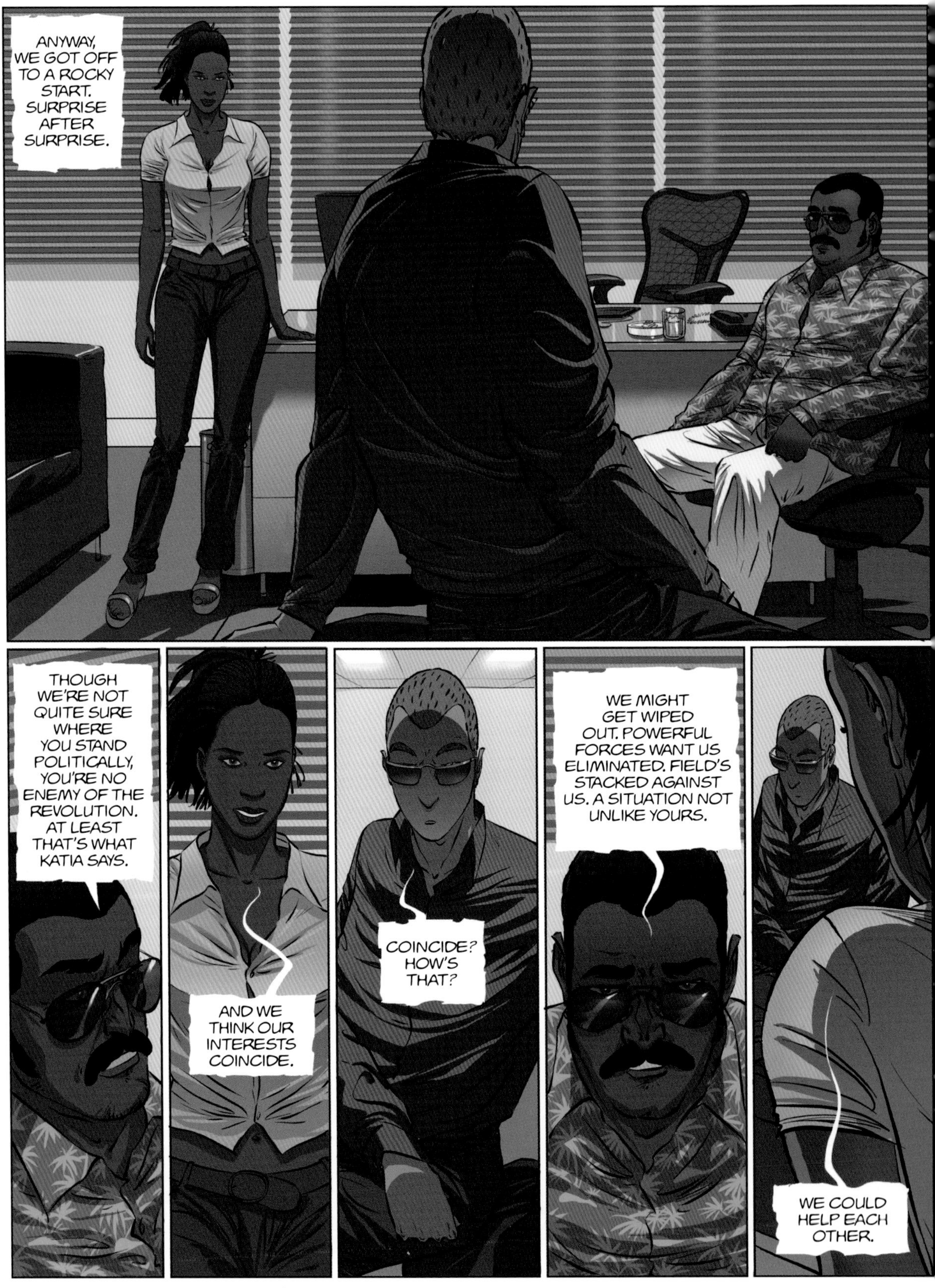
ANYWAY, WE GOT OFF TO A ROCKY START. SURPRISE AFTER SURPRISE.
THOUGH WE'RE NOT QUITE SURE WHERE YOU STAND POLITICALLY, YOU'RE NO ENEMY OF THE REVOLUTION. AT LEAST THAT'S WHAT KATIA SAYS.
AND WE THINK OUR INTERESTS COINCIDE.
COINCIDE? HOW'S THAT?
WE MIGHT GET WIPED OUT. POWERFUL FORCES WANT US ELIMINATED. FIELD'S STACKED AGAINST US. A SITUATION NOT UNLIKE YOURS.
WE COULD HELP EACH OTHER.

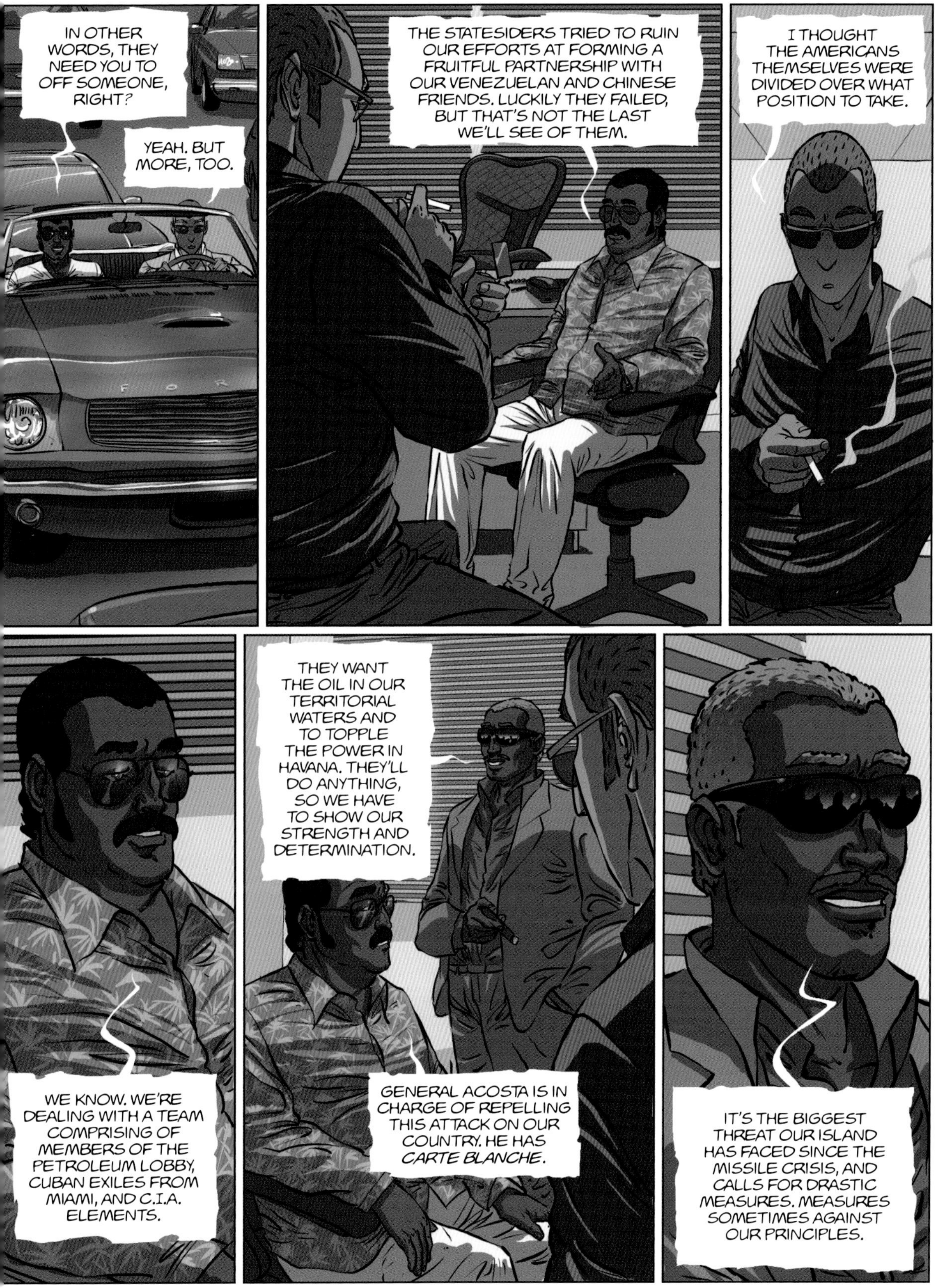
IN OTHER WORDS, THEY NEED YOU TO OFF SOMEONE, RIGHT?
YEAH. BUT MORE, TOO.
THE STATESIDERS TRIED TO RUIN OUR EFFORTS AT FORMING A FRUITFUL PARTNERSHIP WITH OUR VENEZUELAN AND CHINESE FRIENDS. LUCKILY THEY FAILED, BUT THAT'S NOT THE LAST WE'LL SEE OF THEM.
I THOUGHT THE AMERICANS THEMSELVES WERE DIVIDED OVER WHAT POSITION TO TAKE.
WE KNOW. WE'RE DEALING WITH A TEAM COMPRISING OF MEMBERS OF THE PETROLEUM LOBBY, CUBAN EXILES FROM MIAMI, AND C.I.A. ELEMENTS.
THEY WANT THE OIL IN OUR TERRITORIAL WATERS AND TO TOPPLE THE POWER IN HAVANA. THEY'LL DO ANYTHING, SO WE HAVE TO SHOW OUR STRENGTH AND DETERMINATION.
GENERAL ACOSTA IS IN CHARGE OF REPELLING THIS ATTACK ON OUR COUNTRY. HE HAS *CARTE BLANCHE*.
IT'S THE BIGGEST THREAT OUR ISLAND HAS FACED SINCE THE MISSILE CRISIS, AND CALLS FOR DRASTIC MEASURES. MEASURES SOMETIMES AGAINST OUR PRINCIPLES.

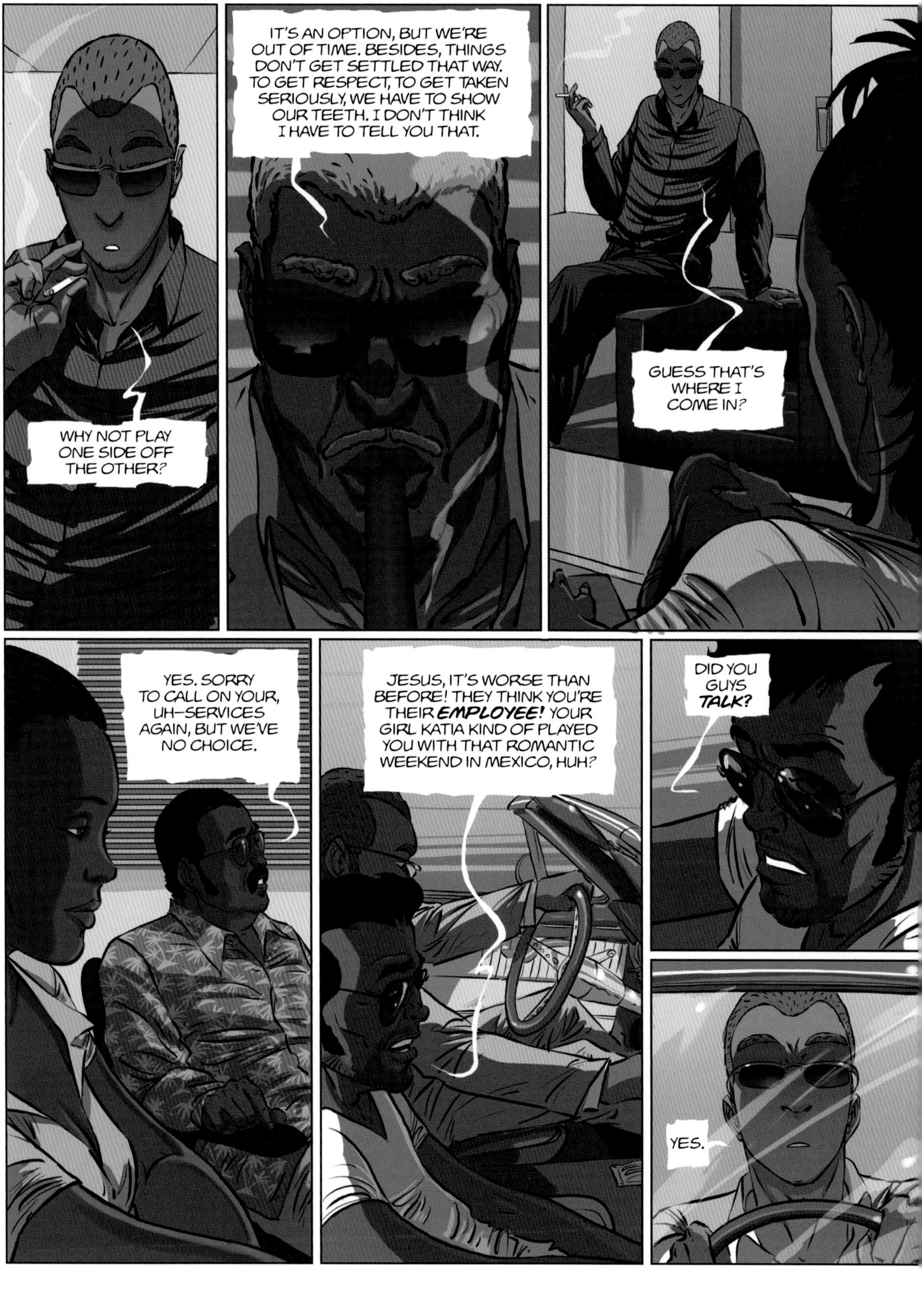
WHY NOT PLAY ONE SIDE OFF THE OTHER?
IT'S AN OPTION, BUT WE'RE OUT OF TIME. BESIDES, THINGS DON'T GET SETTLED THAT WAY. TO GET RESPECT, TO GET TAKEN SERIOUSLY, WE HAVE TO SHOW OUR TEETH. I DON'T THINK I HAVE TO TELL YOU THAT.
GUESS THAT'S WHERE I COME IN?
YES. SORRY TO CALL ON YOUR, UH–SERVICES AGAIN, BUT WE'VE NO CHOICE.
JESUS, IT'S WORSE THAN BEFORE! THEY THINK YOU'RE THEIR ***EMPLOYEE!*** YOUR GIRL KATIA KIND OF PLAYED YOU WITH THAT ROMANTIC WEEKEND IN MEXICO, HUH?
DID YOU GUYS ***TALK?***
YES.

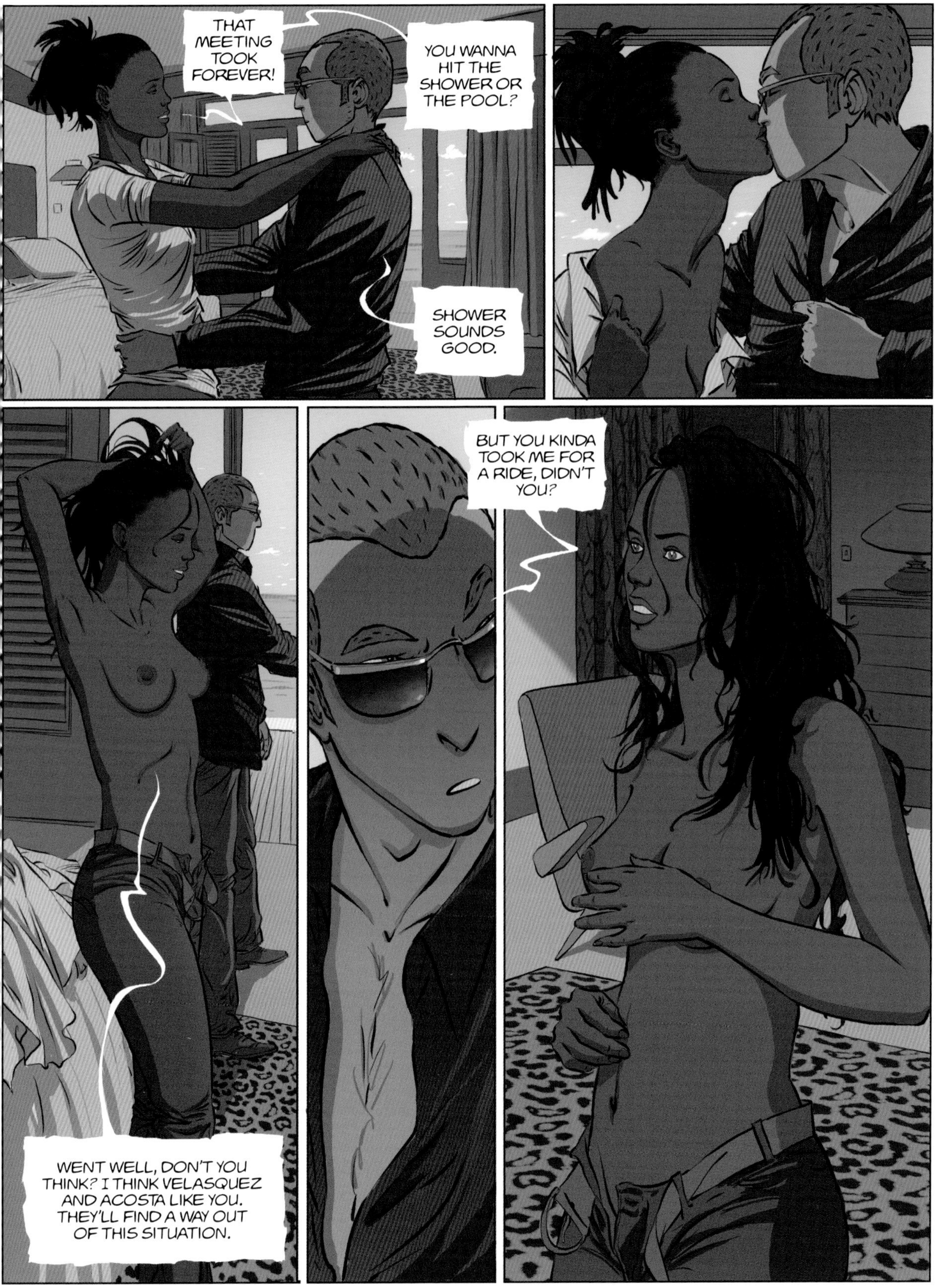
THAT MEETING TOOK FOREVER!
YOU WANNA HIT THE SHOWER OR THE POOL?
SHOWER SOUNDS GOOD.
WENT WELL, DON'T YOU THINK? I THINK VELASQUEZ AND ACOSTA LIKE YOU. THEY'LL FIND A WAY OUT OF THIS SITUATION.
BUT YOU KINDA TOOK ME FOR A RIDE, DIDN'T YOU?

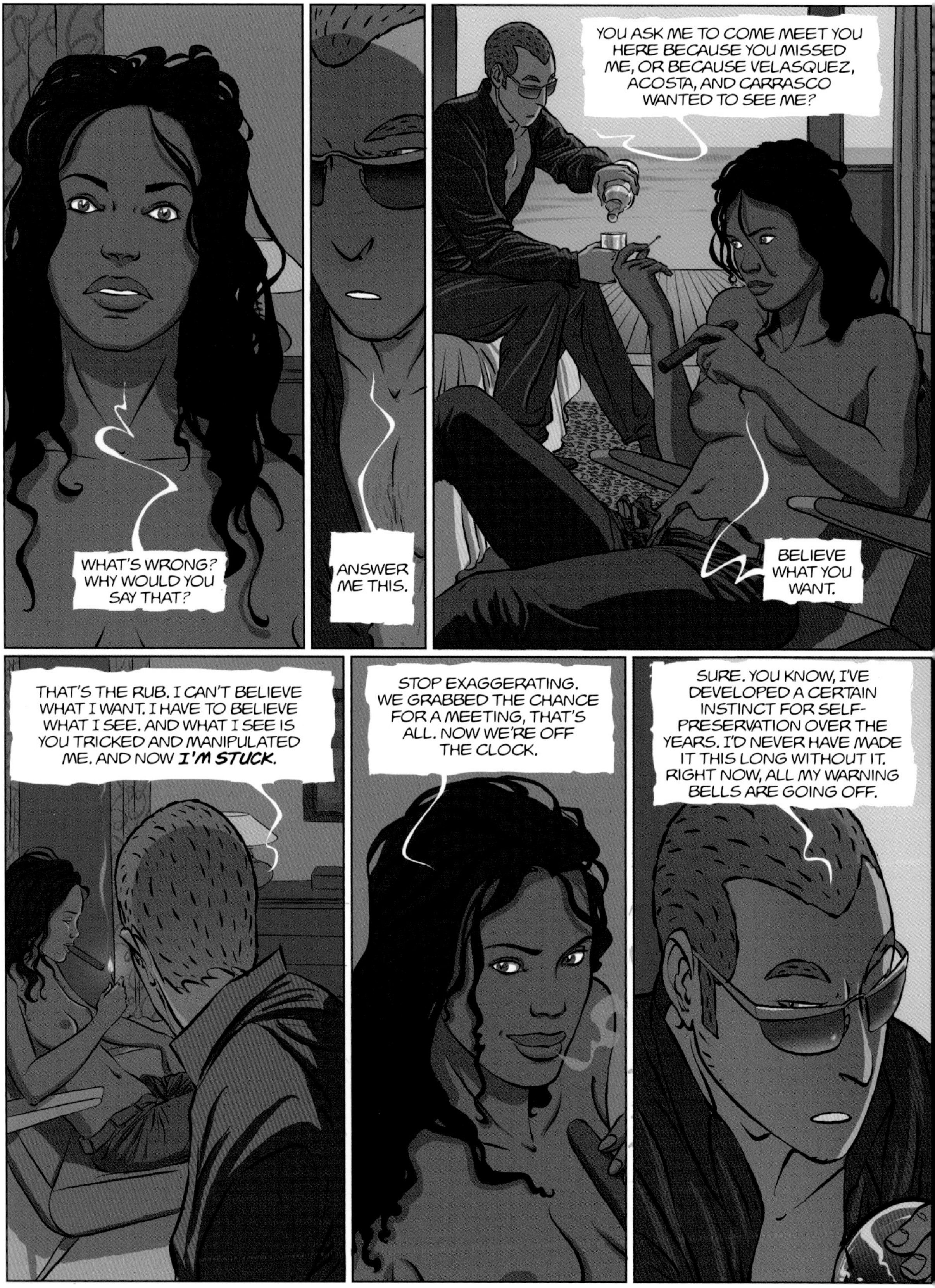
WHAT'S WRONG? WHY WOULD YOU SAY THAT?
ANSWER ME THIS.
YOU ASK ME TO COME MEET YOU HERE BECAUSE YOU MISSED ME, OR BECAUSE VELASQUEZ, ACOSTA, AND CARRASCO WANTED TO SEE ME?
BELIEVE WHAT YOU WANT.
THAT'S THE RUB. I CAN'T BELIEVE WHAT I WANT. I HAVE TO BELIEVE WHAT I SEE. AND WHAT I SEE IS YOU TRICKED AND MANIPULATED ME. AND NOW ***I'M STUCK***.
STOP EXAGGERATING. WE GRABBED THE CHANCE FOR A MEETING, THAT'S ALL. NOW WE'RE OFF THE CLOCK.
SURE. YOU KNOW, I'VE DEVELOPED A CERTAIN INSTINCT FOR SELF-PRESERVATION OVER THE YEARS. I'D NEVER HAVE MADE IT THIS LONG WITHOUT IT. RIGHT NOW, ALL MY WARNING BELLS ARE GOING OFF.

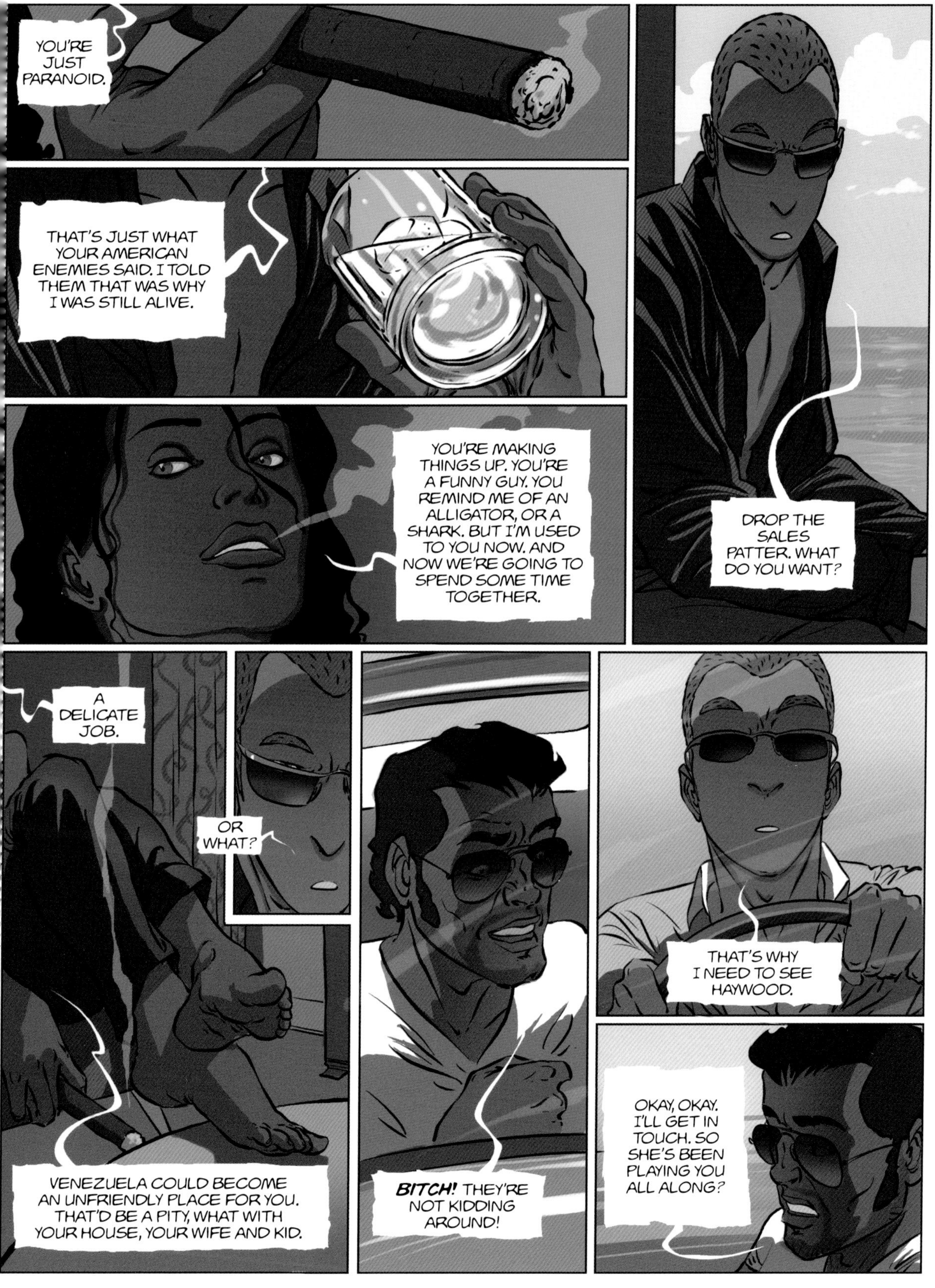
YOU'RE JUST PARANOID.
THAT'S JUST WHAT YOUR AMERICAN ENEMIES SAID. I TOLD THEM THAT WAS WHY I WAS STILL ALIVE.
YOU'RE MAKING THINGS UP. YOU'RE A FUNNY GUY. YOU REMIND ME OF AN ALLIGATOR, OR A SHARK. BUT I'M USED TO YOU NOW. AND NOW WE'RE GOING TO SPEND SOME TIME TOGETHER.
DROP THE SALES PATTER. WHAT DO YOU WANT?
A DELICATE JOB.
OR WHAT?
VENEZUELA COULD BECOME AN UNFRIENDLY PLACE FOR YOU. THAT'D BE A PITY, WHAT WITH YOUR HOUSE, YOUR WIFE AND KID.
BITCH! THEY'RE NOT KIDDING AROUND!
THAT'S WHY I NEED TO SEE HAYWOOD.
OKAY, OKAY. I'LL GET IN TOUCH. SO SHE'S BEEN PLAYING YOU ALL ALONG?

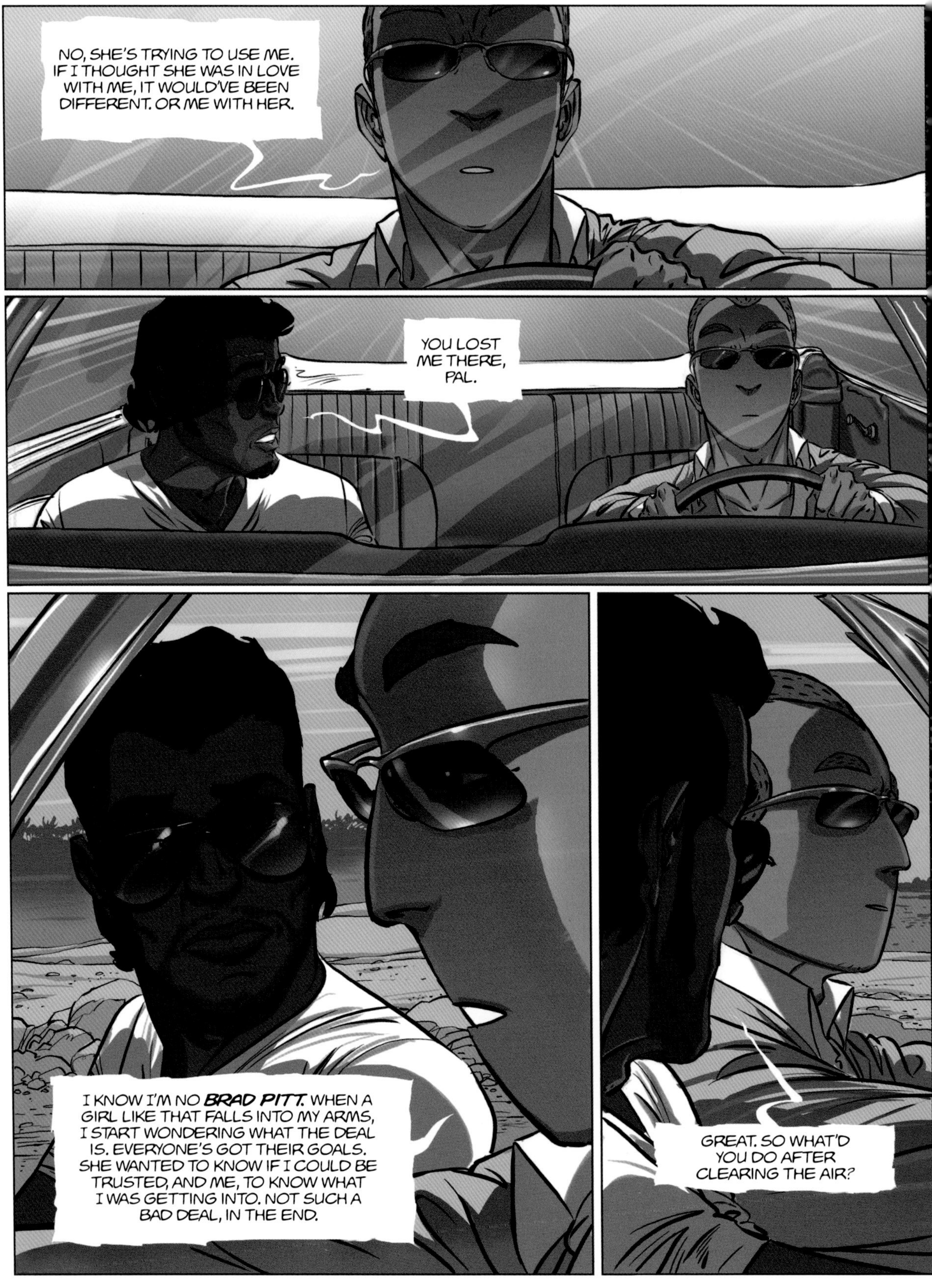
NO, SHE'S TRYING TO USE ME. IF I THOUGHT SHE WAS IN LOVE WITH ME, IT WOULD'VE BEEN DIFFERENT. OR ME WITH HER.
YOU LOST ME THERE, PAL.
I KNOW I'M NO **BRAD PITT**. WHEN A GIRL LIKE THAT FALLS INTO MY ARMS, I START WONDERING WHAT THE DEAL IS. EVERYONE'S GOT THEIR GOALS. SHE WANTED TO KNOW IF I COULD BE TRUSTED, AND ME, TO KNOW WHAT I WAS GETTING INTO. NOT SUCH A BAD DEAL, IN THE END.
GREAT. SO WHAT'D YOU DO AFTER CLEARING THE AIR?

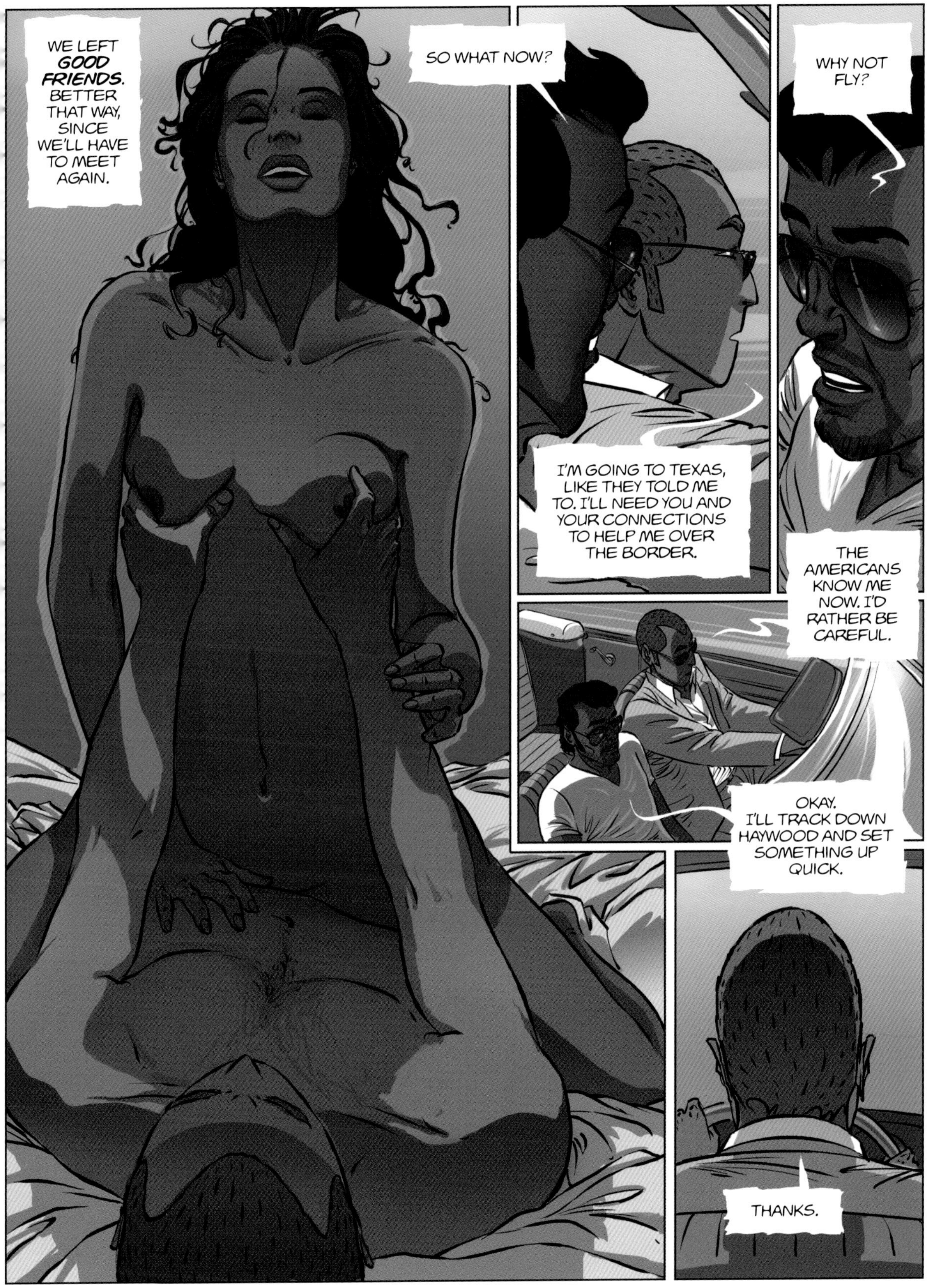
WE LEFT **GOOD FRIENDS**. BETTER THAT WAY, SINCE WE'LL HAVE TO MEET AGAIN.
SO WHAT NOW?
I'M GOING TO TEXAS, LIKE THEY TOLD ME TO. I'LL NEED YOU AND YOUR CONNECTIONS TO HELP ME OVER THE BORDER.
WHY NOT FLY?
THE AMERICANS KNOW ME NOW. I'D RATHER BE CAREFUL.
OKAY. I'LL TRACK DOWN HAYWOOD AND SET SOMETHING UP QUICK.
THANKS.

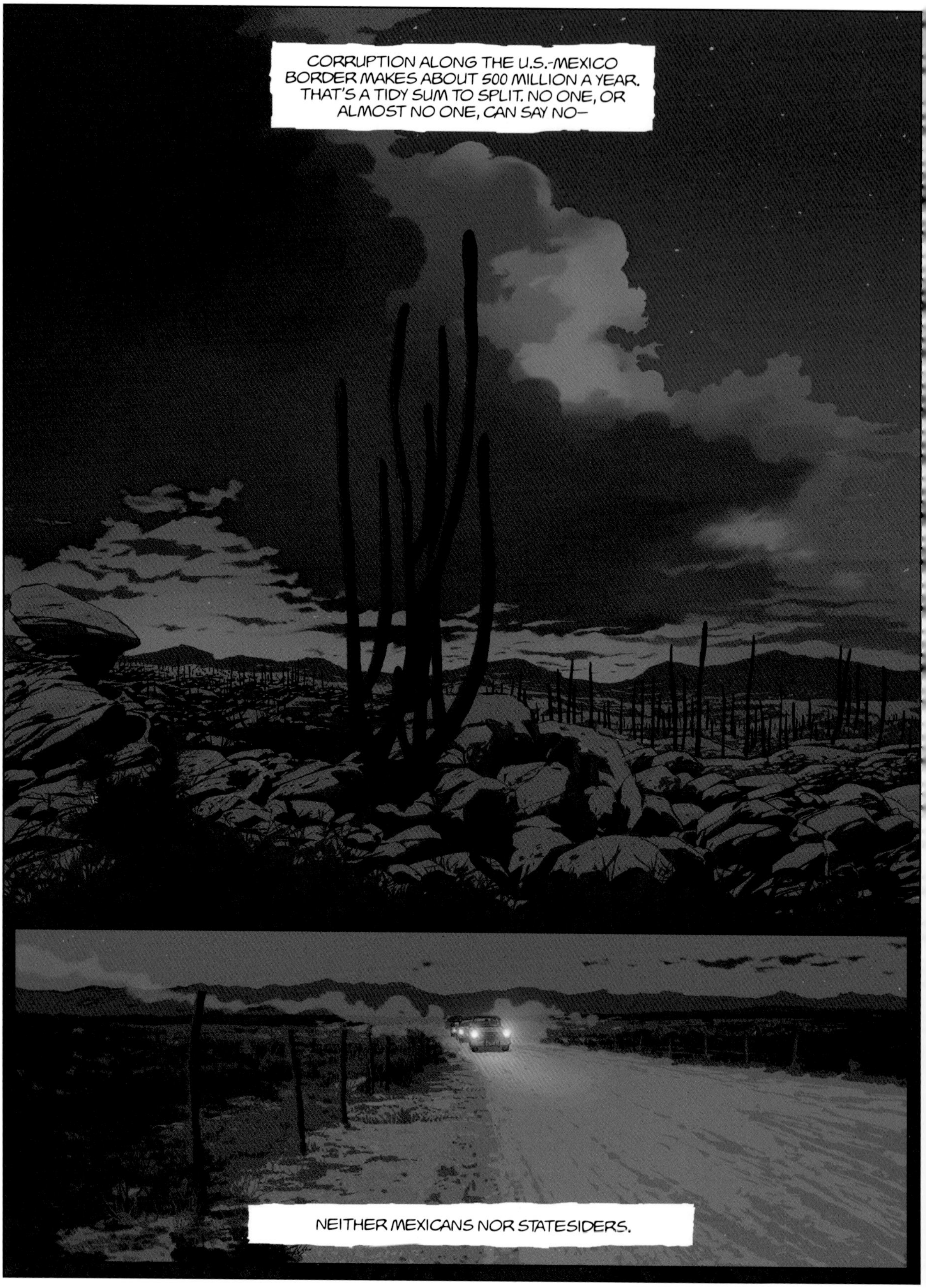
CORRUPTION ALONG THE U.S.-MEXICO BORDER MAKES ABOUT 500 MILLION A YEAR. THAT'S A TIDY SUM TO SPLIT. NO ONE, OR ALMOST NO ONE, CAN SAY NO—
NEITHER MEXICANS NOR STATESIDERS.

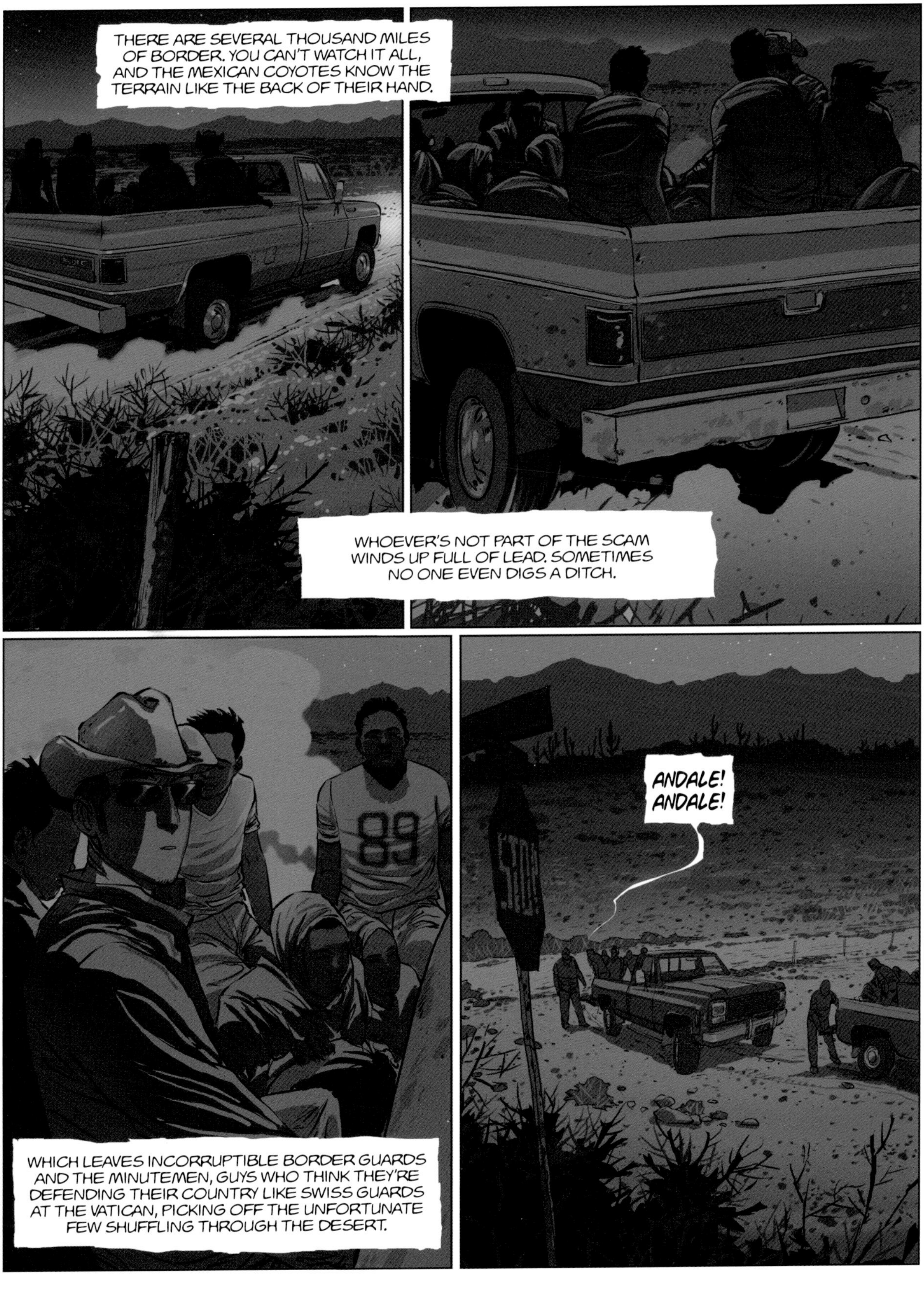
THERE ARE SEVERAL THOUSAND MILES OF BORDER. YOU CAN'T WATCH IT ALL, AND THE MEXICAN COYOTES KNOW THE TERRAIN LIKE THE BACK OF THEIR HAND.
WHOEVER'S NOT PART OF THE SCAM WINDS UP FULL OF LEAD. SOMETIMES NO ONE EVEN DIGS A DITCH.
WHICH LEAVES INCORRUPTIBLE BORDER GUARDS AND THE MINUTEMEN, GUYS WHO THINK THEY'RE DEFENDING THEIR COUNTRY LIKE SWISS GUARDS AT THE VATICAN, PICKING OFF THE UNFORTUNATE FEW SHUFFLING THROUGH THE DESERT.
ANDALE! ANDALE!
89

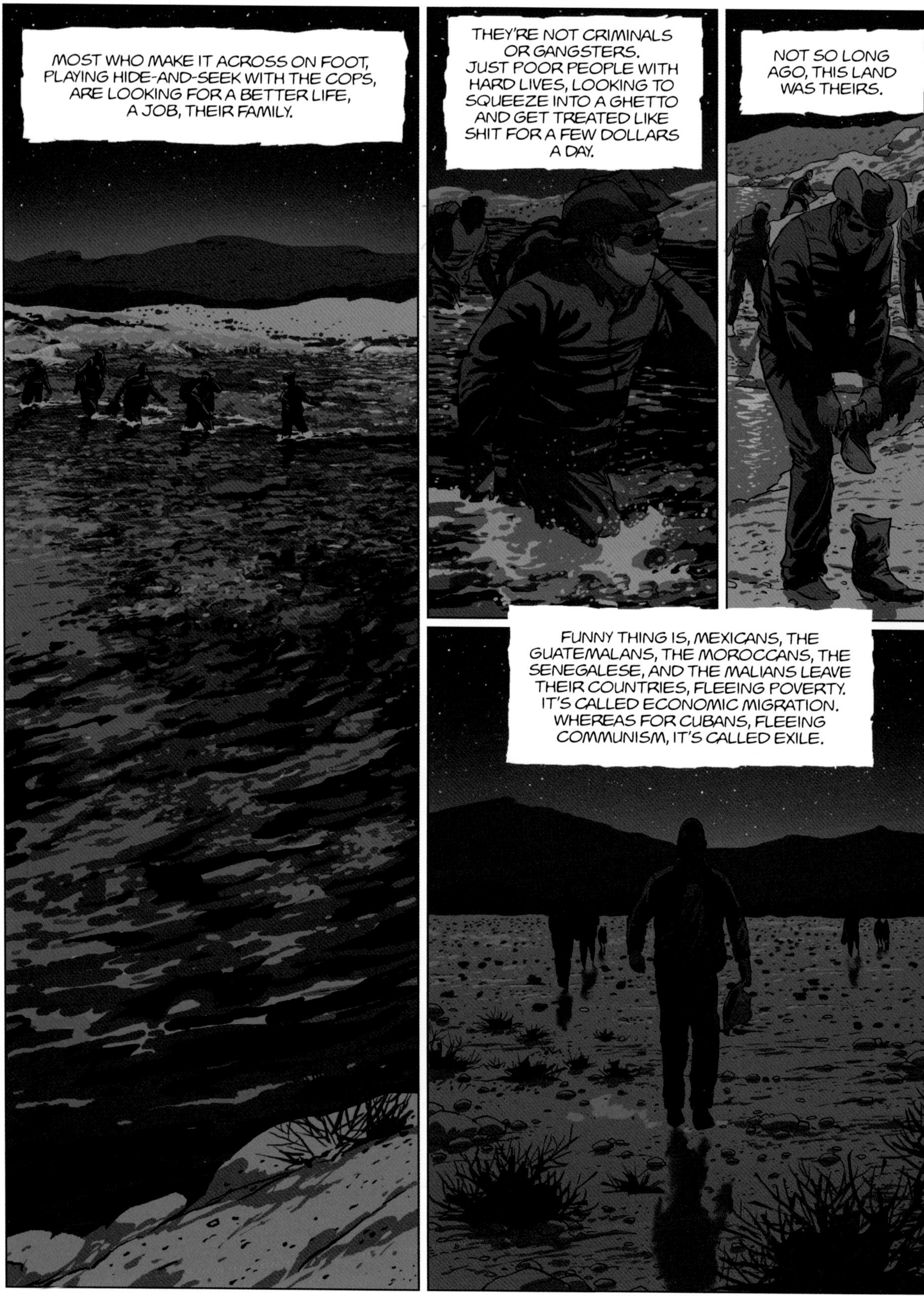
MOST WHO MAKE IT ACROSS ON FOOT, PLAYING HIDE-AND-SEEK WITH THE COPS, ARE LOOKING FOR A BETTER LIFE, A JOB, THEIR FAMILY.
THEY'RE NOT CRIMINALS OR GANGSTERS. JUST POOR PEOPLE WITH HARD LIVES, LOOKING TO SQUEEZE INTO A GHETTO AND GET TREATED LIKE SHIT FOR A FEW DOLLARS A DAY.
NOT SO LONG AGO, THIS LAND WAS THEIRS.
FUNNY THING IS, MEXICANS, THE GUATEMALANS, THE MOROCCANS, THE SENEGALESE, AND THE MALIANS LEAVE THEIR COUNTRIES, FLEEING POVERTY. IT'S CALLED ECONOMIC MIGRATION. WHEREAS FOR CUBANS, FLEEING COMMUNISM, IT'S CALLED EXILE.

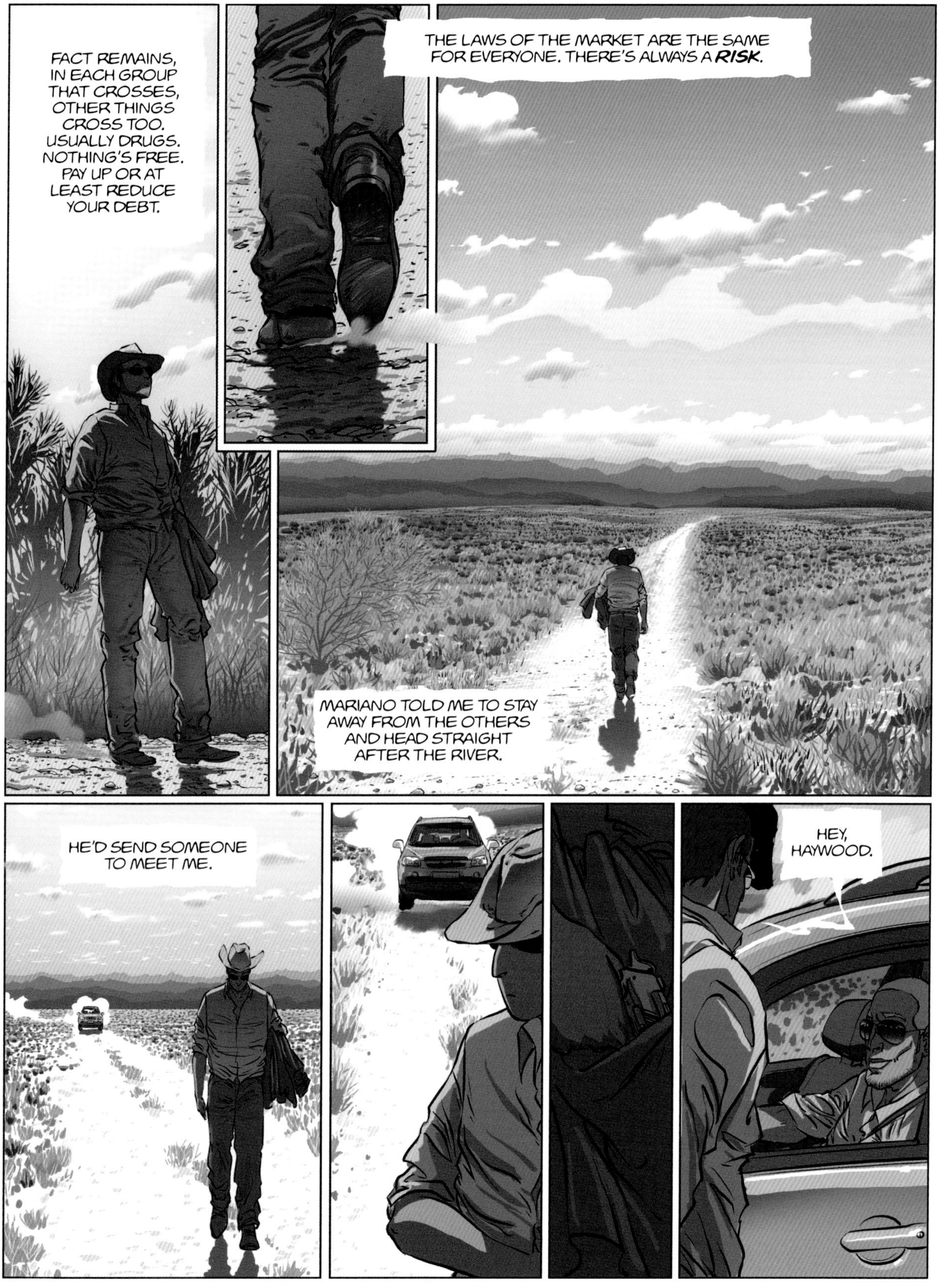
FACT REMAINS, IN EACH GROUP THAT CROSSES, OTHER THINGS CROSS TOO. USUALLY DRUGS. NOTHING'S FREE. PAY UP OR AT LEAST REDUCE YOUR DEBT.
THE LAWS OF THE MARKET ARE THE SAME FOR EVERYONE. THERE'S ALWAYS A **RISK**.
MARIANO TOLD ME TO STAY AWAY FROM THE OTHERS AND HEAD STRAIGHT AFTER THE RIVER.
HE'D SEND SOMEONE TO MEET ME.
HEY, HAYWOOD.

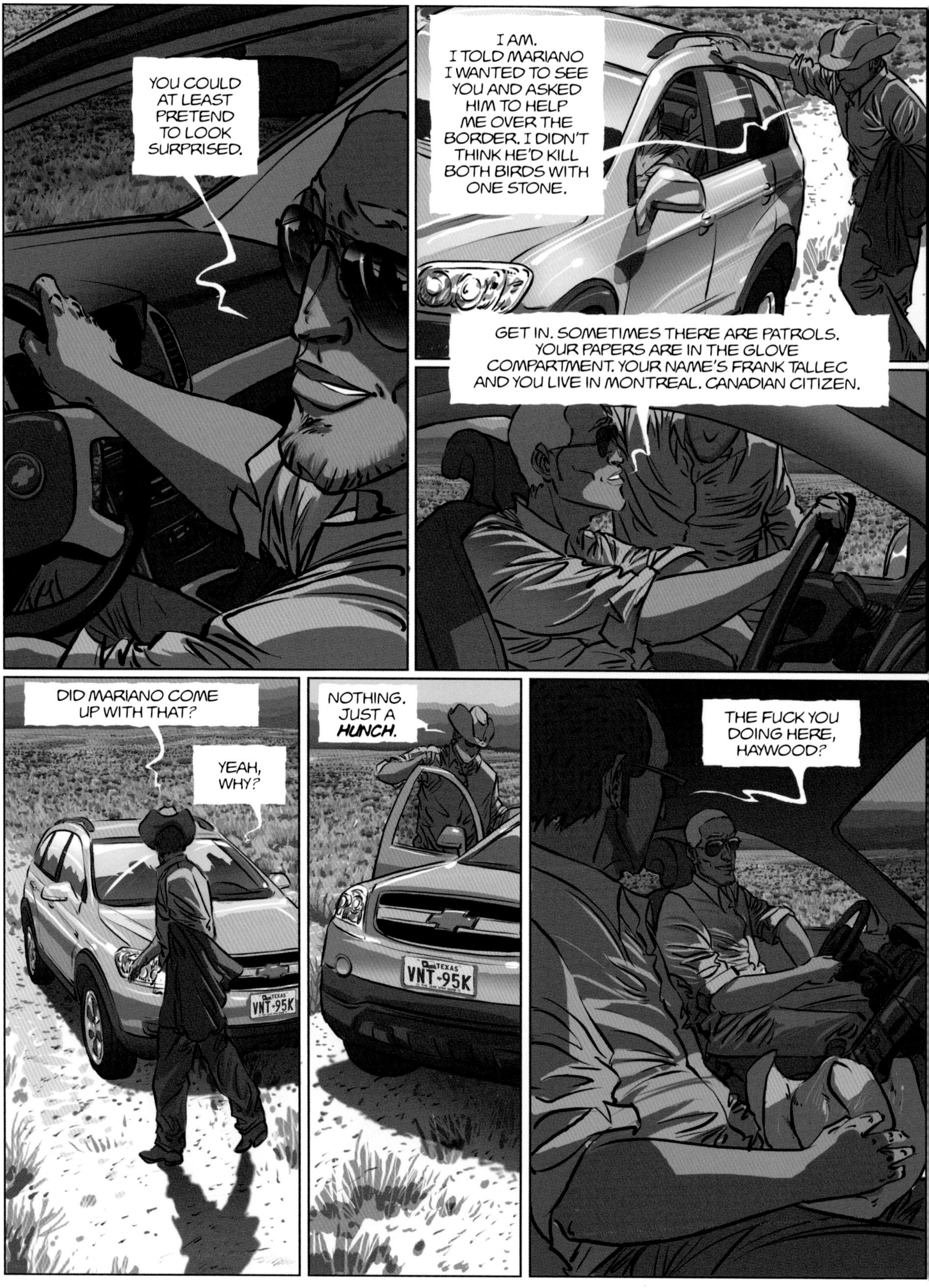
YOU COULD AT LEAST PRETEND TO LOOK SURPRISED.
I AM. I TOLD MARIANO I WANTED TO SEE YOU AND ASKED HIM TO HELP ME OVER THE BORDER. I DIDN'T THINK HE'D KILL BOTH BIRDS WITH ONE STONE.
GET IN. SOMETIMES THERE ARE PATROLS. YOUR PAPERS ARE IN THE GLOVE COMPARTMENT. YOUR NAME'S FRANK TALLEC AND YOU LIVE IN MONTREAL. CANADIAN CITIZEN.
DID MARIANO COME UP WITH THAT?
YEAH, WHY?
NOTHING. JUST A HUNCH.
THE FUCK YOU DOING HERE, HAYWOOD?
TEXAS
VNT-95K

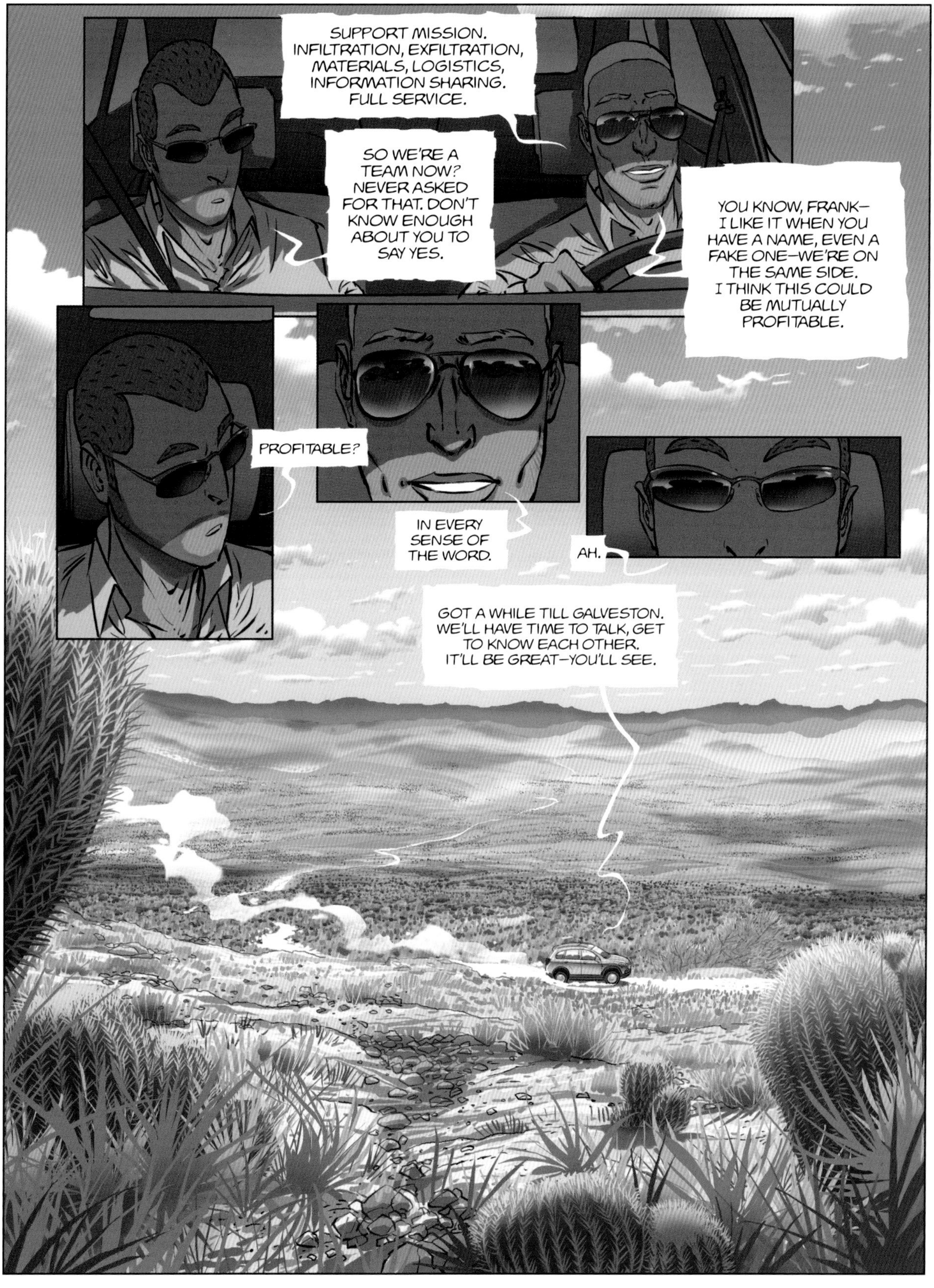
SUPPORT MISSION. INFILTRATION, EXFILTRATION, MATERIALS, LOGISTICS, INFORMATION SHARING. FULL SERVICE.
SO WE'RE A TEAM NOW? NEVER ASKED FOR THAT. DON'T KNOW ENOUGH ABOUT YOU TO SAY YES.
YOU KNOW, FRANK— I LIKE IT WHEN YOU HAVE A NAME, EVEN A FAKE ONE—WE'RE ON THE SAME SIDE. I THINK THIS COULD BE MUTUALLY PROFITABLE.
PROFITABLE?
IN EVERY SENSE OF THE WORD.
AH.
GOT A WHILE TILL GALVESTON. WE'LL HAVE TIME TO TALK, GET TO KNOW EACH OTHER. IT'LL BE GREAT—YOU'LL SEE.

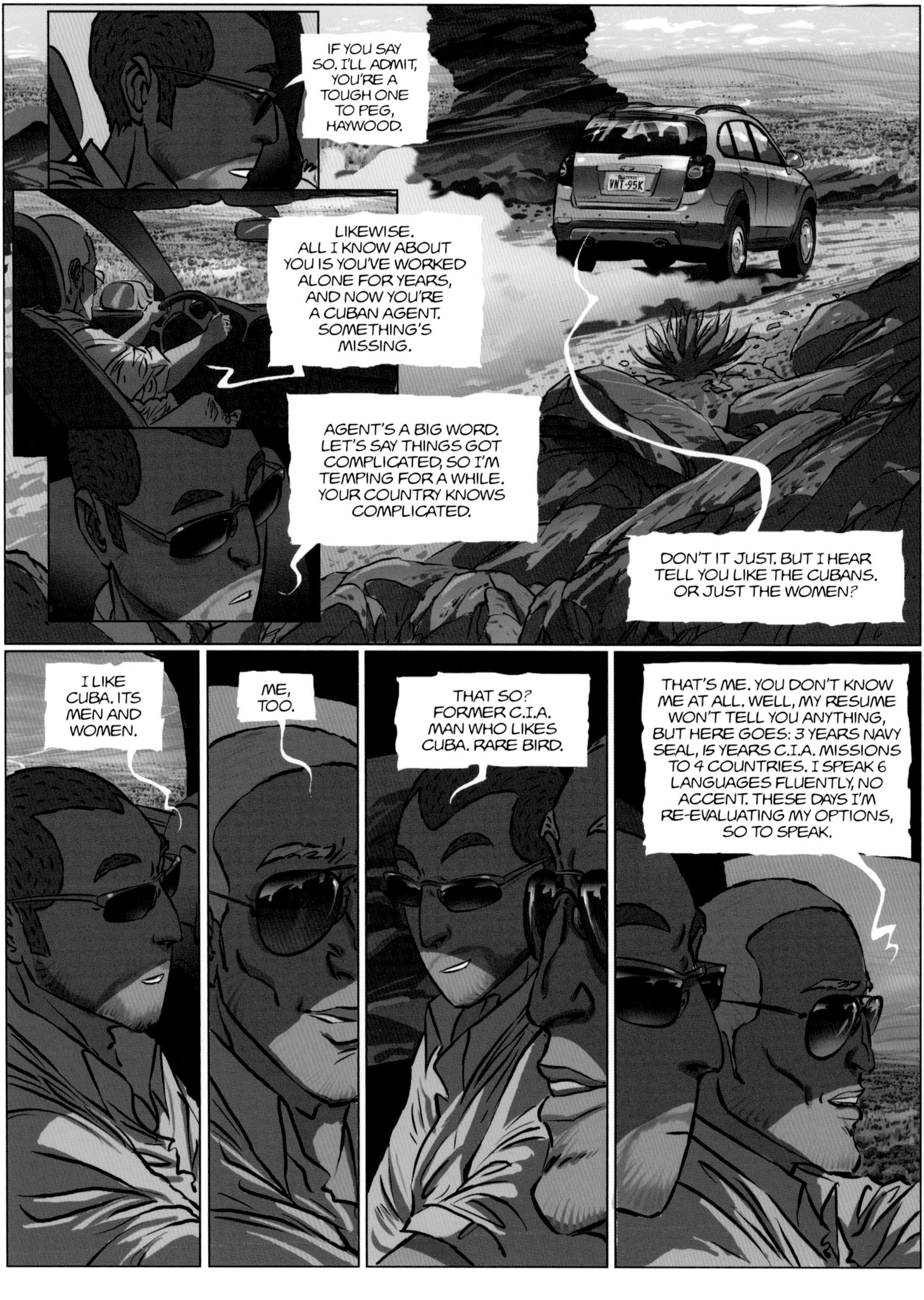
IF YOU SAY SO. I'LL ADMIT, YOU'RE A TOUGH ONE TO PEG, HAYWOOD.
LIKEWISE. ALL I KNOW ABOUT YOU IS YOU'VE WORKED ALONE FOR YEARS, AND NOW YOU'RE A CUBAN AGENT. SOMETHING'S MISSING.
AGENT'S A BIG WORD. LET'S SAY THINGS GOT COMPLICATED, SO I'M TEMPING FOR A WHILE. YOUR COUNTRY KNOWS COMPLICATED.
DON'T IT JUST. BUT I HEAR TELL YOU LIKE THE CUBANS. OR JUST THE WOMEN?
I LIKE CUBA. ITS MEN AND WOMEN.
ME, TOO.
THAT SO? FORMER C.I.A. MAN WHO LIKES CUBA. RARE BIRD.
THAT'S ME. YOU DON'T KNOW ME AT ALL. WELL, MY RESUME WON'T TELL YOU ANYTHING, BUT HERE GOES: 3 YEARS NAVY SEAL, 15 YEARS C.I.A. MISSIONS TO 4 COUNTRIES. I SPEAK 6 LANGUAGES FLUENTLY, NO ACCENT. THESE DAYS I'M RE-EVALUATING MY OPTIONS, SO TO SPEAK.

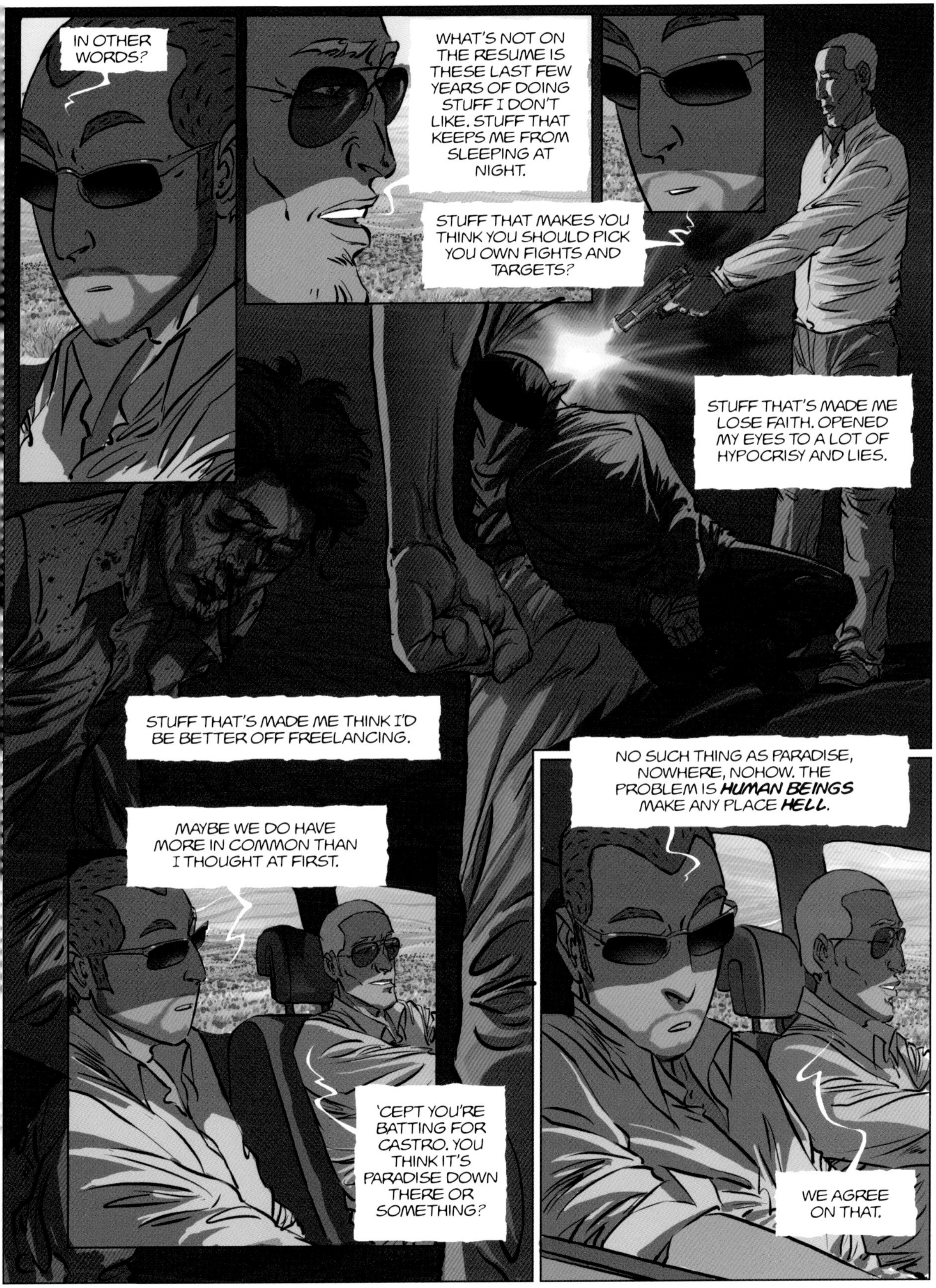
IN OTHER WORDS?
WHAT'S NOT ON THE RESUME IS THESE LAST FEW YEARS OF DOING STUFF I DON'T LIKE. STUFF THAT KEEPS ME FROM SLEEPING AT NIGHT.
STUFF THAT MAKES YOU THINK YOU SHOULD PICK YOU OWN FIGHTS AND TARGETS?
STUFF THAT'S MADE ME LOSE FAITH. OPENED MY EYES TO A LOT OF HYPOCRISY AND LIES.
STUFF THAT'S MADE ME THINK I'D BE BETTER OFF FREELANCING.
MAYBE WE DO HAVE MORE IN COMMON THAN I THOUGHT AT FIRST.
'CEPT YOU'RE BATTING FOR CASTRO. YOU THINK IT'S PARADISE DOWN THERE OR SOMETHING?
NO SUCH THING AS PARADISE, NOWHERE, NOHOW. THE PROBLEM IS **HUMAN BEINGS** MAKE ANY PLACE **HELL**.
WE AGREE ON THAT.

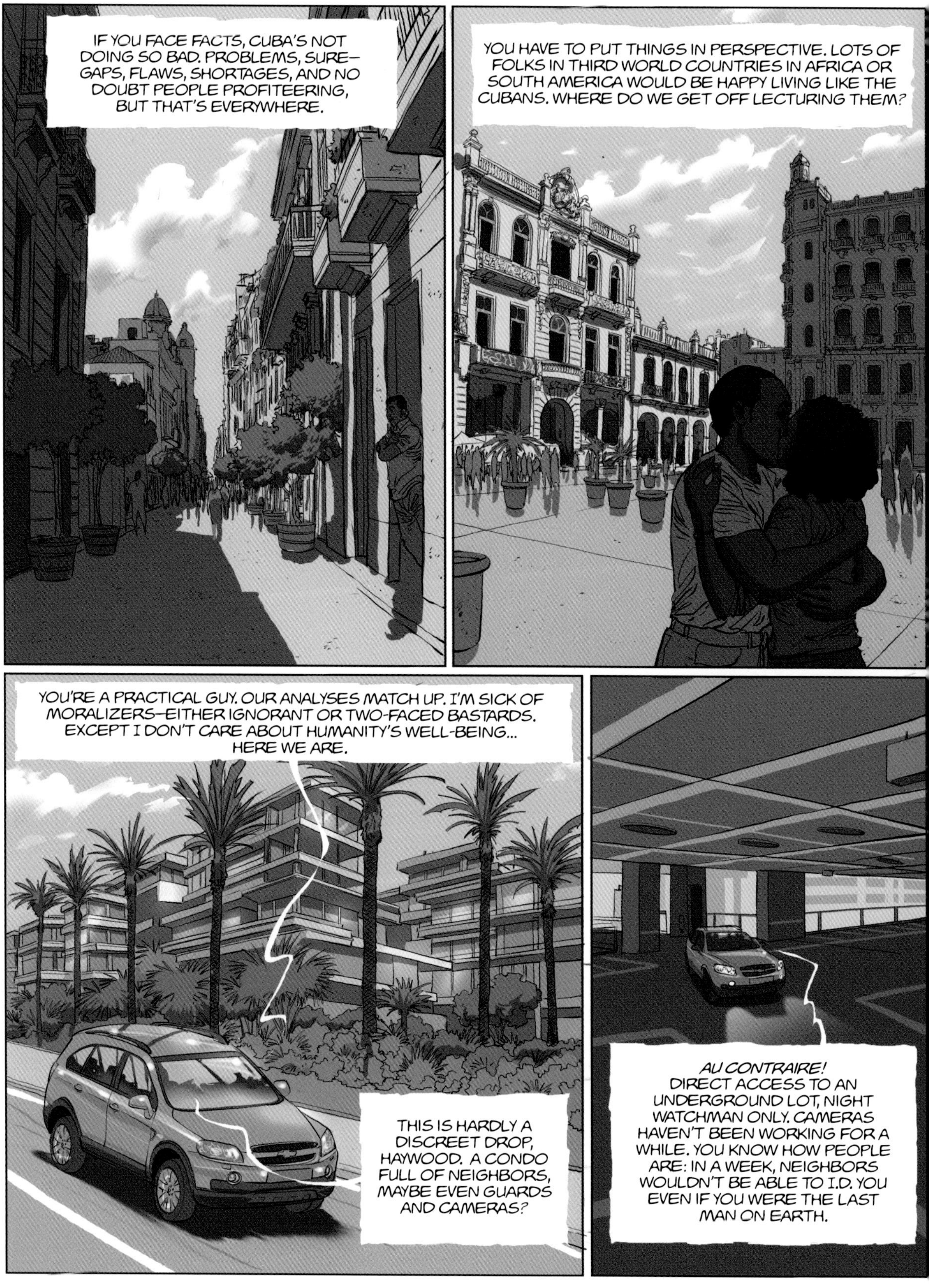
IF YOU FACE FACTS, CUBA'S NOT DOING SO BAD. PROBLEMS, SURE—GAPS, FLAWS, SHORTAGES, AND NO DOUBT PEOPLE PROFITEERING, BUT THAT'S EVERYWHERE.
YOU HAVE TO PUT THINGS IN PERSPECTIVE. LOTS OF FOLKS IN THIRD WORLD COUNTRIES IN AFRICA OR SOUTH AMERICA WOULD BE HAPPY LIVING LIKE THE CUBANS. WHERE DO WE GET OFF LECTURING THEM?
YOU'RE A PRACTICAL GUY. OUR ANALYSES MATCH UP. I'M SICK OF MORALIZERS—EITHER IGNORANT OR TWO-FACED BASTARDS. EXCEPT I DON'T CARE ABOUT HUMANITY'S WELL-BEING... HERE WE ARE.
THIS IS HARDLY A DISCREET DROP, HAYWOOD. A CONDO FULL OF NEIGHBORS, MAYBE EVEN GUARDS AND CAMERAS?
AU CONTRAIRE! DIRECT ACCESS TO AN UNDERGROUND LOT, NIGHT WATCHMAN ONLY. CAMERAS HAVEN'T BEEN WORKING FOR A WHILE. YOU KNOW HOW PEOPLE ARE: IN A WEEK, NEIGHBORS WOULDN'T BE ABLE TO I.D. YOU EVEN IF YOU WERE THE LAST MAN ON EARTH.

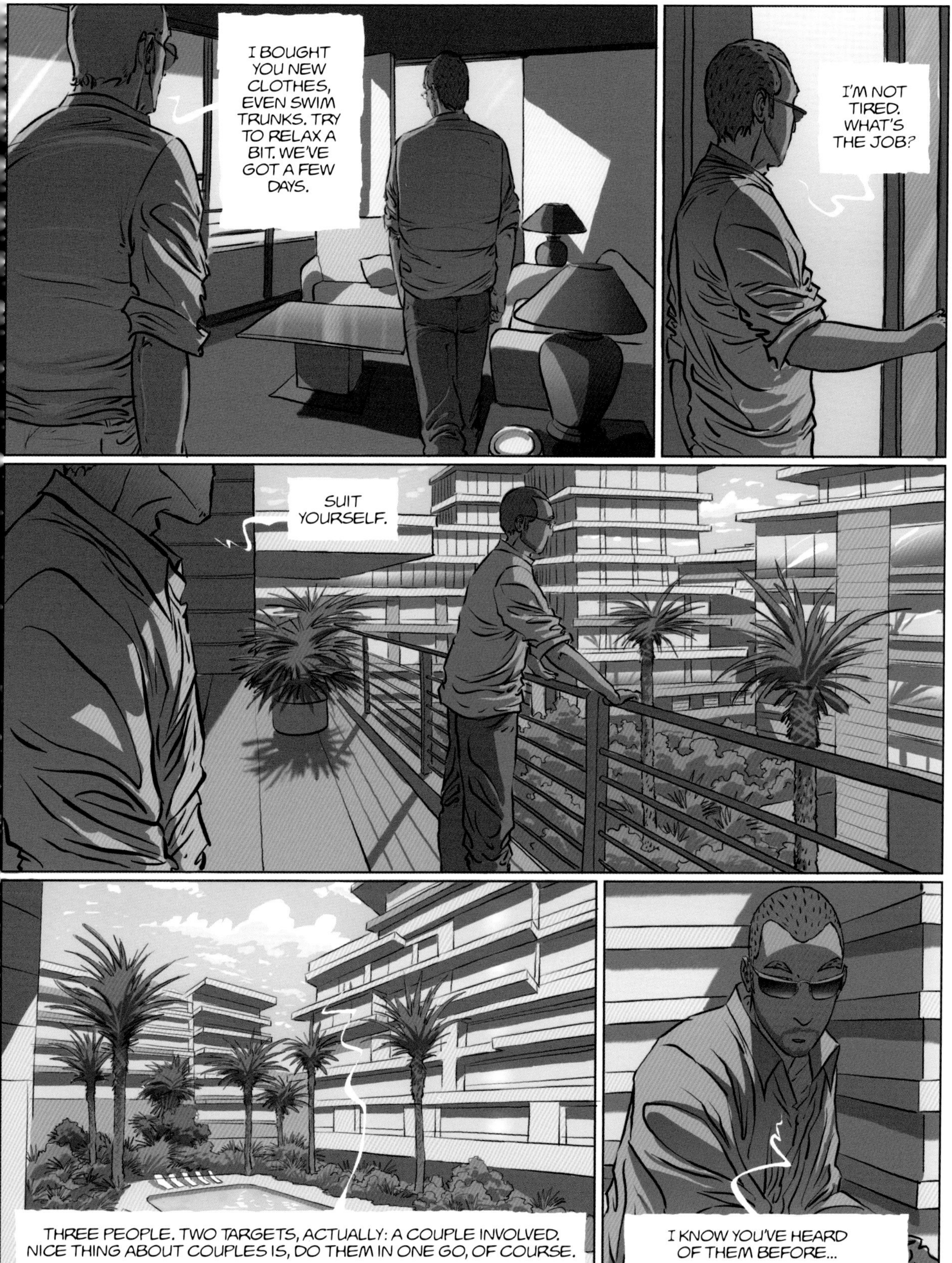
I BOUGHT YOU NEW CLOTHES, EVEN SWIM TRUNKS. TRY TO RELAX A BIT. WE'VE GOT A FEW DAYS.
I'M NOT TIRED. WHAT'S THE JOB?
SUIT YOURSELF.
THREE PEOPLE. TWO TARGETS, ACTUALLY: A COUPLE INVOLVED. NICE THING ABOUT COUPLES IS, DO THEM IN ONE GO, OF COURSE.
I KNOW YOU'VE HEARD OF THEM BEFORE...

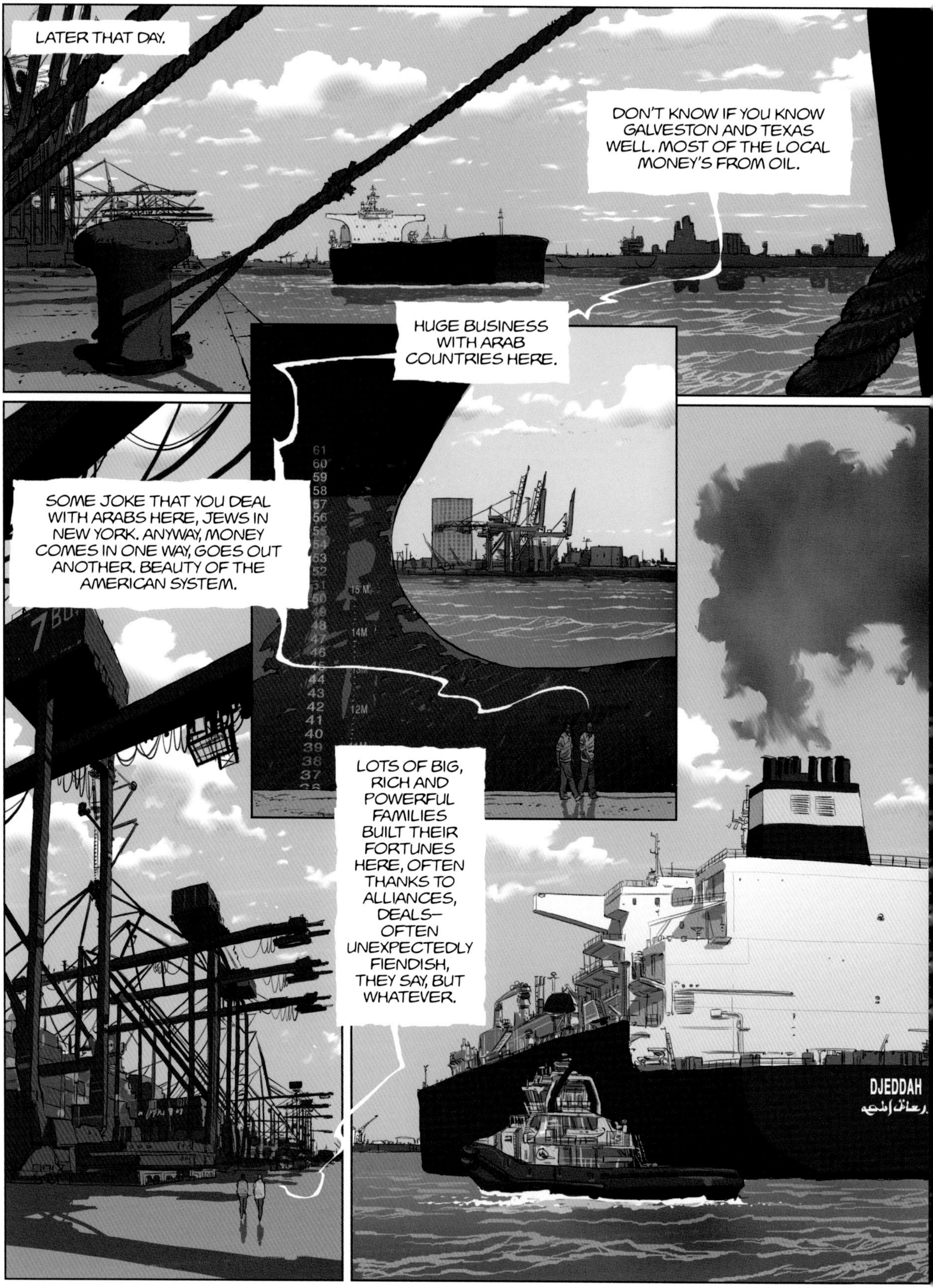
LATER THAT DAY.
DON'T KNOW IF YOU KNOW GALVESTON AND TEXAS WELL. MOST OF THE LOCAL MONEY'S FROM OIL.
HUGE BUSINESS WITH ARAB COUNTRIES HERE.
SOME JOKE THAT YOU DEAL WITH ARABS HERE, JEWS IN NEW YORK. ANYWAY, MONEY COMES IN ONE WAY, GOES OUT ANOTHER. BEAUTY OF THE AMERICAN SYSTEM.
LOTS OF BIG, RICH AND POWERFUL FAMILIES BUILT THEIR FORTUNES HERE, OFTEN THANKS TO ALLIANCES, DEALS— OFTEN UNEXPECTEDLY FIENDISH, THEY SAY, BUT WHATEVER.
DJEDDAH

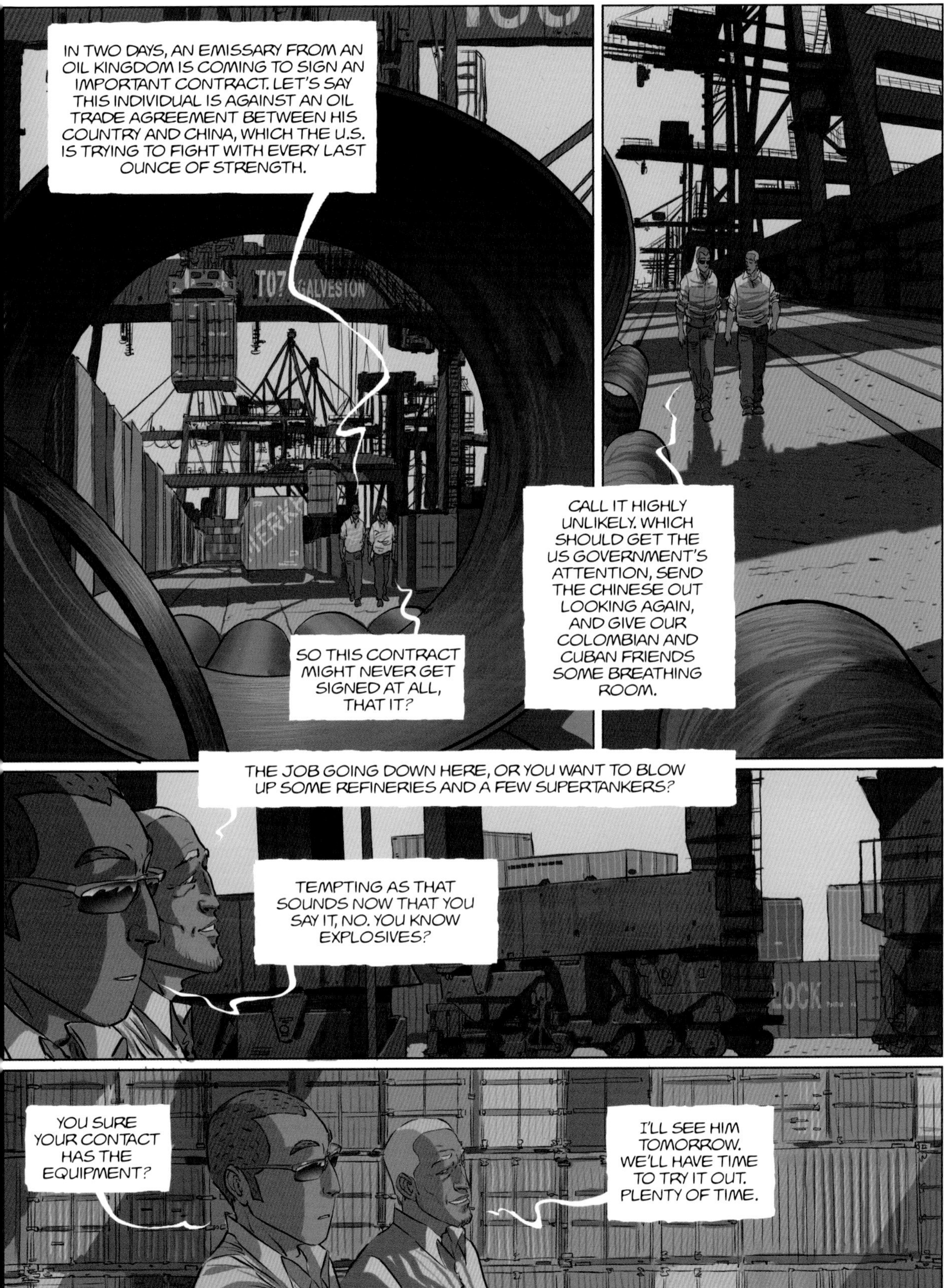
IN TWO DAYS, AN EMISSARY FROM AN OIL KINGDOM IS COMING TO SIGN AN IMPORTANT CONTRACT. LET'S SAY THIS INDIVIDUAL IS AGAINST AN OIL TRADE AGREEMENT BETWEEN HIS COUNTRY AND CHINA, WHICH THE U.S. IS TRYING TO FIGHT WITH EVERY LAST OUNCE OF STRENGTH.
T07 GALVESTON
SO THIS CONTRACT MIGHT NEVER GET SIGNED AT ALL, THAT IT?
CALL IT HIGHLY UNLIKELY. WHICH SHOULD GET THE US GOVERNMENT'S ATTENTION, SEND THE CHINESE OUT LOOKING AGAIN, AND GIVE OUR COLOMBIAN AND CUBAN FRIENDS SOME BREATHING ROOM.
THE JOB GOING DOWN HERE, OR YOU WANT TO BLOW UP SOME REFINERIES AND A FEW SUPERTANKERS?
TEMPTING AS THAT SOUNDS NOW THAT YOU SAY IT, NO. YOU KNOW EXPLOSIVES?
YOU SURE YOUR CONTACT HAS THE EQUIPMENT?
I'LL SEE HIM TOMORROW. WE'LL HAVE TIME TO TRY IT OUT. PLENTY OF TIME.

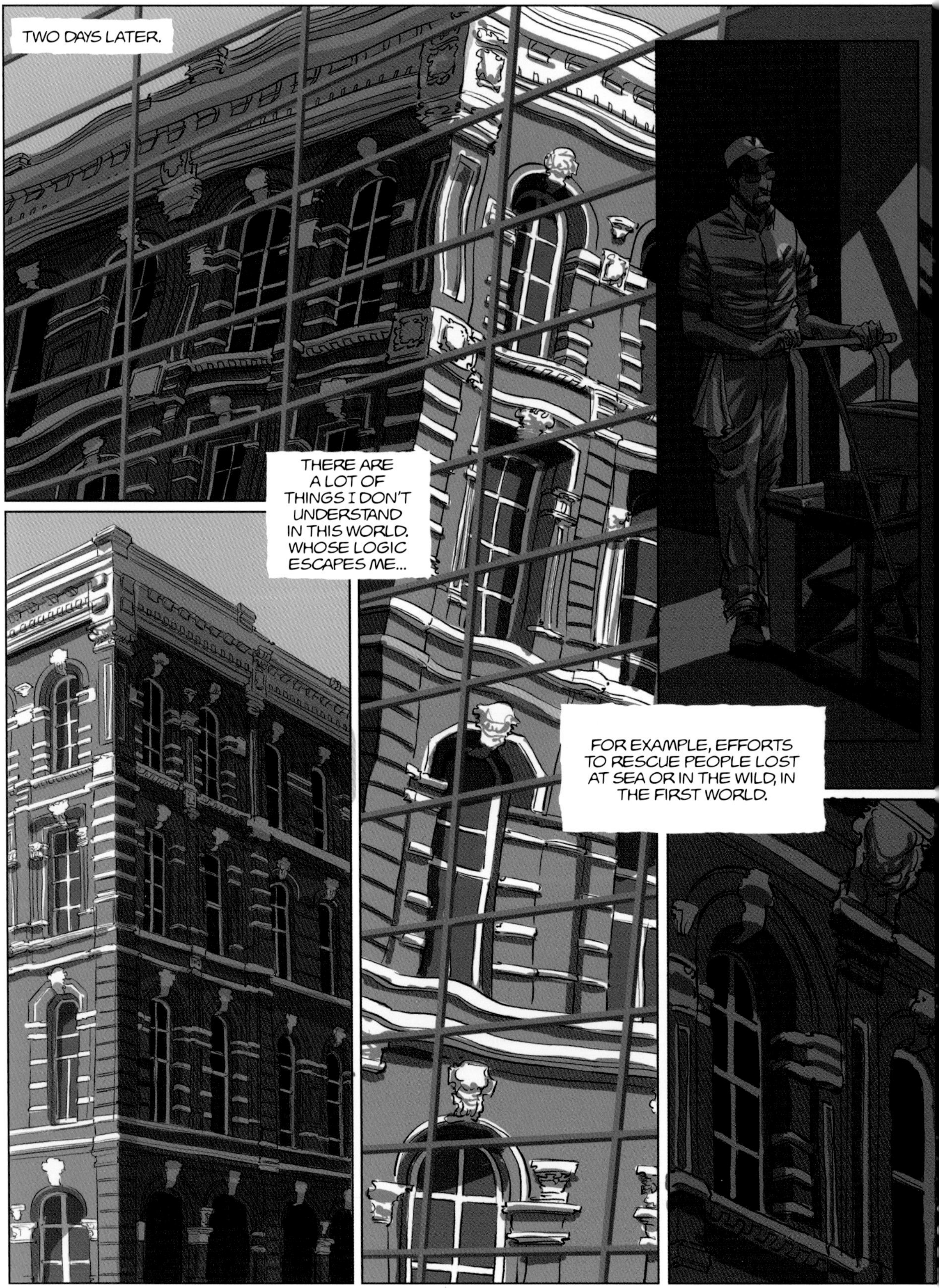
TWO DAYS LATER.
THERE ARE A LOT OF THINGS I DON'T UNDERSTAND IN THIS WORLD. WHOSE LOGIC ESCAPES ME...
FOR EXAMPLE, EFFORTS TO RESCUE PEOPLE LOST AT SEA OR IN THE WILD, IN THE FIRST WORLD.

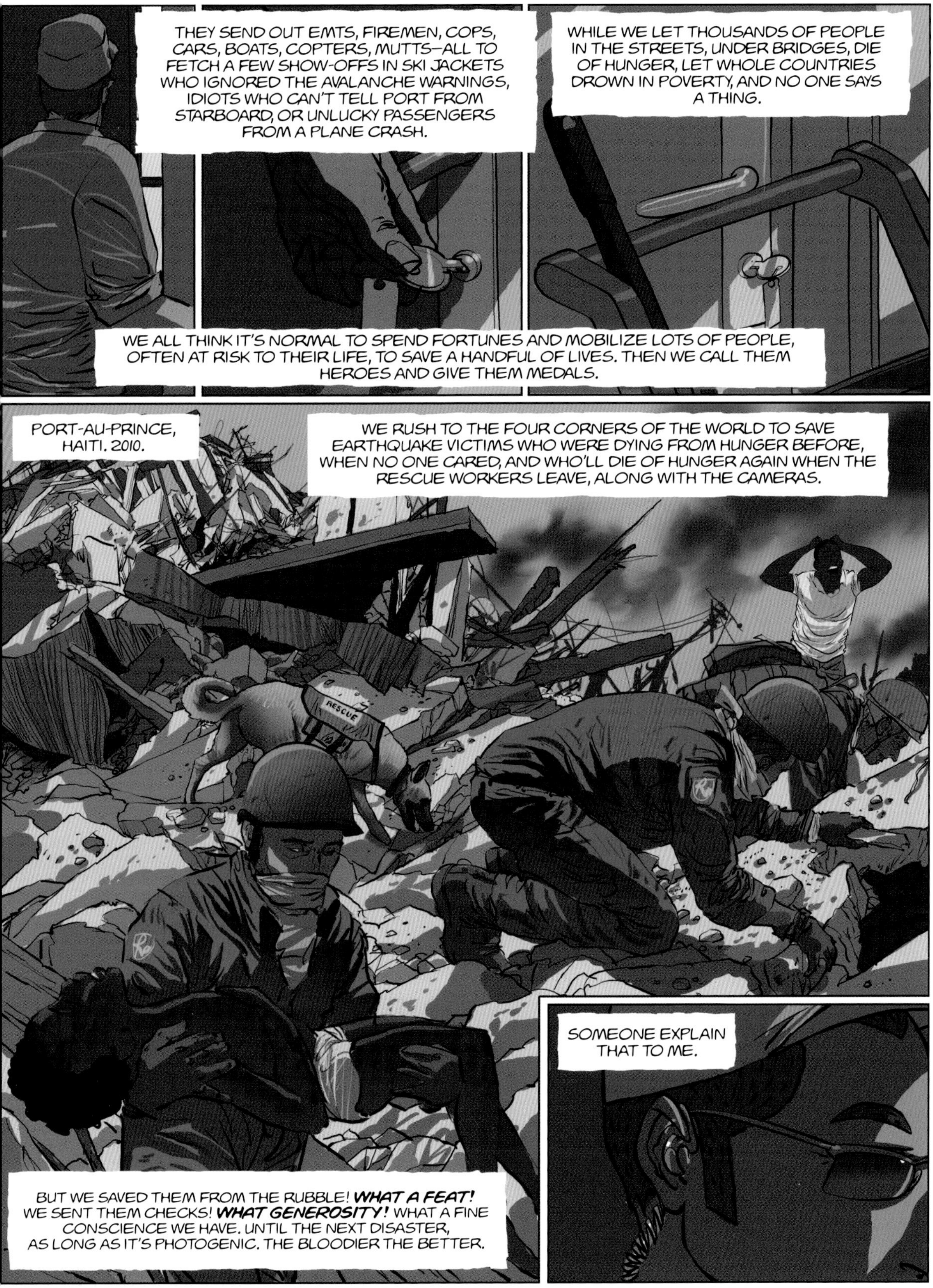
THEY SEND OUT EMTS, FIREMEN, COPS, CARS, BOATS, COPTERS, MUTTS—ALL TO FETCH A FEW SHOW-OFFS IN SKI JACKETS WHO IGNORED THE AVALANCHE WARNINGS, IDIOTS WHO CAN'T TELL PORT FROM STARBOARD, OR UNLUCKY PASSENGERS FROM A PLANE CRASH.
WHILE WE LET THOUSANDS OF PEOPLE IN THE STREETS, UNDER BRIDGES, DIE OF HUNGER, LET WHOLE COUNTRIES DROWN IN POVERTY, AND NO ONE SAYS A THING.
WE ALL THINK IT'S NORMAL TO SPEND FORTUNES AND MOBILIZE LOTS OF PEOPLE, OFTEN AT RISK TO THEIR LIFE, TO SAVE A HANDFUL OF LIVES. THEN WE CALL THEM HEROES AND GIVE THEM MEDALS.
PORT-AU-PRINCE, HAITI. 2010.
WE RUSH TO THE FOUR CORNERS OF THE WORLD TO SAVE EARTHQUAKE VICTIMS WHO WERE DYING FROM HUNGER BEFORE, WHEN NO ONE CARED, AND WHO'LL DIE OF HUNGER AGAIN WHEN THE RESCUE WORKERS LEAVE, ALONG WITH THE CAMERAS.
RESCUE
BUT WE SAVED THEM FROM THE RUBBLE! **WHAT A FEAT!** WE SENT THEM CHECKS! **WHAT GENEROSITY!** WHAT A FINE CONSCIENCE WE HAVE. UNTIL THE NEXT DISASTER, AS LONG AS IT'S PHOTOGENIC. THE BLOODIER THE BETTER.
SOMEONE EXPLAIN THAT TO ME.

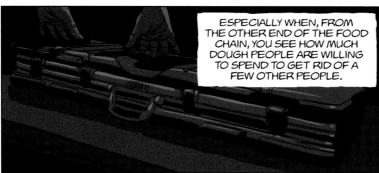

ESPECIALLY WHEN, FROM THE OTHER END OF THE FOOD CHAIN, YOU SEE HOW MUCH DOUGH PEOPLE ARE WILLING TO SPEND TO GET RID OF A FEW OTHER PEOPLE.

I WOULD KNOW.

I REALLY DO WONDER IF THERE'S ANY POINT TO LOOKING FOR SOME LOGIC IN HOW THINGS GO DOWN IN THIS WORLD, IN HUMAN BEHAVIOR.

ANOTHER THING THAT SURPRISES ME IS THAT THERE AREN'T MORE SUICIDES. SEEMS LIKE IT'S MOSTLY TEENAGERS. THE AGE OF LUCIDITY, APPARENTLY.

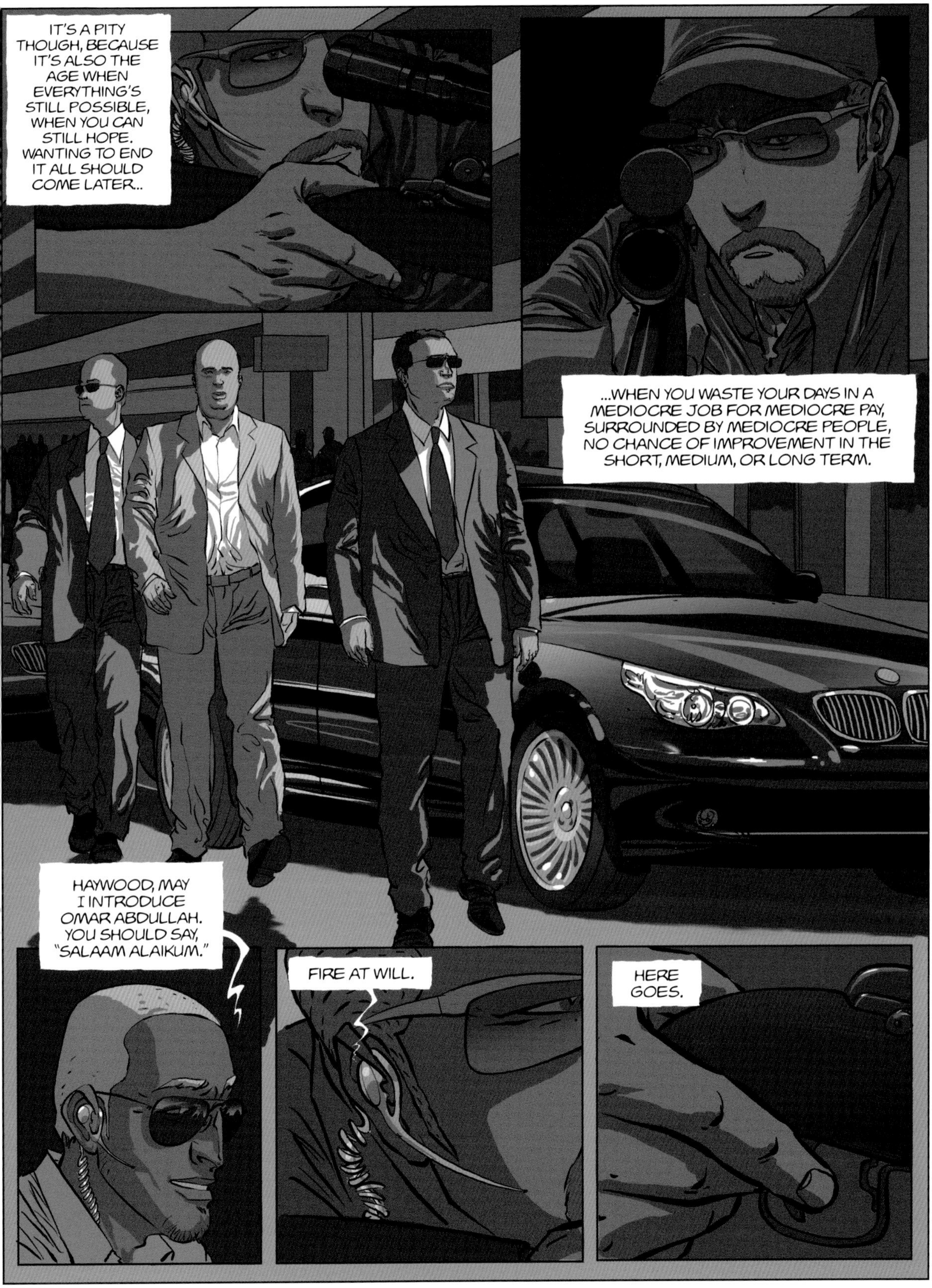
IT'S A PITY THOUGH, BECAUSE IT'S ALSO THE AGE WHEN EVERYTHING'S STILL POSSIBLE, WHEN YOU CAN STILL HOPE. WANTING TO END IT ALL SHOULD COME LATER...
...WHEN YOU WASTE YOUR DAYS IN A MEDIOCRE JOB FOR MEDIOCRE PAY, SURROUNDED BY MEDIOCRE PEOPLE, NO CHANCE OF IMPROVEMENT IN THE SHORT, MEDIUM, OR LONG TERM.
HAYWOOD, MAY I INTRODUCE OMAR ABDULLAH. YOU SHOULD SAY, "SALAAM ALAIKUM."
FIRE AT WILL.
HERE GOES.

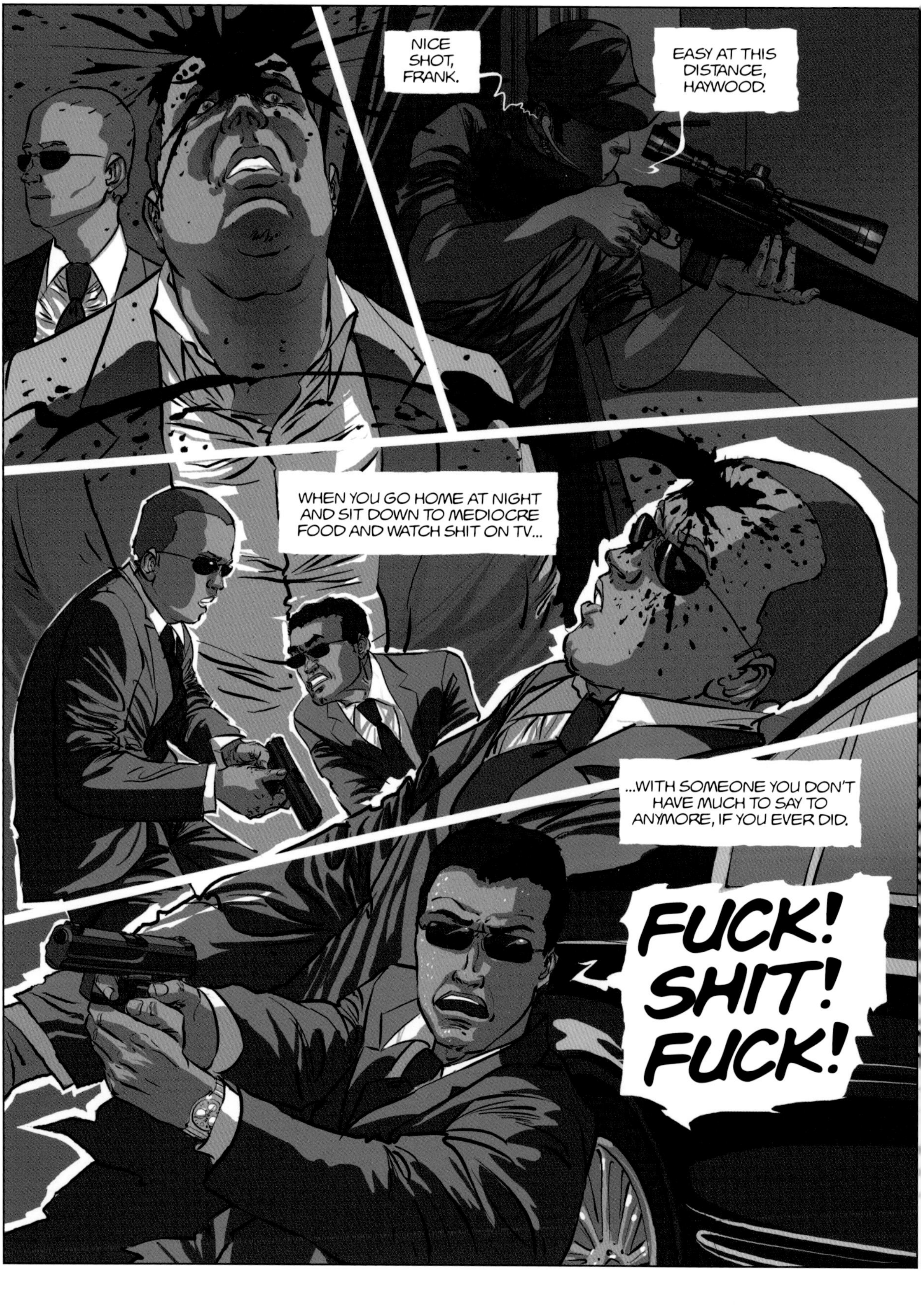
NICE SHOT, FRANK.
EASY AT THIS DISTANCE, HAYWOOD.
WHEN YOU GO HOME AT NIGHT AND SIT DOWN TO MEDIOCRE FOOD AND WATCH SHIT ON TV...
...WITH SOMEONE YOU DON'T HAVE MUCH TO SAY TO ANYMORE, IF YOU EVER DID.
FUCK! SHIT! FUCK!

AND YET, THE OLDER YOU GET, THE SHORTER LIFE SEEMS; THE MORE YOU HOPE IT LASTS, THE HARDER YOU HANG ON. BUT IF THAT'S HOW YOU'RE GOING TO LIVE, WHAT'S THE DIFFERENCE IF YOU DIE AT 90, 60, OR EVEN 40?

OF COURSE, THERE'S ALWAYS THAT NEW CAR, THE COUNTRY HOUSE, KIDS, THE LATEST FASHIONABLE GADGET FOR LISTENING TO TUNES OR WATCHING FLICKS...

... ANOTHER CORNER OF THE WORLD TO TOUR, WHERE YOU CAN TAKE MEDIOCRE PHOTOS WITH A CAMERA. THE MONEY YOU PAID FOR IT COULD SUPPORT A THIRD WORLD FAMILY FOR WEEKS.

YOU PUT THE PHOTOS ONLINE TO SHOW OFF TO YOUR FRIENDS.

OR YOU SLAVE AWAY ON A BLOG THAT, WITH IMPRECISE LANGUAGE AND DEFICIENT SPELLING, DOCUMENTS YOUR LITTLE ADVENTURES— ANECDOTES MEANT TO BE CUTE AND MOVING—BUT WHICH ARE MORE OR LESS **BORING**, CONVINCED AS YOU ARE THAT THE NET'S A BASIC NEED AND FUNDAMENTAL HUMAN RIGHT.

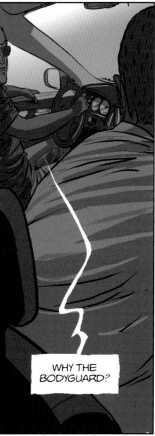

WHY THE BODYGUARD?

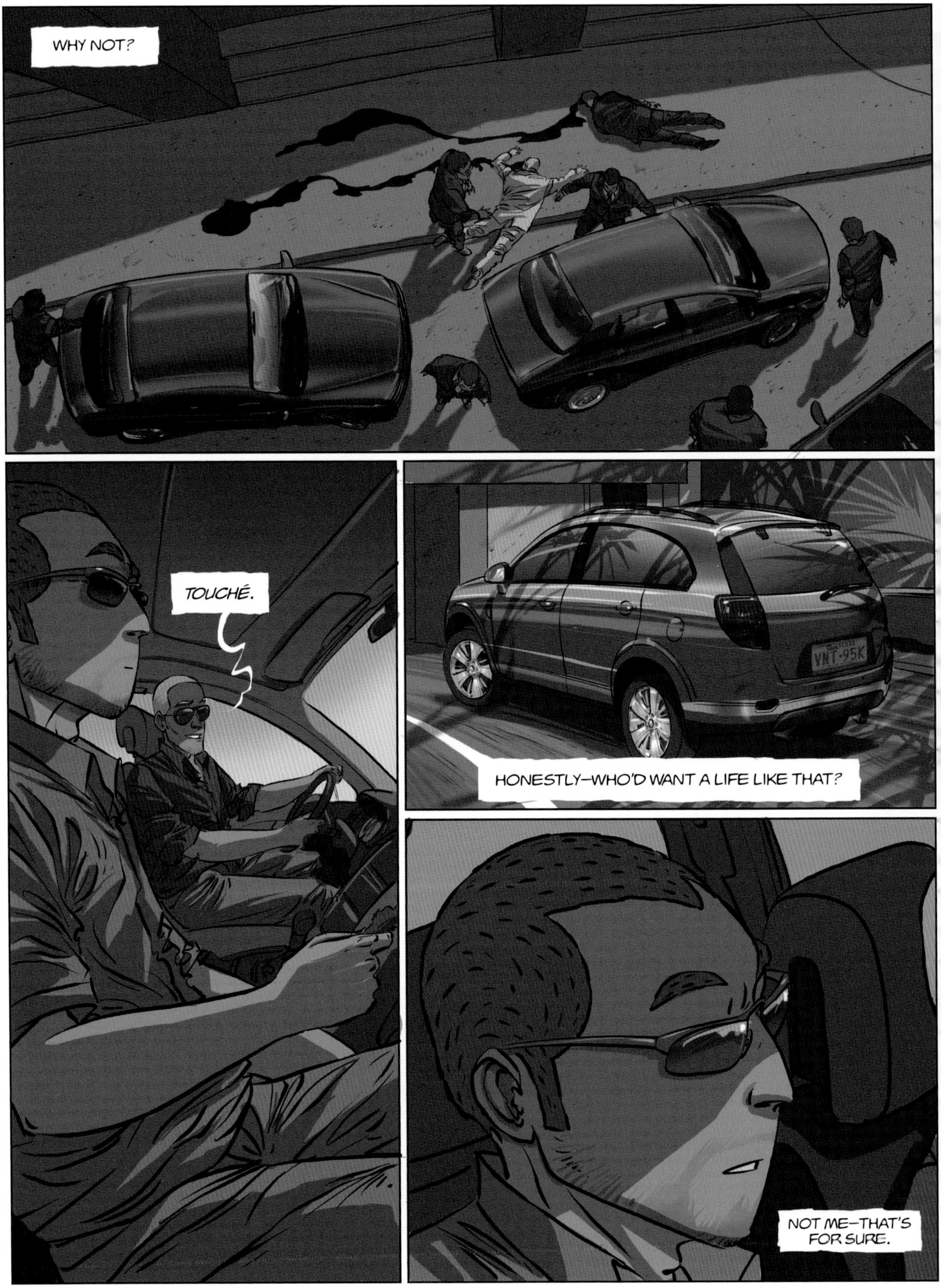
WHY NOT?
TOUCHÉ.
HONESTLY—WHO'D WANT A LIFE LIKE THAT?
NOT ME—THAT'S FOR SURE.

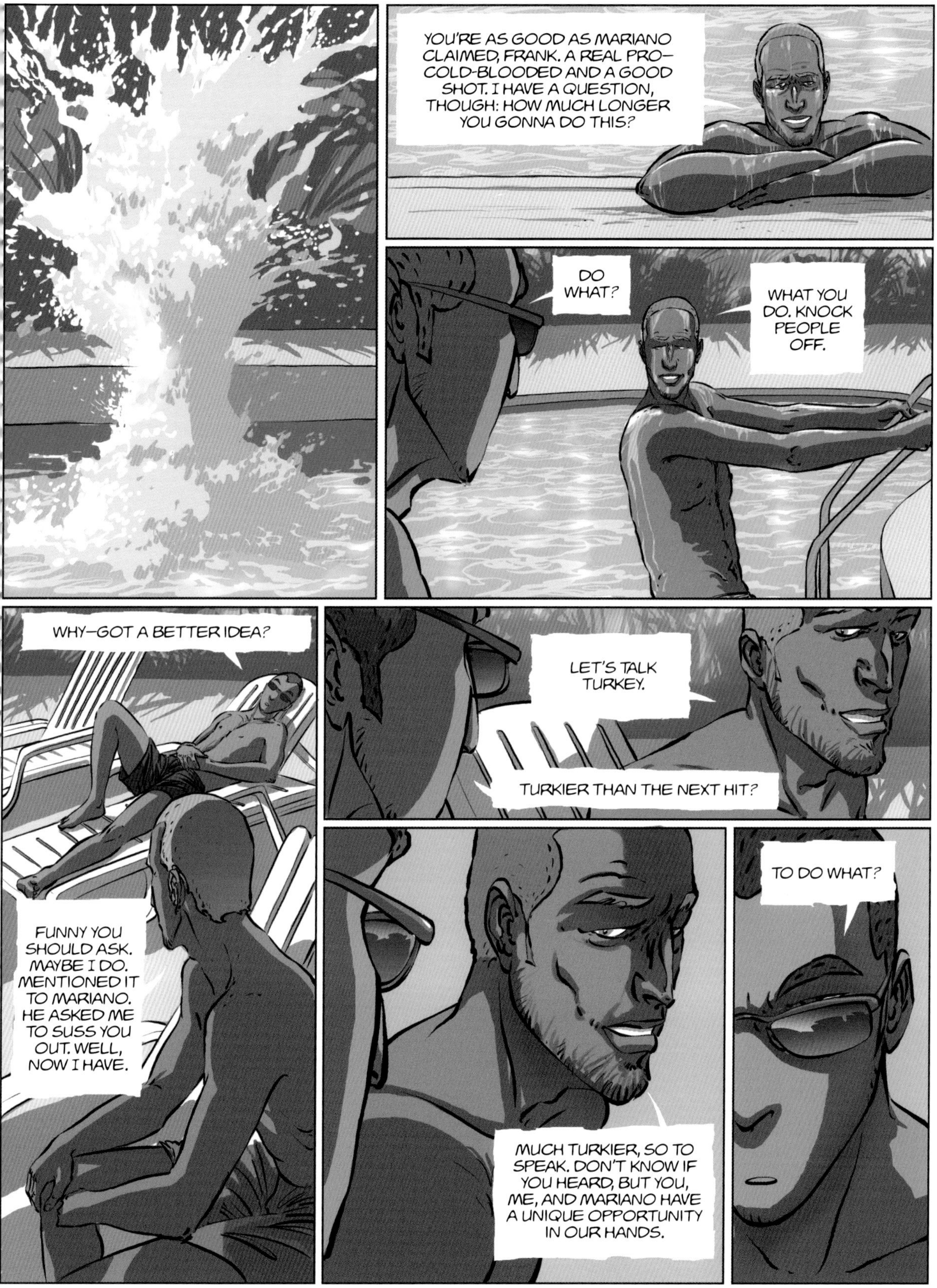
YOU'RE AS GOOD AS MARIANO CLAIMED, FRANK. A REAL PRO—COLD-BLOODED AND A GOOD SHOT. I HAVE A QUESTION, THOUGH: HOW MUCH LONGER YOU GONNA DO THIS?
DO WHAT?
WHAT YOU DO. KNOCK PEOPLE OFF.
WHY—GOT A BETTER IDEA?
FUNNY YOU SHOULD ASK. MAYBE I DO. MENTIONED IT TO MARIANO. HE ASKED ME TO SUSS YOU OUT. WELL, NOW I HAVE.
LET'S TALK TURKEY.
TURKIER THAN THE NEXT HIT?
MUCH TURKIER, SO TO SPEAK. DON'T KNOW IF YOU HEARD, BUT YOU, ME, AND MARIANO HAVE A UNIQUE OPPORTUNITY IN OUR HANDS.
TO DO WHAT?

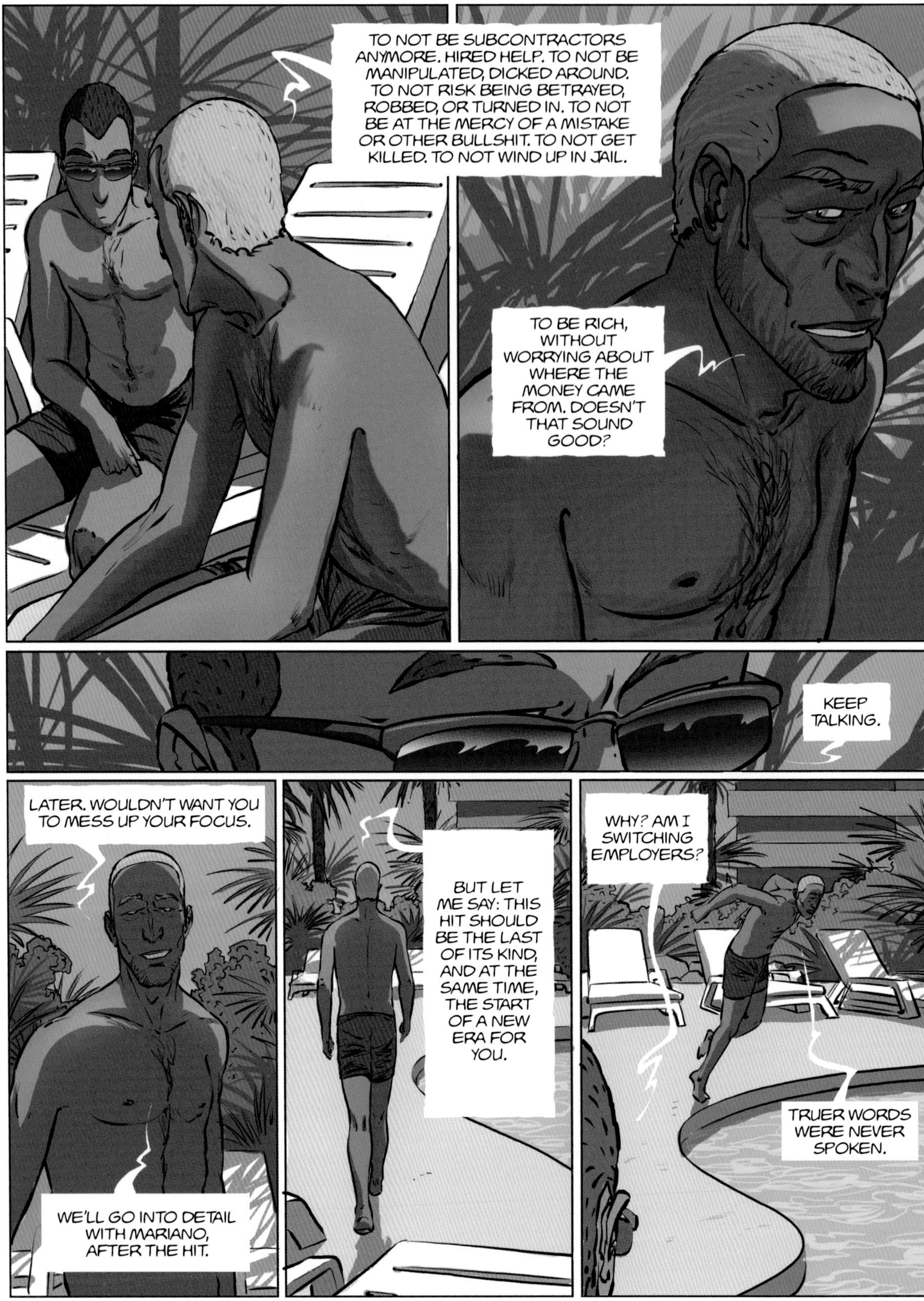
TO NOT BE SUBCONTRACTORS ANYMORE. HIRED HELP. TO NOT BE MANIPULATED, DICKED AROUND. TO NOT RISK BEING BETRAYED, ROBBED, OR TURNED IN. TO NOT BE AT THE MERCY OF A MISTAKE OR OTHER BULLSHIT. TO NOT GET KILLED. TO NOT WIND UP IN JAIL.
TO BE RICH, WITHOUT WORRYING ABOUT WHERE THE MONEY CAME FROM. DOESN'T THAT SOUND GOOD?
KEEP TALKING.
LATER. WOULDN'T WANT YOU TO MESS UP YOUR FOCUS.
WE'LL GO INTO DETAIL WITH MARIANO, AFTER THE HIT.
BUT LET ME SAY: THIS HIT SHOULD BE THE LAST OF ITS KIND, AND AT THE SAME TIME, THE START OF A NEW ERA FOR YOU.
WHY? AM I SWITCHING EMPLOYERS?
TRUER WORDS WERE NEVER SPOKEN.

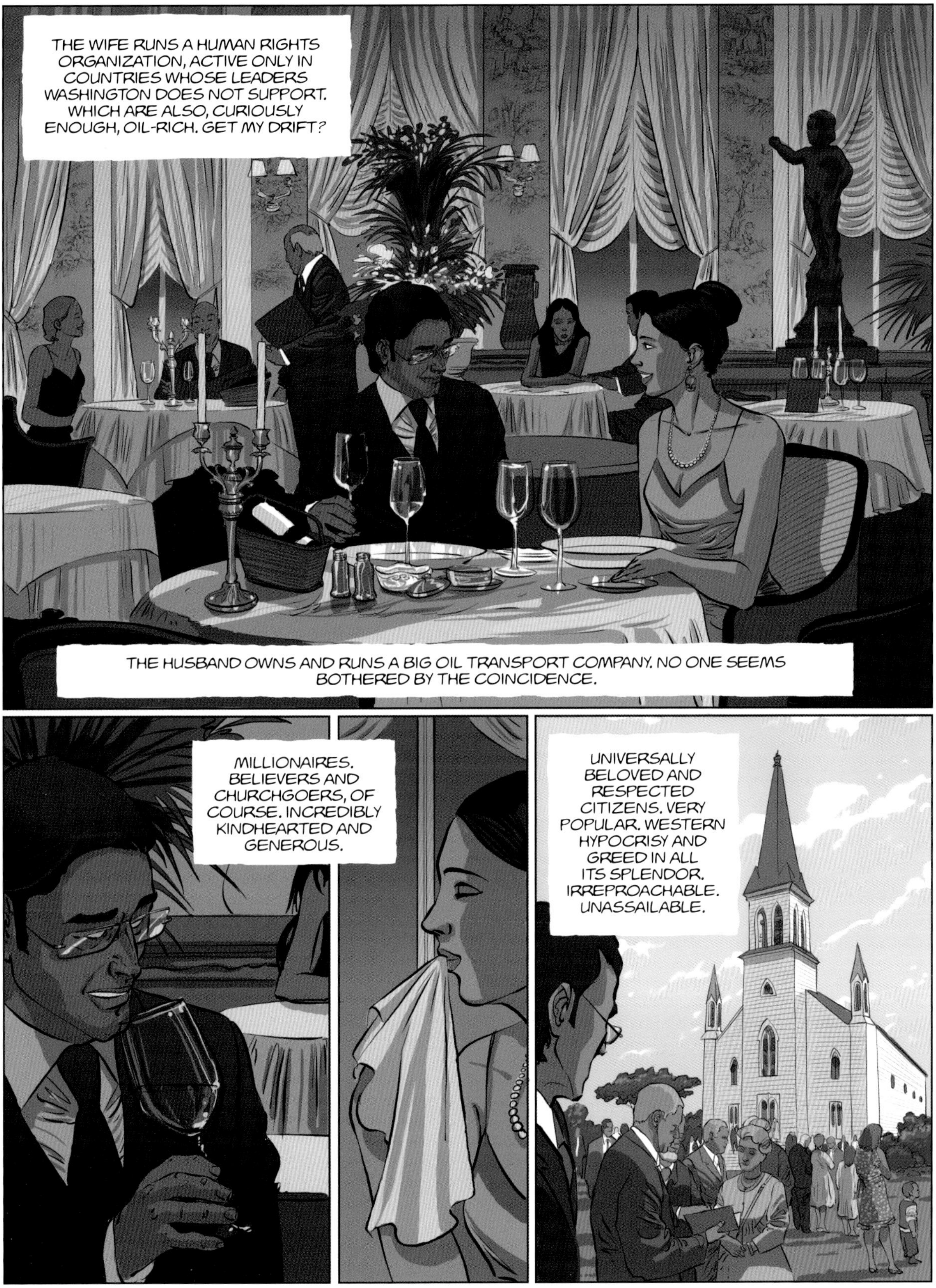
THE WIFE RUNS A HUMAN RIGHTS ORGANIZATION, ACTIVE ONLY IN COUNTRIES WHOSE LEADERS WASHINGTON DOES NOT SUPPORT. WHICH ARE ALSO, CURIOUSLY ENOUGH, OIL-RICH. GET MY DRIFT?
THE HUSBAND OWNS AND RUNS A BIG OIL TRANSPORT COMPANY. NO ONE SEEMS BOTHERED BY THE COINCIDENCE.
MILLIONAIRES. BELIEVERS AND CHURCHGOERS, OF COURSE. INCREDIBLY KINDHEARTED AND GENEROUS.
UNIVERSALLY BELOVED AND RESPECTED CITIZENS. VERY POPULAR. WESTERN HYPOCRISY AND GREED IN ALL ITS SPLENDOR. IRREPROACHABLE. UNASSAILABLE.

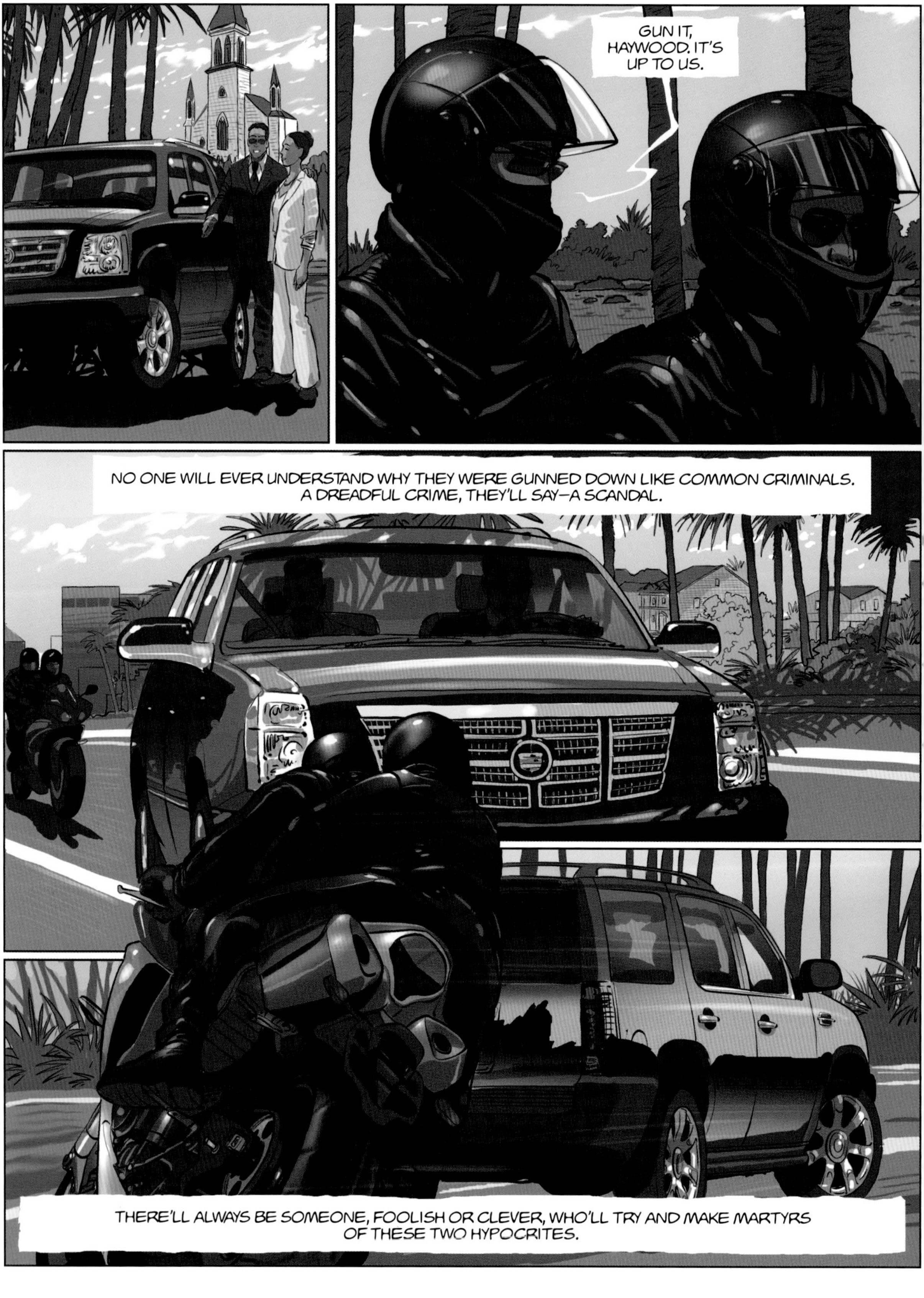
GUN IT, HAYWOOD. IT'S UP TO US.
NO ONE WILL EVER UNDERSTAND WHY THEY WERE GUNNED DOWN LIKE COMMON CRIMINALS. A DREADFUL CRIME, THEY'LL SAY—A SCANDAL.
THERE'LL ALWAYS BE SOMEONE, FOOLISH OR CLEVER, WHO'LL TRY AND MAKE MARTYRS OF THESE TWO HYPOCRITES.

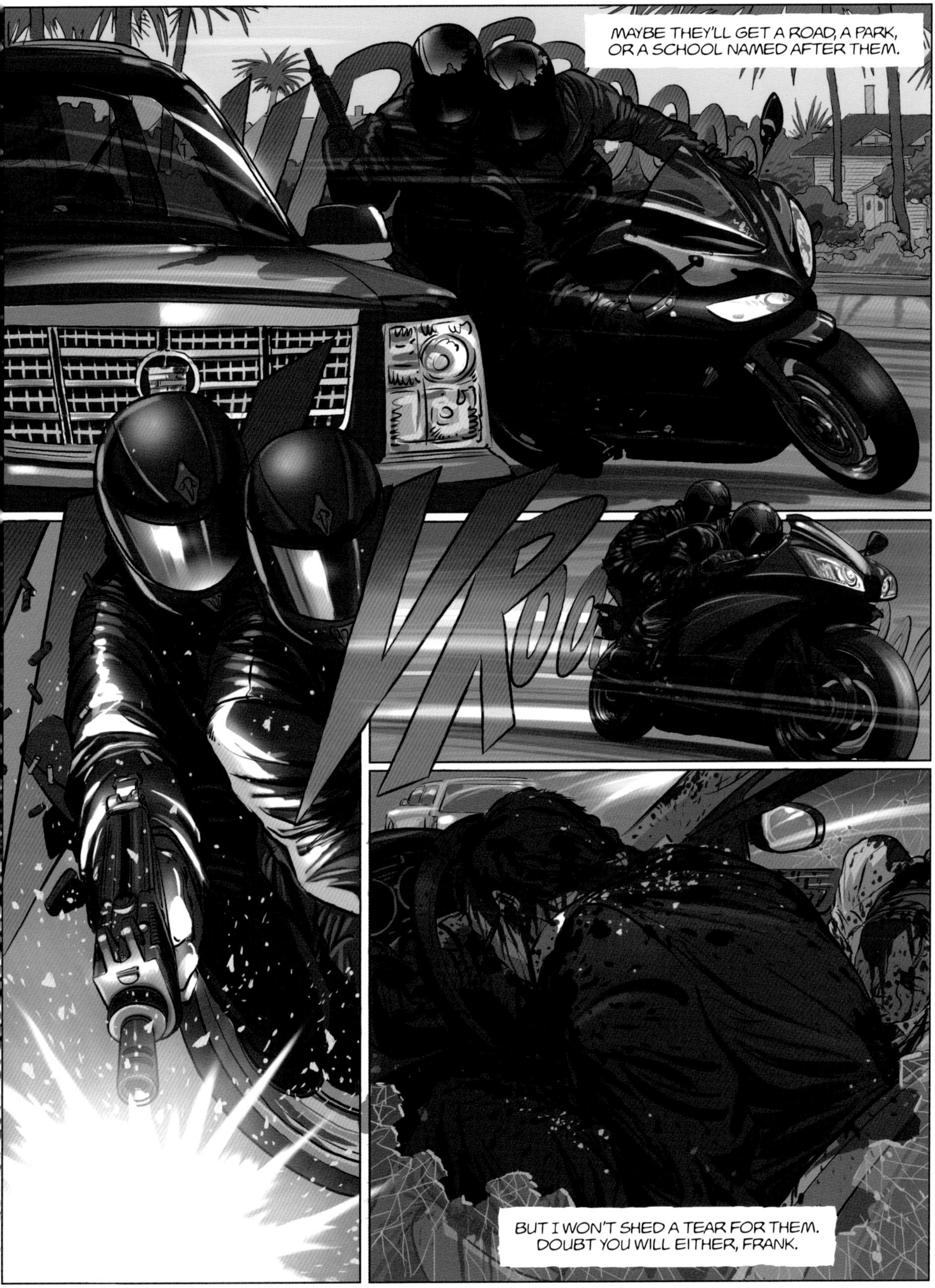
MAYBE THEY'LL GET A ROAD, A PARK, OR A SCHOOL NAMED AFTER THEM.
BUT I WON'T SHED A TEAR FOR THEM. DOUBT YOU WILL EITHER, FRANK.

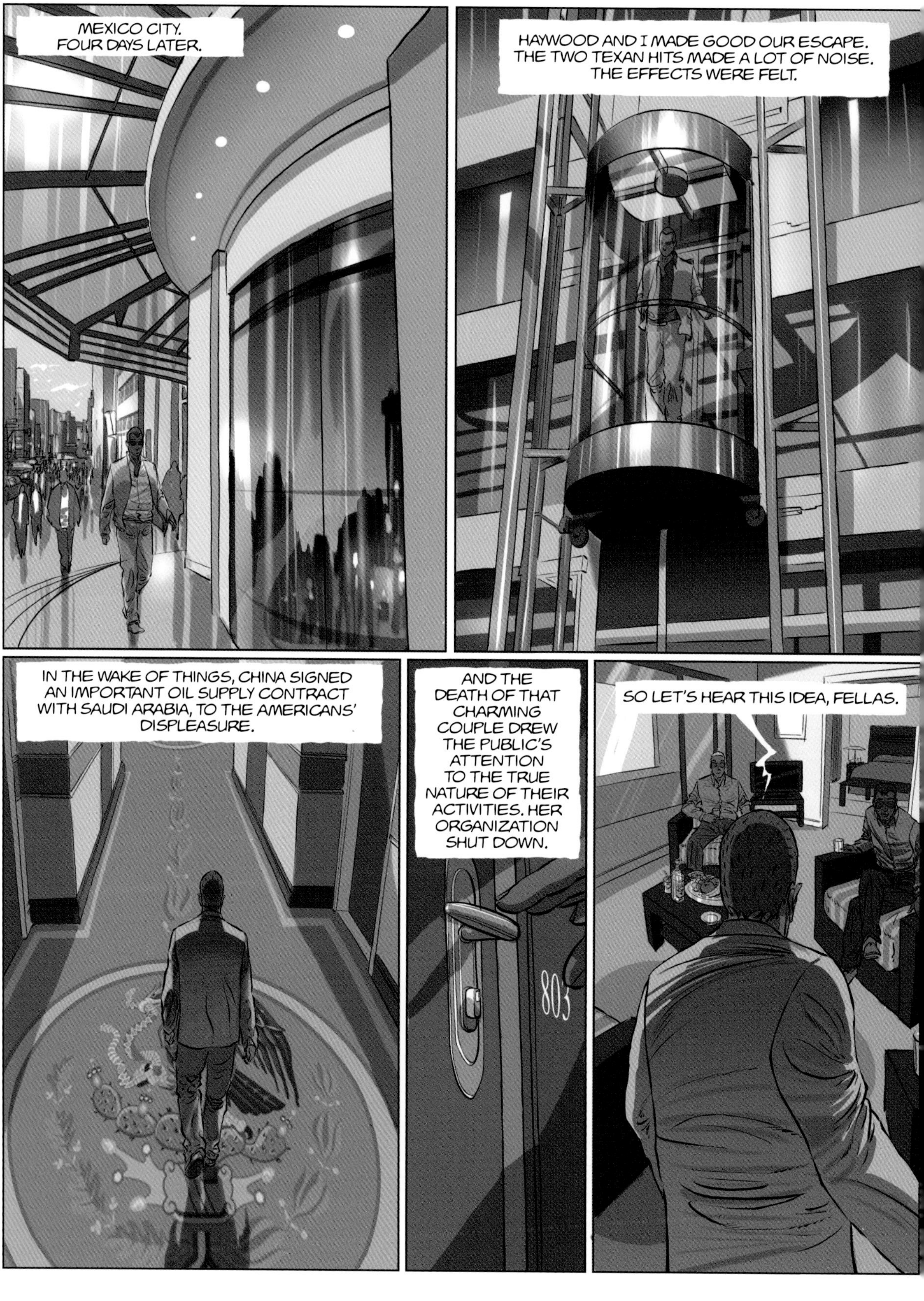
MEXICO CITY.
FOUR DAYS LATER.
HAYWOOD AND I MADE GOOD OUR ESCAPE. THE TWO TEXAN HITS MADE A LOT OF NOISE. THE EFFECTS WERE FELT.
IN THE WAKE OF THINGS, CHINA SIGNED AN IMPORTANT OIL SUPPLY CONTRACT WITH SAUDI ARABIA, TO THE AMERICANS' DISPLEASURE.
AND THE DEATH OF THAT CHARMING COUPLE DREW THE PUBLIC'S ATTENTION TO THE TRUE NATURE OF THEIR ACTIVITIES. HER ORGANIZATION SHUT DOWN.
803
SO LET'S HEAR THIS IDEA, FELLAS.

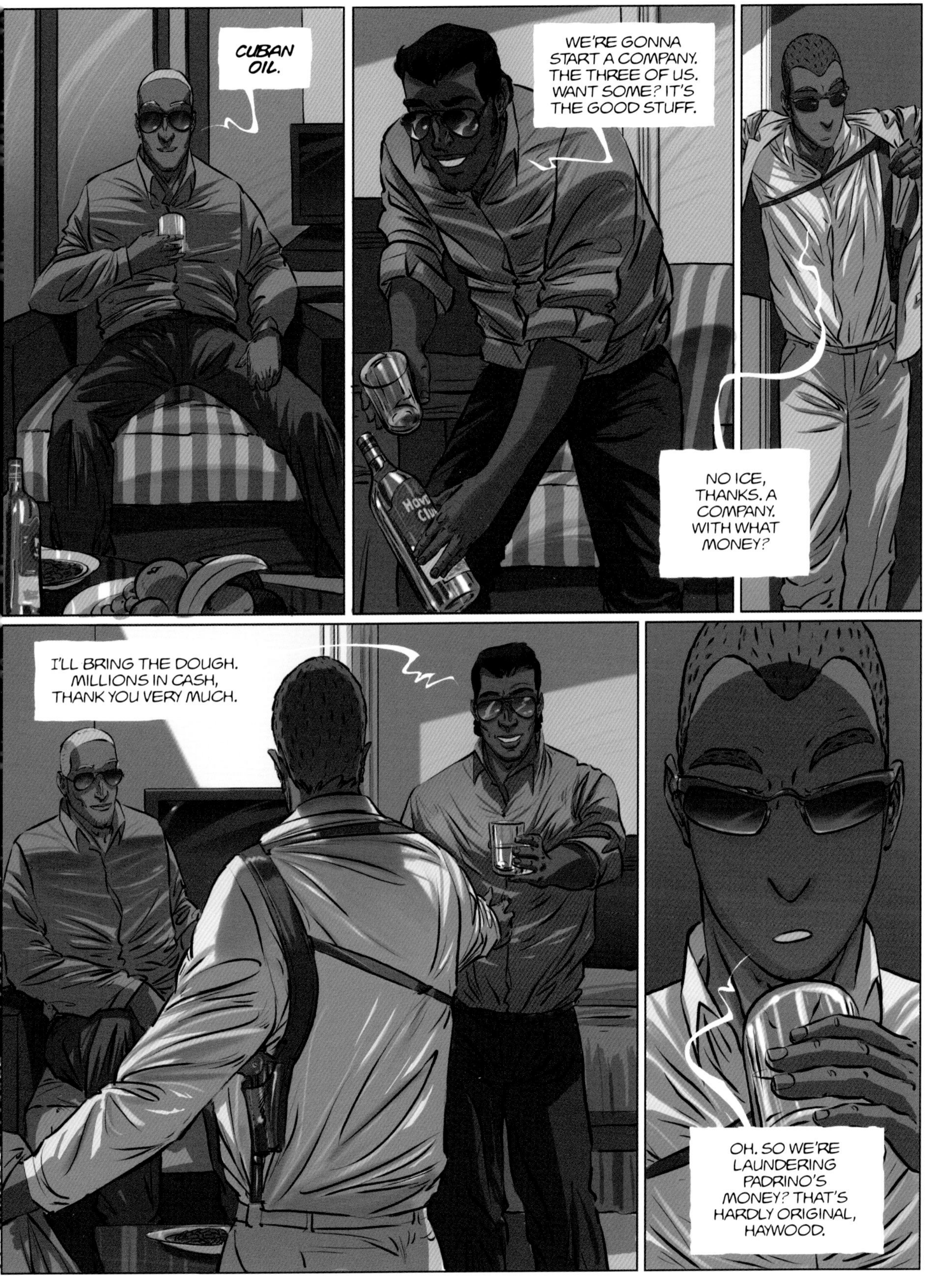
CUBAN OIL.
WE'RE GONNA START A COMPANY. THE THREE OF US. WANT SOME? IT'S THE GOOD STUFF.
NO ICE, THANKS. A COMPANY. WITH WHAT MONEY?
I'LL BRING THE DOUGH. MILLIONS IN CASH, THANK YOU VERY MUCH.
OH. SO WE'RE LAUNDERING PADRINO'S MONEY? THAT'S HARDLY ORIGINAL, HAYWOOD.

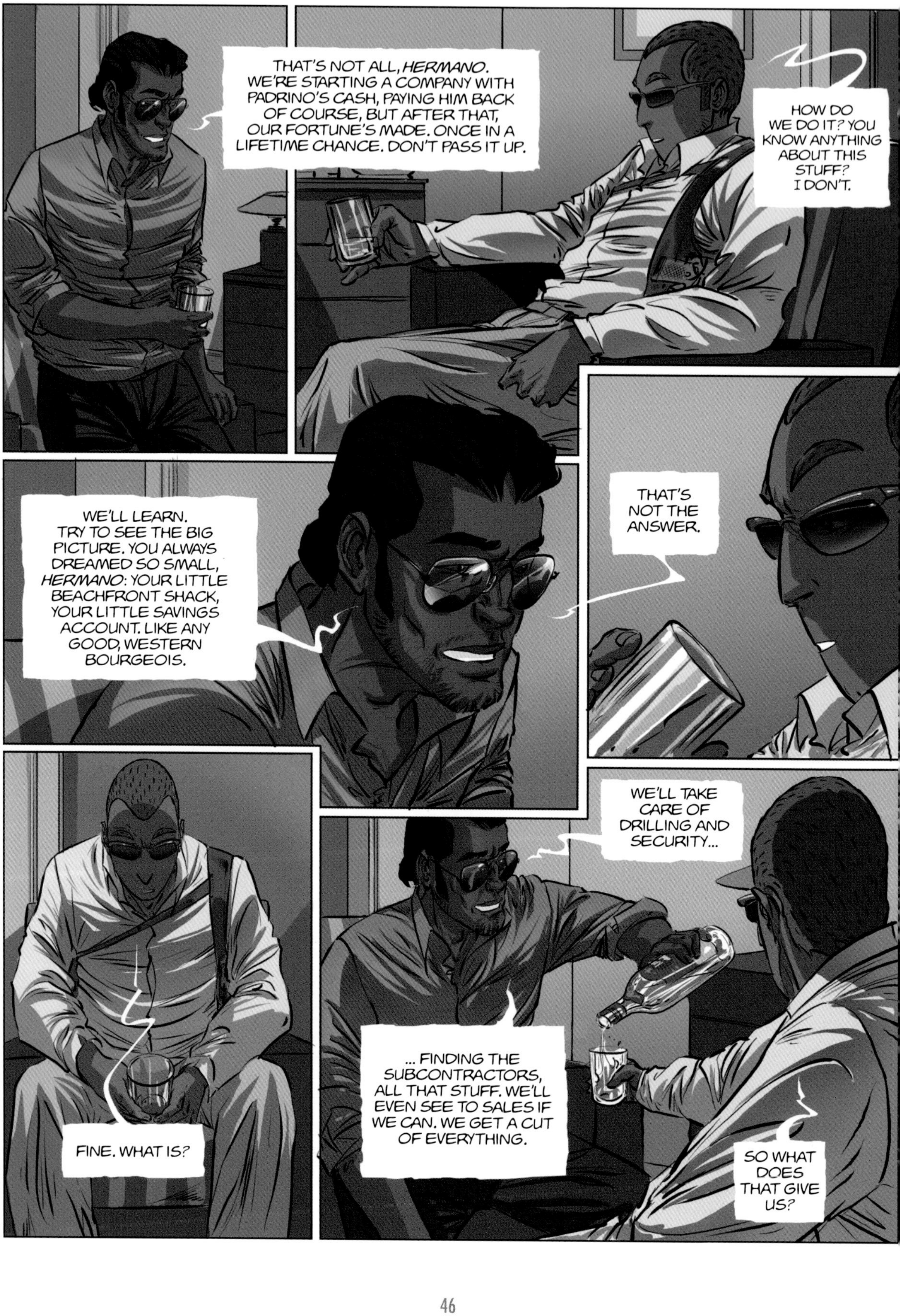
THAT'S NOT ALL, *HERMANO*. WE'RE STARTING A COMPANY WITH PADRINO'S CASH, PAYING HIM BACK OF COURSE, BUT AFTER THAT, OUR FORTUNE'S MADE. ONCE IN A LIFETIME CHANCE. DON'T PASS IT UP.
HOW DO WE DO IT? YOU KNOW ANYTHING ABOUT THIS STUFF? I DON'T.
WE'LL LEARN. TRY TO SEE THE BIG PICTURE. YOU ALWAYS DREAMED SO SMALL, *HERMANO*: YOUR LITTLE BEACHFRONT SHACK, YOUR LITTLE SAVINGS ACCOUNT. LIKE ANY GOOD, WESTERN BOURGEOIS.
THAT'S NOT THE ANSWER.
FINE. WHAT IS?
WE'LL TAKE CARE OF DRILLING AND SECURITY...
... FINDING THE SUBCONTRACTORS, ALL THAT STUFF. WE'LL EVEN SEE TO SALES IF WE CAN. WE GET A CUT OF EVERYTHING.
SO WHAT DOES THAT GIVE US?

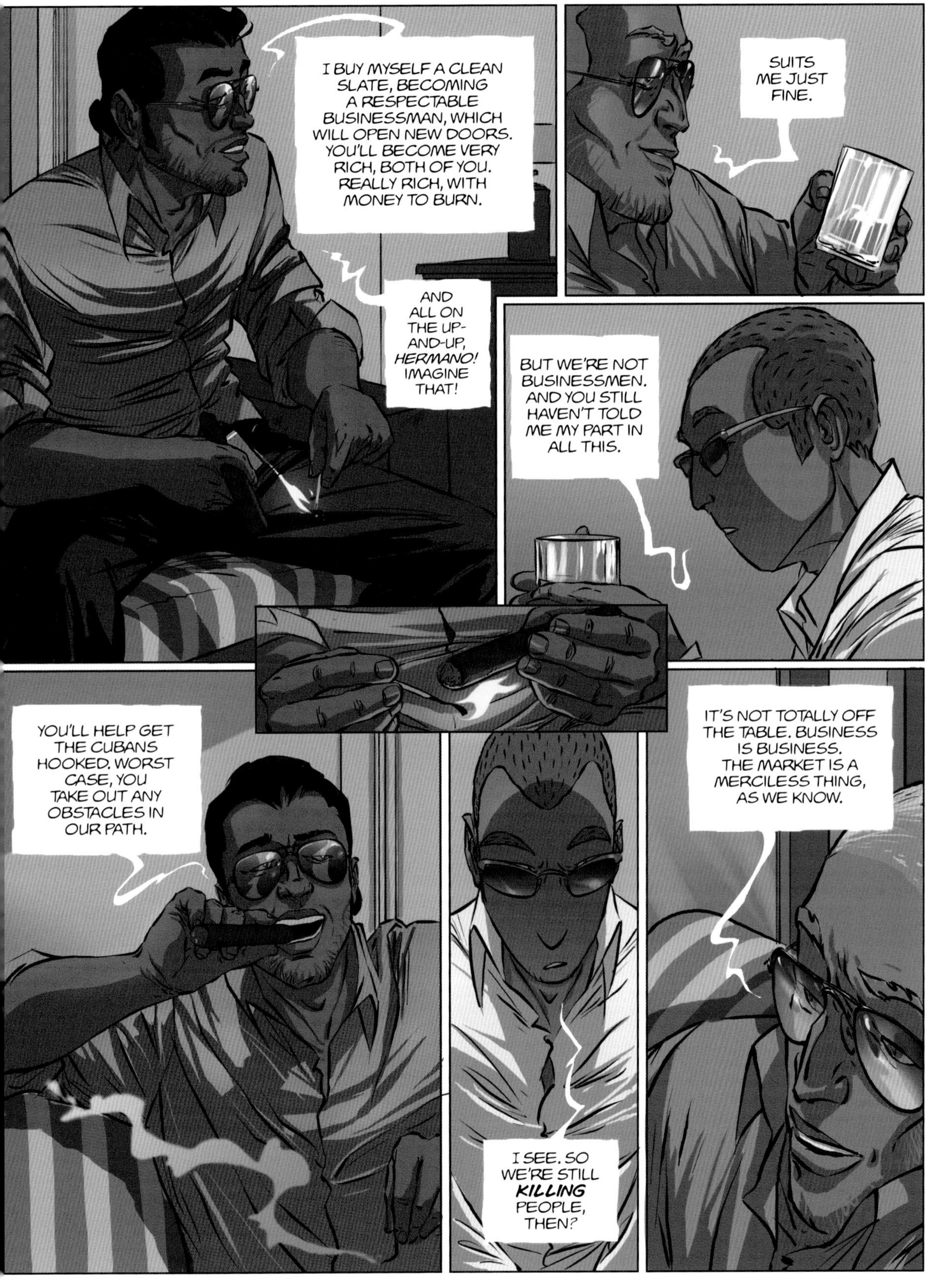
I BUY MYSELF A CLEAN SLATE, BECOMING A RESPECTABLE BUSINESSMAN, WHICH WILL OPEN NEW DOORS. YOU'LL BECOME VERY RICH, BOTH OF YOU. REALLY RICH, WITH MONEY TO BURN.
SUITS ME JUST FINE.
AND ALL ON THE UP-AND-UP, *HERMANO!* IMAGINE THAT!
BUT WE'RE NOT BUSINESSMEN. AND YOU STILL HAVEN'T TOLD ME MY PART IN ALL THIS.
YOU'LL HELP GET THE CUBANS HOOKED. WORST CASE, YOU TAKE OUT ANY OBSTACLES IN OUR PATH.
I SEE. SO WE'RE STILL ***KILLING*** PEOPLE, THEN?
IT'S NOT TOTALLY OFF THE TABLE. BUSINESS IS BUSINESS. THE MARKET IS A MERCILESS THING, AS WE KNOW.

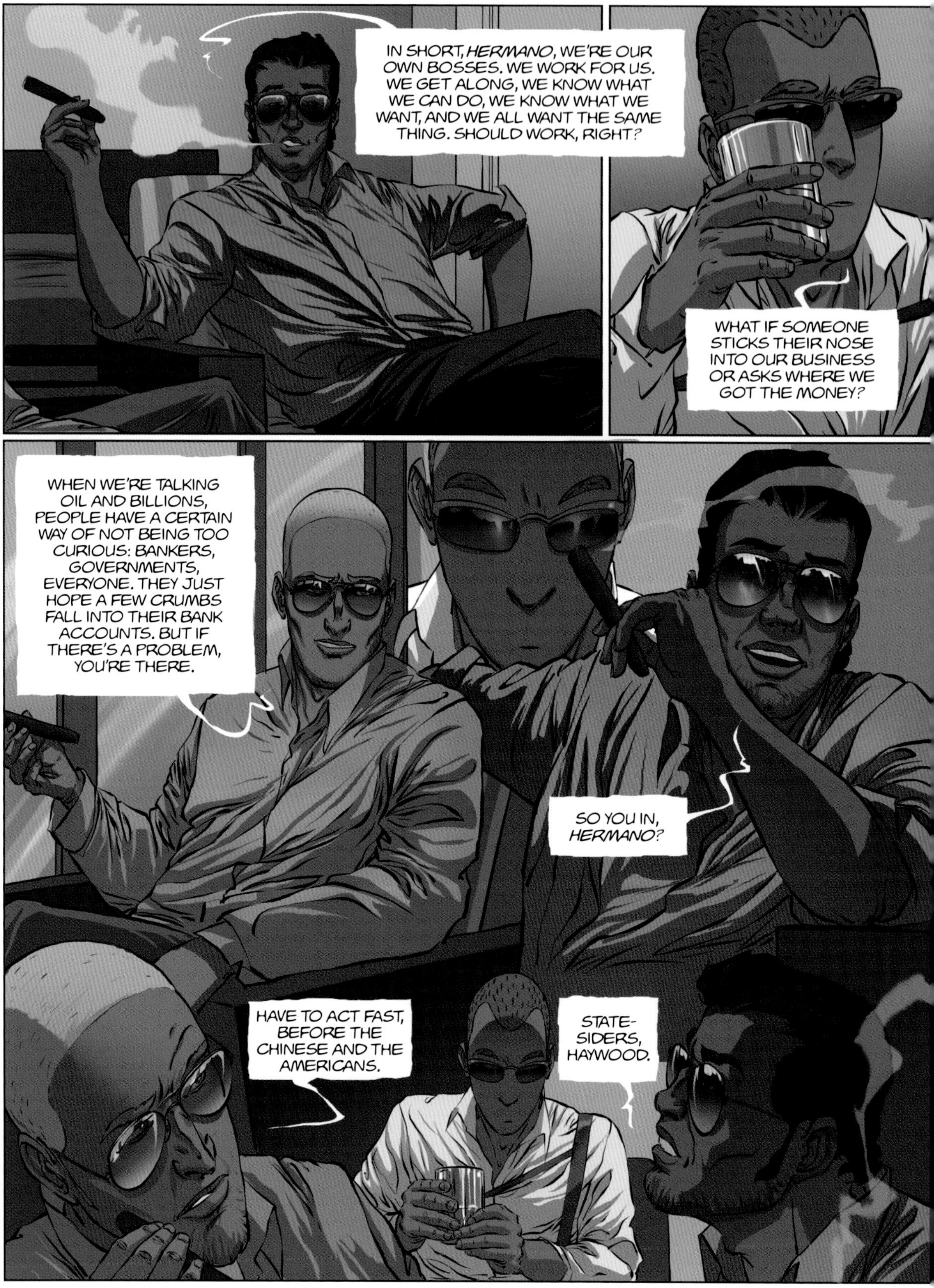
IN SHORT, *HERMANO*, WE'RE OUR OWN BOSSES. WE WORK FOR US. WE GET ALONG, WE KNOW WHAT WE CAN DO, WE KNOW WHAT WE WANT, AND WE ALL WANT THE SAME THING. SHOULD WORK, RIGHT?
WHAT IF SOMEONE STICKS THEIR NOSE INTO OUR BUSINESS OR ASKS WHERE WE GOT THE MONEY?
WHEN WE'RE TALKING OIL AND BILLIONS, PEOPLE HAVE A CERTAIN WAY OF NOT BEING TOO CURIOUS: BANKERS, GOVERNMENTS, EVERYONE. THEY JUST HOPE A FEW CRUMBS FALL INTO THEIR BANK ACCOUNTS. BUT IF THERE'S A PROBLEM, YOU'RE THERE.
SO YOU IN, *HERMANO*?
HAVE TO ACT FAST, BEFORE THE CHINESE AND THE AMERICANS.
STATE-SIDERS, HAYWOOD.

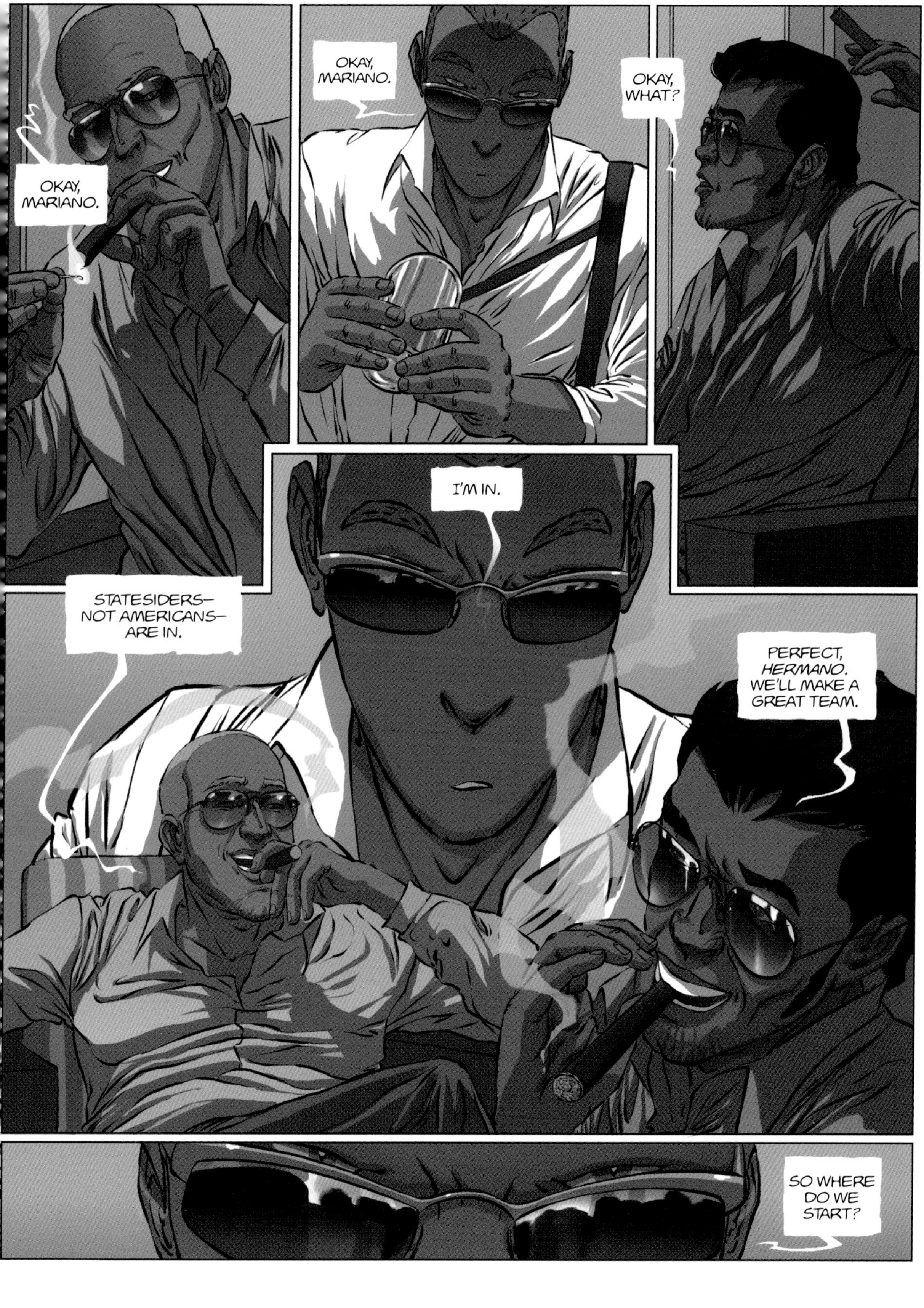
OKAY, MARIANO.
OKAY, MARIANO.
OKAY, WHAT?
I'M IN.
STATESIDERS— NOT AMERICANS— ARE IN.
PERFECT, *HERMANO.* WE'LL MAKE A GREAT TEAM.
SO WHERE DO WE START?

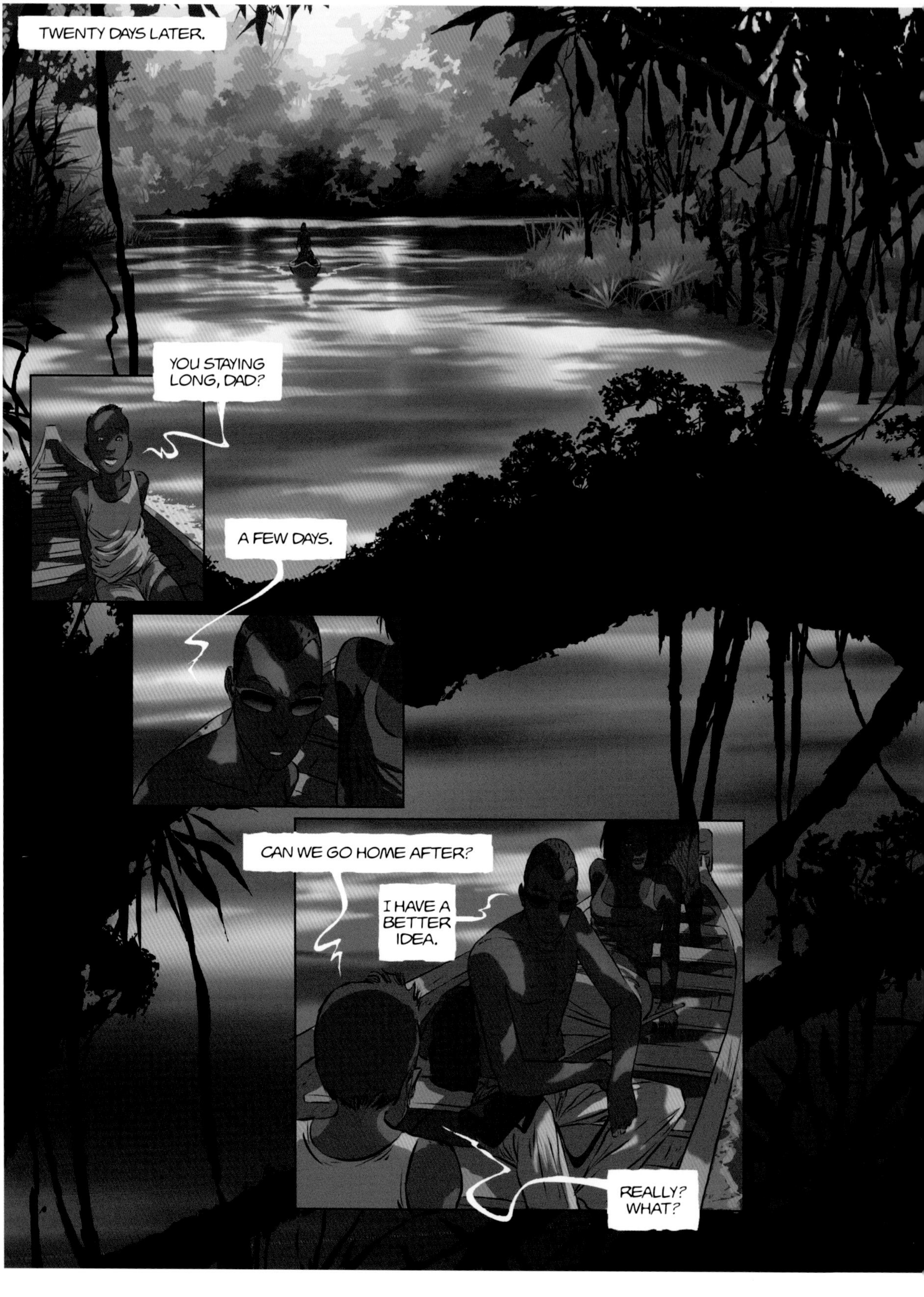
TWENTY DAYS LATER.
YOU STAYING LONG, DAD?
A FEW DAYS.
CAN WE GO HOME AFTER?
I HAVE A BETTER IDEA.
REALLY? WHAT?

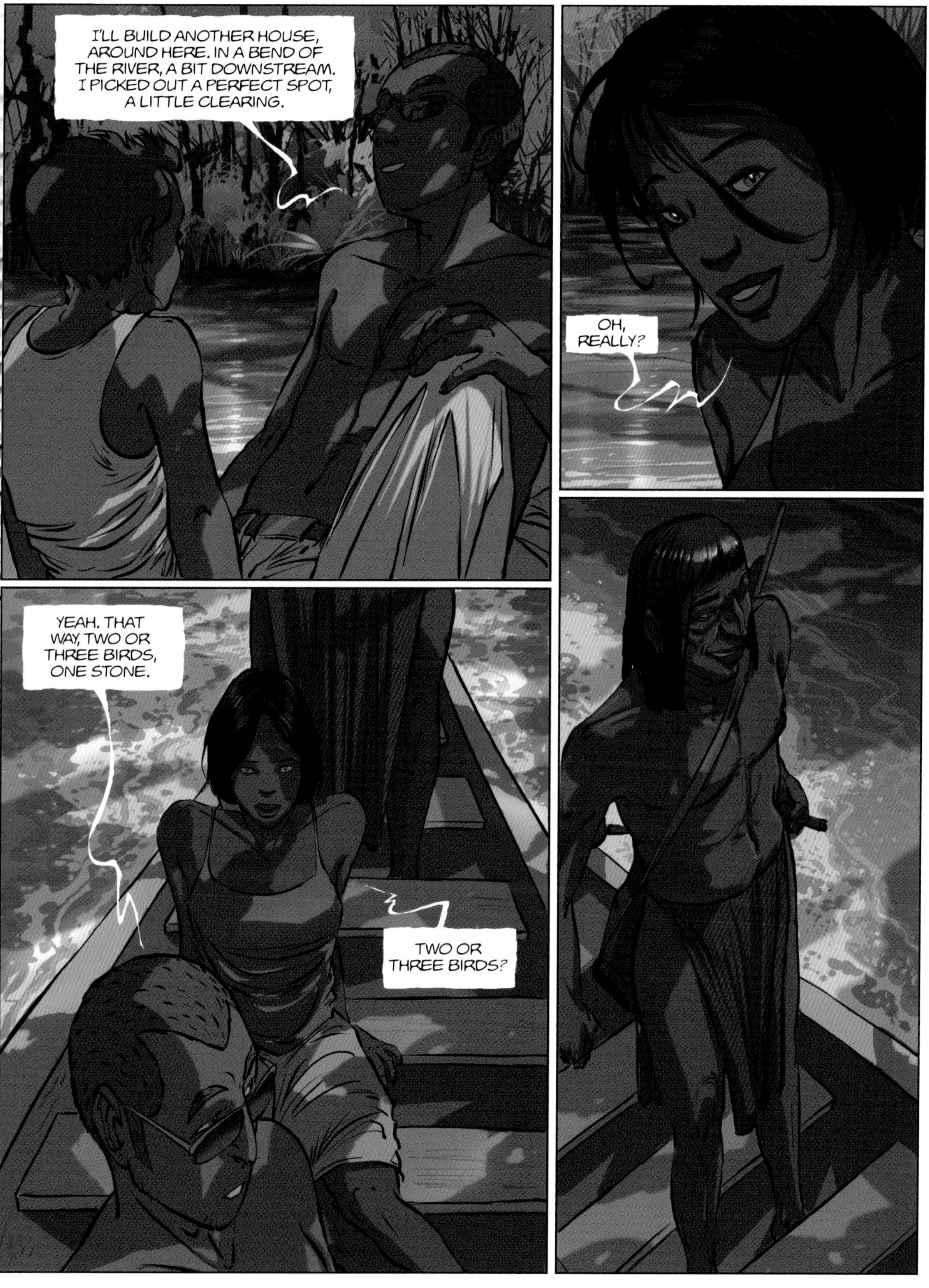
I'LL BUILD ANOTHER HOUSE, AROUND HERE. IN A BEND OF THE RIVER, A BIT DOWNSTREAM. I PICKED OUT A PERFECT SPOT, A LITTLE CLEARING.
OH, REALLY?
YEAH. THAT WAY, TWO OR THREE BIRDS, ONE STONE.
TWO OR THREE BIRDS?

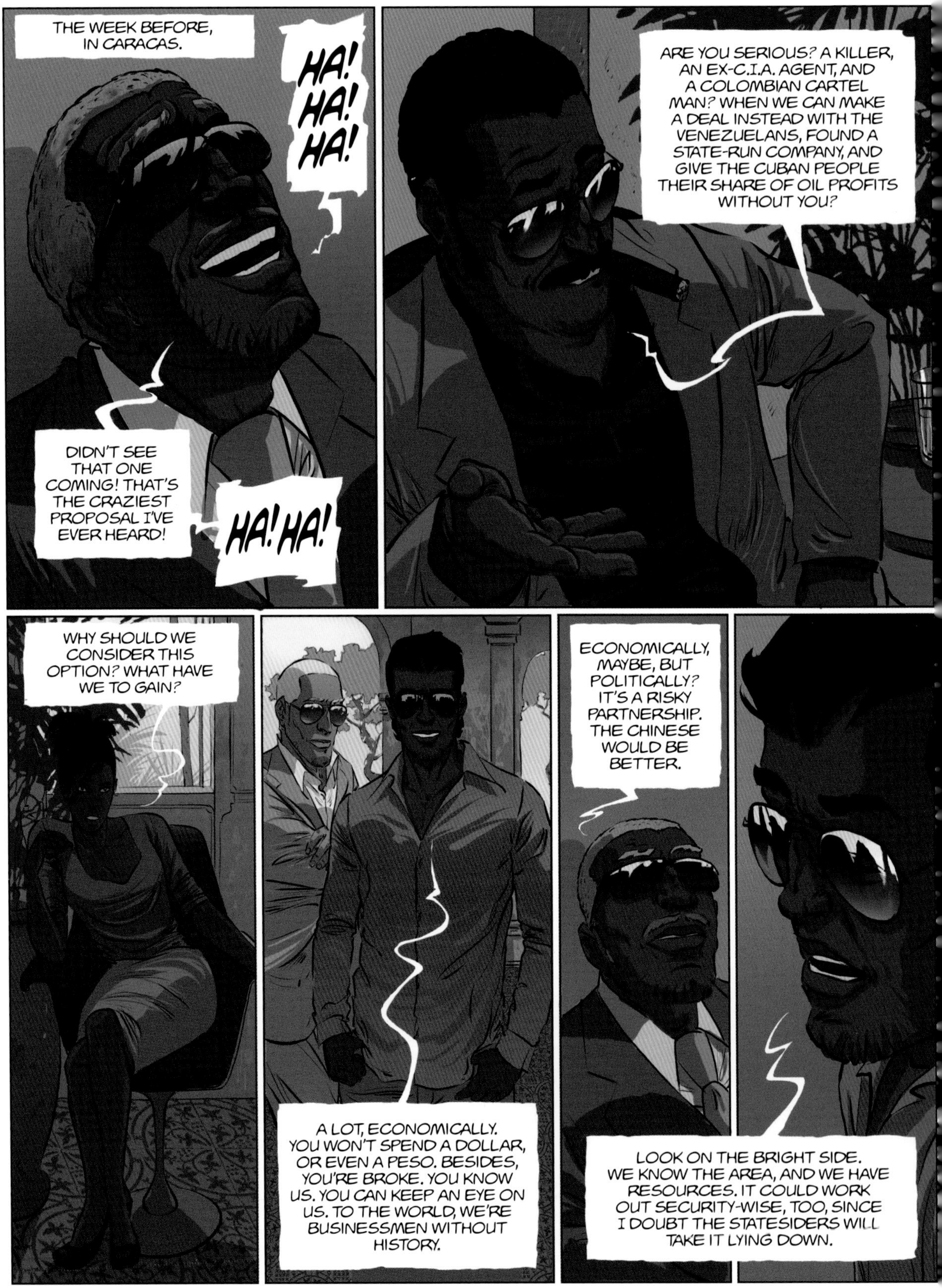
THE WEEK BEFORE, IN CARACAS.
HA! HA! HA!
DIDN'T SEE THAT ONE COMING! THAT'S THE CRAZIEST PROPOSAL I'VE EVER HEARD!
HA! HA!
ARE YOU SERIOUS? A KILLER, AN EX-C.I.A. AGENT, AND A COLOMBIAN CARTEL MAN? WHEN WE CAN MAKE A DEAL INSTEAD WITH THE VENEZUELANS, FOUND A STATE-RUN COMPANY, AND GIVE THE CUBAN PEOPLE THEIR SHARE OF OIL PROFITS WITHOUT YOU?
WHY SHOULD WE CONSIDER THIS OPTION? WHAT HAVE WE TO GAIN?
A LOT, ECONOMICALLY. YOU WON'T SPEND A DOLLAR, OR EVEN A PESO. BESIDES, YOU'RE BROKE. YOU KNOW US. YOU CAN KEEP AN EYE ON US. TO THE WORLD, WE'RE BUSINESSMEN WITHOUT HISTORY.
ECONOMICALLY, MAYBE, BUT POLITICALLY? IT'S A RISKY PARTNERSHIP. THE CHINESE WOULD BE BETTER.
LOOK ON THE BRIGHT SIDE. WE KNOW THE AREA, AND WE HAVE RESOURCES. IT COULD WORK OUT SECURITY-WISE, TOO, SINCE I DOUBT THE STATESIDERS WILL TAKE IT LYING DOWN.

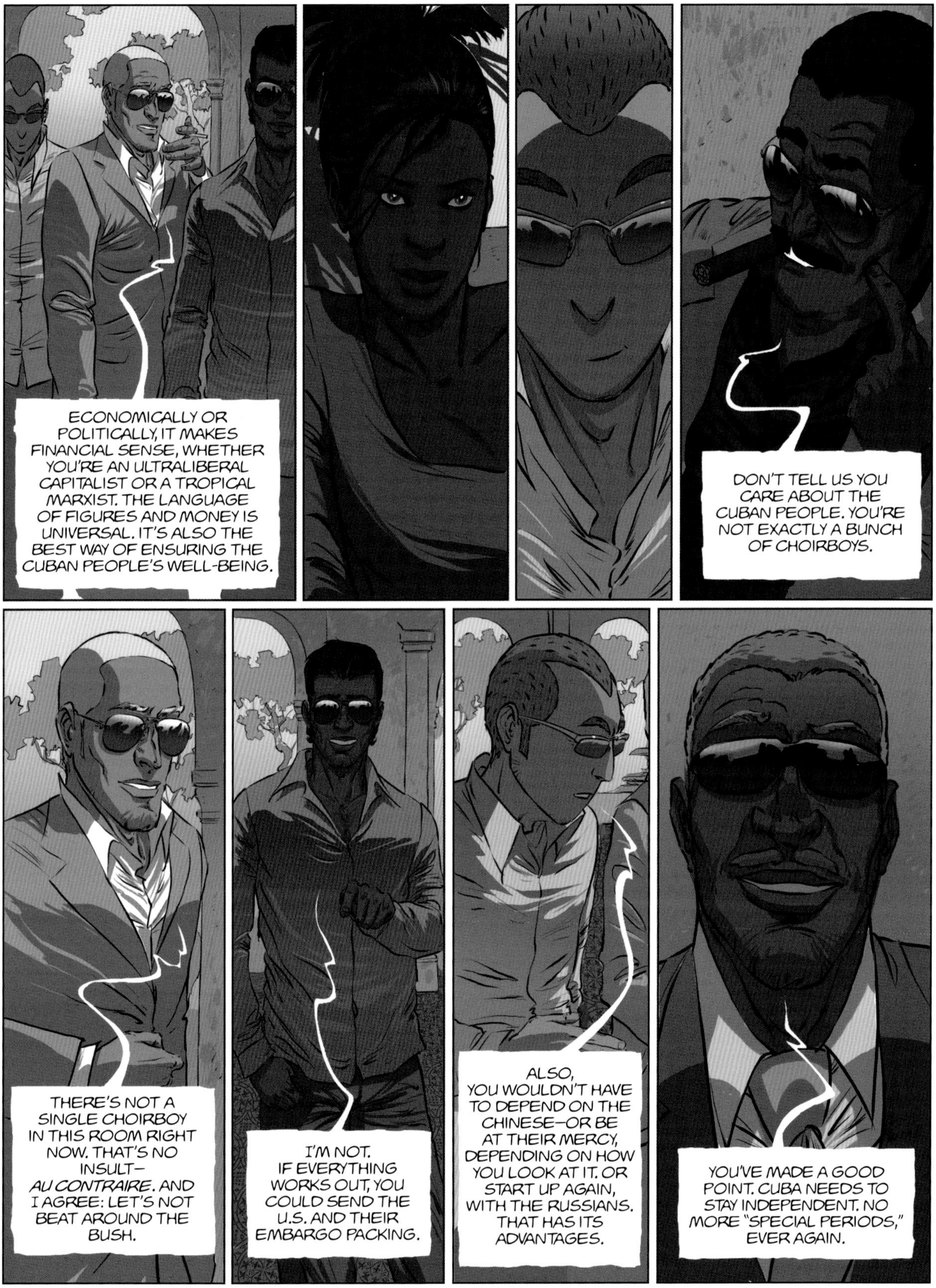
ECONOMICALLY OR POLITICALLY, IT MAKES FINANCIAL SENSE, WHETHER YOU'RE AN ULTRALIBERAL CAPITALIST OR A TROPICAL MARXIST. THE LANGUAGE OF FIGURES AND MONEY IS UNIVERSAL. IT'S ALSO THE BEST WAY OF ENSURING THE CUBAN PEOPLE'S WELL-BEING.
DON'T TELL US YOU CARE ABOUT THE CUBAN PEOPLE. YOU'RE NOT EXACTLY A BUNCH OF CHOIRBOYS.
THERE'S NOT A SINGLE CHOIRBOY IN THIS ROOM RIGHT NOW. THAT'S NO INSULT— *AU CONTRAIRE*. AND I AGREE: LET'S NOT BEAT AROUND THE BUSH.
I'M NOT. IF EVERYTHING WORKS OUT, YOU COULD SEND THE U.S. AND THEIR EMBARGO PACKING.
ALSO, YOU WOULDN'T HAVE TO DEPEND ON THE CHINESE—OR BE AT THEIR MERCY, DEPENDING ON HOW YOU LOOK AT IT. OR START UP AGAIN, WITH THE RUSSIANS. THAT HAS ITS ADVANTAGES.
YOU'VE MADE A GOOD POINT. CUBA NEEDS TO STAY INDEPENDENT. NO MORE "SPECIAL PERIODS," EVER AGAIN.

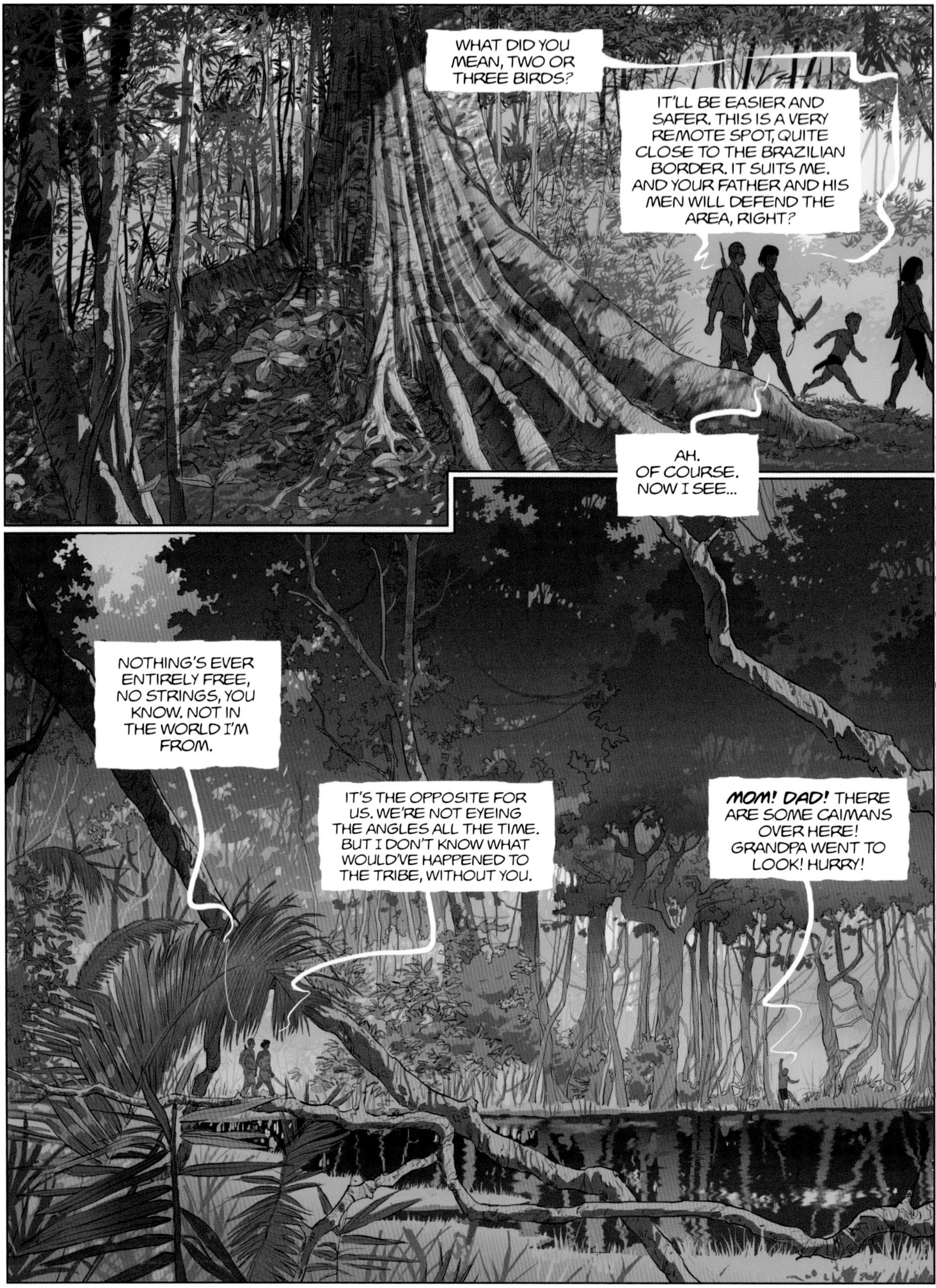
WHAT DID YOU MEAN, TWO OR THREE BIRDS?
IT'LL BE EASIER AND SAFER. THIS IS A VERY REMOTE SPOT, QUITE CLOSE TO THE BRAZILIAN BORDER. IT SUITS ME. AND YOUR FATHER AND HIS MEN WILL DEFEND THE AREA, RIGHT?
AH. OF COURSE. NOW I SEE...
NOTHING'S EVER ENTIRELY FREE, NO STRINGS, YOU KNOW. NOT IN THE WORLD I'M FROM.
IT'S THE OPPOSITE FOR US. WE'RE NOT EYEING THE ANGLES ALL THE TIME. BUT I DON'T KNOW WHAT WOULD'VE HAPPENED TO THE TRIBE, WITHOUT YOU.
MOM! DAD! THERE ARE SOME CAIMANS OVER HERE! GRANDPA WENT TO LOOK! HURRY!

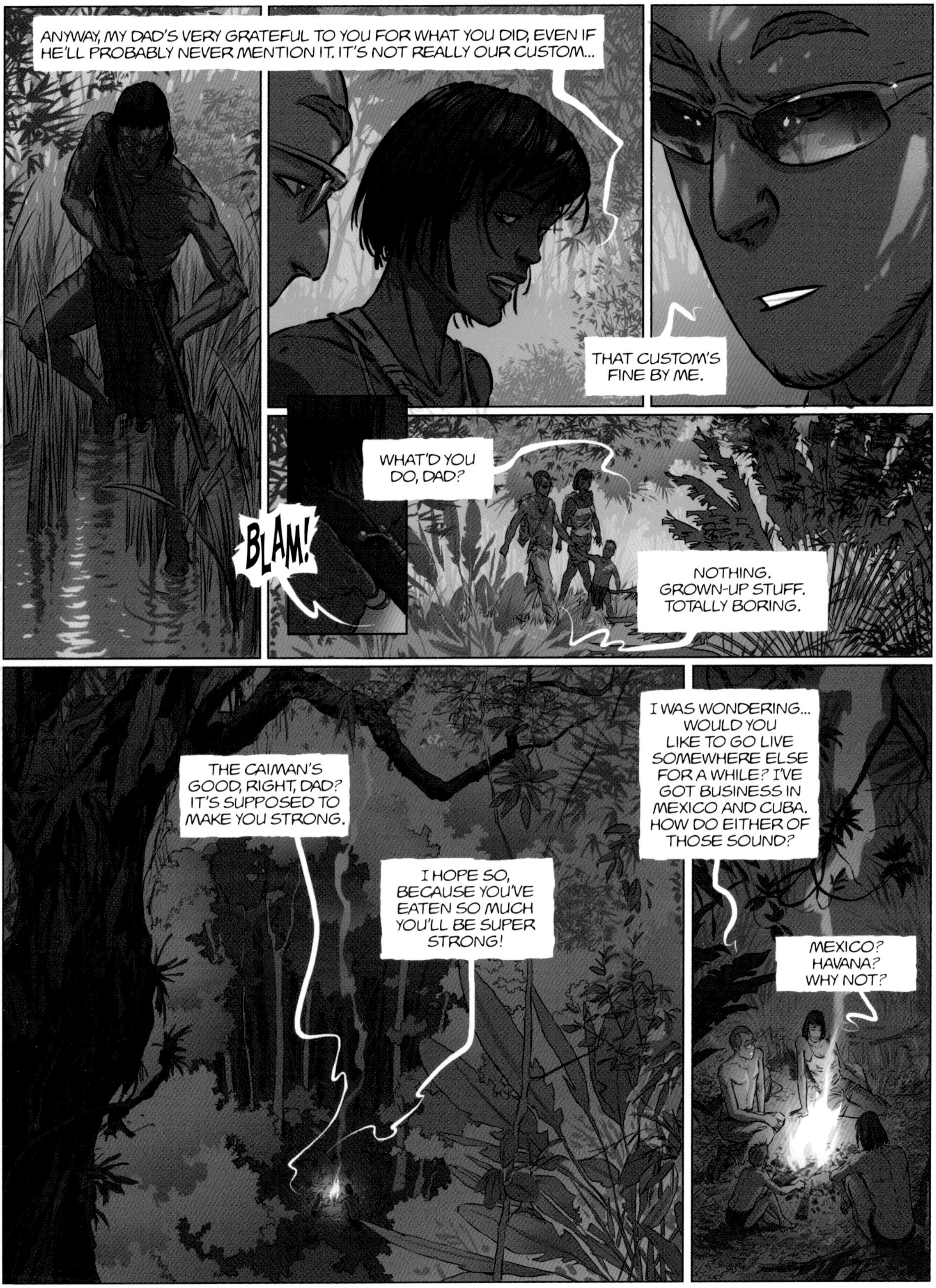
ANYWAY, MY DAD'S VERY GRATEFUL TO YOU FOR WHAT YOU DID, EVEN IF HE'LL PROBABLY NEVER MENTION IT. IT'S NOT REALLY OUR CUSTOM...
THAT CUSTOM'S FINE BY ME.
WHAT'D YOU DO, DAD?
BLAM!
NOTHING. GROWN-UP STUFF. TOTALLY BORING.
THE CAIMAN'S GOOD, RIGHT, DAD? IT'S SUPPOSED TO MAKE YOU STRONG.
I HOPE SO, BECAUSE YOU'VE EATEN SO MUCH YOU'LL BE SUPER STRONG!
I WAS WONDERING... WOULD YOU LIKE TO GO LIVE SOMEWHERE ELSE FOR A WHILE? I'VE GOT BUSINESS IN MEXICO AND CUBA. HOW DO EITHER OF THOSE SOUND?
MEXICO? HAVANA? WHY NOT?

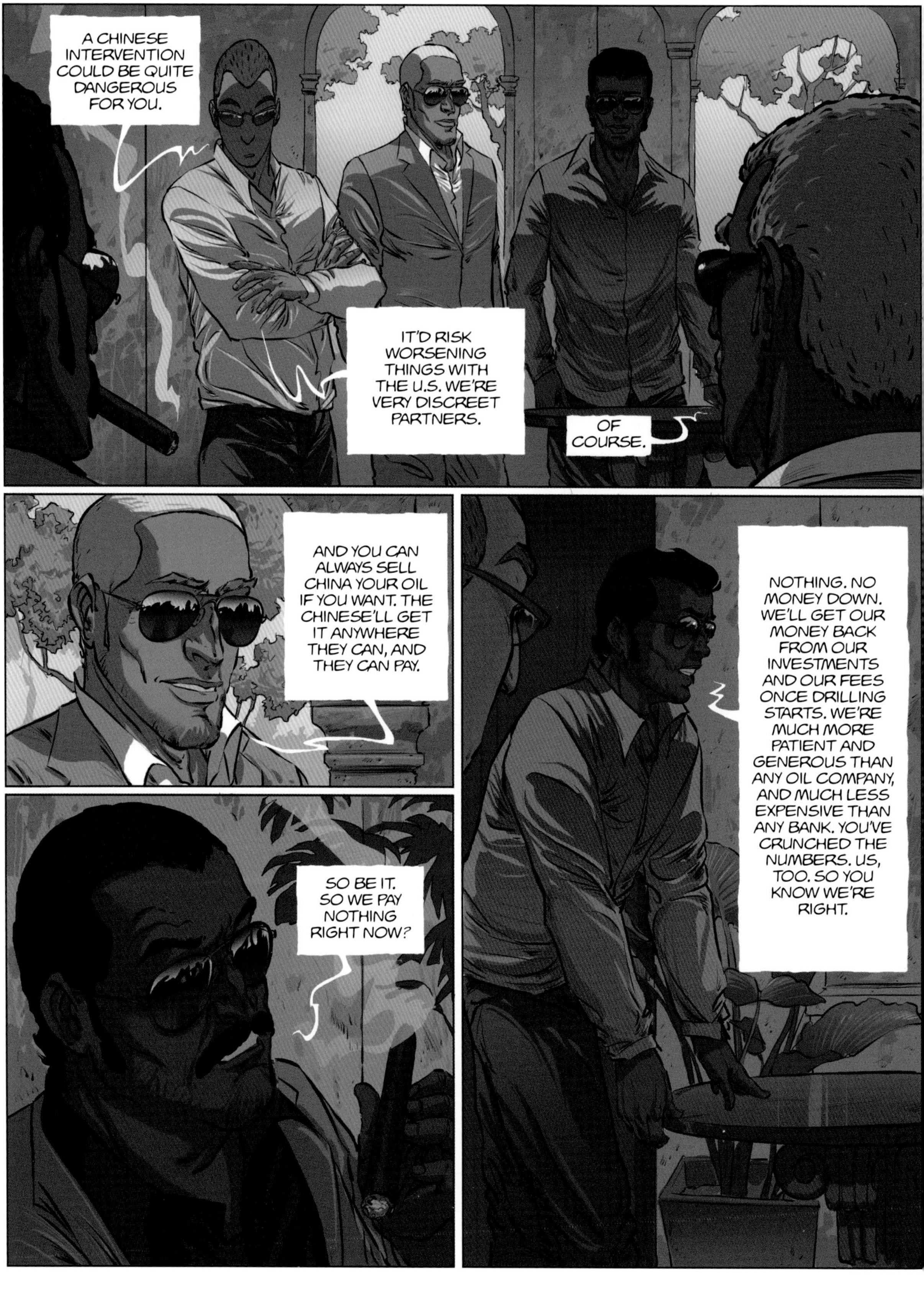
A CHINESE INTERVENTION COULD BE QUITE DANGEROUS FOR YOU.
IT'D RISK WORSENING THINGS WITH THE U.S. WE'RE VERY DISCREET PARTNERS.
OF COURSE.
AND YOU CAN ALWAYS SELL CHINA YOUR OIL IF YOU WANT. THE CHINESE'LL GET IT ANYWHERE THEY CAN, AND THEY CAN PAY.
SO BE IT. SO WE PAY NOTHING RIGHT NOW?
NOTHING. NO MONEY DOWN. WE'LL GET OUR MONEY BACK FROM OUR INVESTMENTS AND OUR FEES ONCE DRILLING STARTS. WE'RE MUCH MORE PATIENT AND GENEROUS THAN ANY OIL COMPANY, AND MUCH LESS EXPENSIVE THAN ANY BANK. YOU'VE CRUNCHED THE NUMBERS. US, TOO. SO YOU KNOW WE'RE RIGHT.

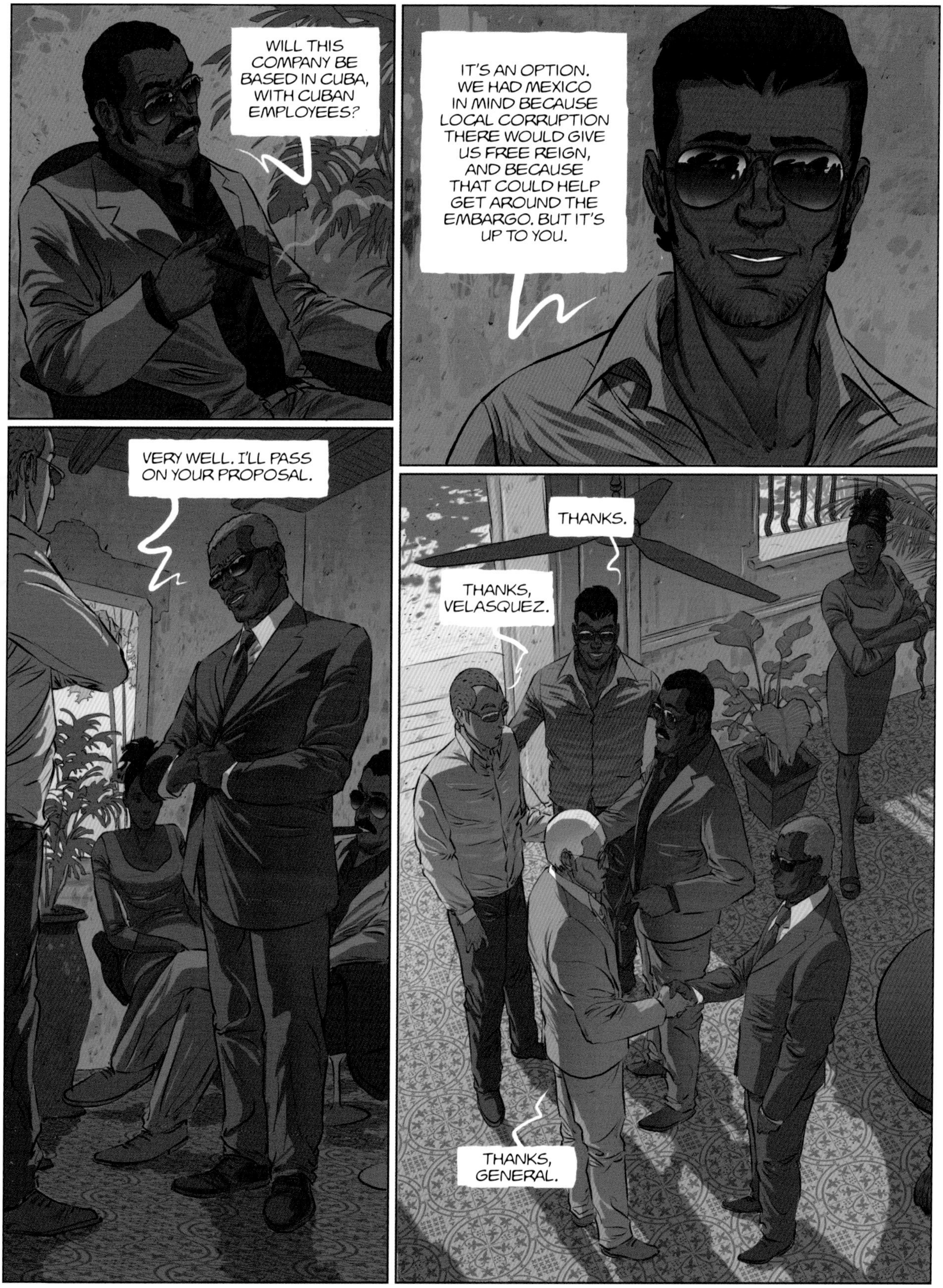
WILL THIS COMPANY BE BASED IN CUBA, WITH CUBAN EMPLOYEES?
IT'S AN OPTION. WE HAD MEXICO IN MIND BECAUSE LOCAL CORRUPTION THERE WOULD GIVE US FREE REIGN, AND BECAUSE THAT COULD HELP GET AROUND THE EMBARGO. BUT IT'S UP TO YOU.
VERY WELL. I'LL PASS ON YOUR PROPOSAL.
THANKS.
THANKS, VELASQUEZ.
THANKS, GENERAL.

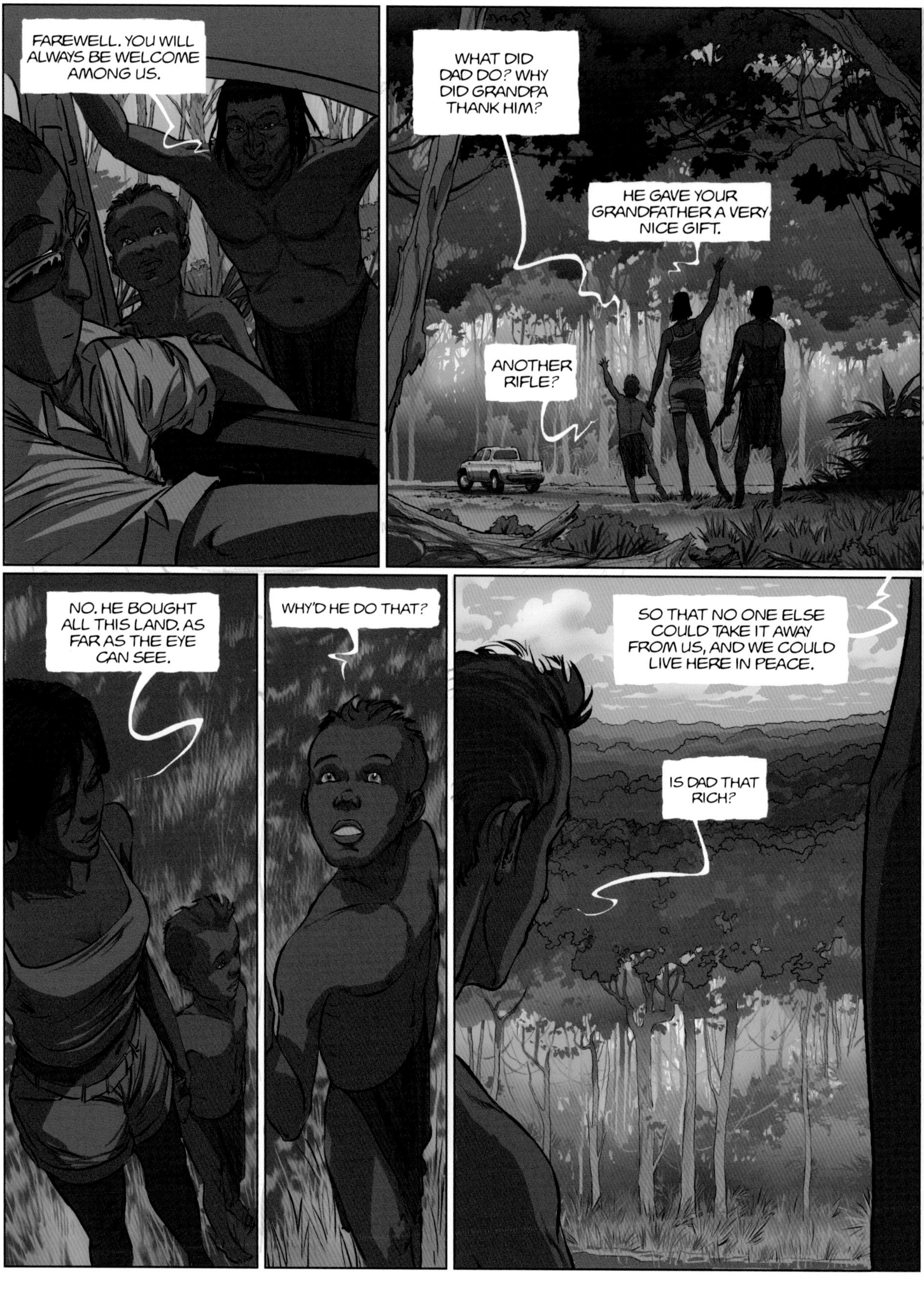
FAREWELL. YOU WILL ALWAYS BE WELCOME AMONG US.
WHAT DID DAD DO? WHY DID GRANDPA THANK HIM?
HE GAVE YOUR GRANDFATHER A VERY NICE GIFT.
ANOTHER RIFLE?
NO. HE BOUGHT ALL THIS LAND. AS FAR AS THE EYE CAN SEE.
WHY'D HE DO THAT?
SO THAT NO ONE ELSE COULD TAKE IT AWAY FROM US, AND WE COULD LIVE HERE IN PEACE.
IS DAD THAT RICH?

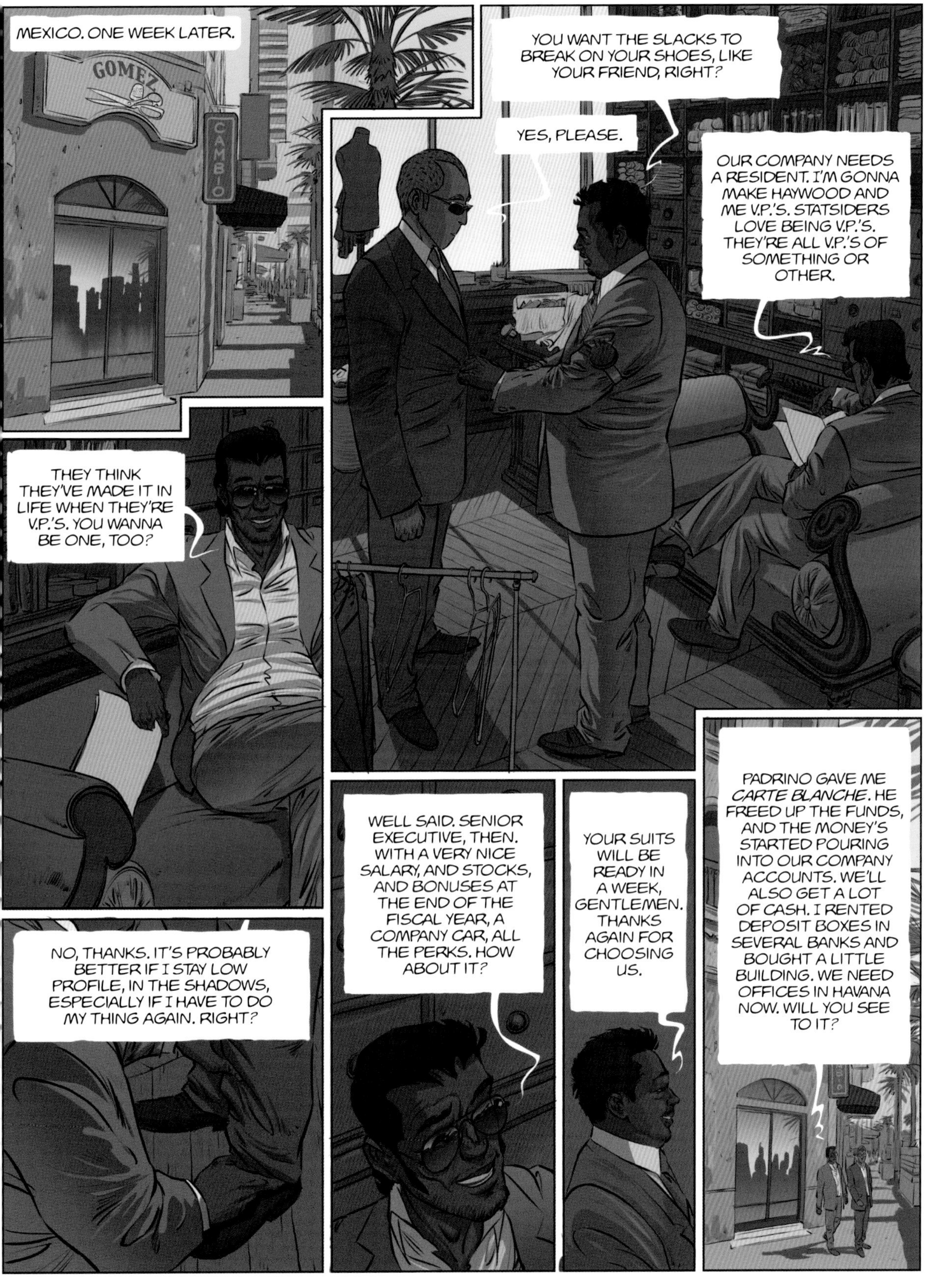
MEXICO. ONE WEEK LATER.
GOMEZ
CAMBIO
YOU WANT THE SLACKS TO BREAK ON YOUR SHOES, LIKE YOUR FRIEND, RIGHT?
YES, PLEASE.
OUR COMPANY NEEDS A RESIDENT. I'M GONNA MAKE HAYWOOD AND ME V.P.'S. STATSIDERS LOVE BEING V.P.'S. THEY'RE ALL V.P.'S OF SOMETHING OR OTHER.
THEY THINK THEY'VE MADE IT IN LIFE WHEN THEY'RE V.P.'S. YOU WANNA BE ONE, TOO?
NO, THANKS. IT'S PROBABLY BETTER IF I STAY LOW PROFILE, IN THE SHADOWS, ESPECIALLY IF I HAVE TO DO MY THING AGAIN. RIGHT?
WELL SAID. SENIOR EXECUTIVE, THEN. WITH A VERY NICE SALARY, AND STOCKS, AND BONUSES AT THE END OF THE FISCAL YEAR, A COMPANY CAR, ALL THE PERKS. HOW ABOUT IT?
YOUR SUITS WILL BE READY IN A WEEK, GENTLEMEN. THANKS AGAIN FOR CHOOSING US.
PADRINO GAVE ME *CARTE BLANCHE*. HE FREED UP THE FUNDS, AND THE MONEY'S STARTED POURING INTO OUR COMPANY ACCOUNTS. WE'LL ALSO GET A LOT OF CASH. I RENTED DEPOSIT BOXES IN SEVERAL BANKS AND BOUGHT A LITTLE BUILDING. WE NEED OFFICES IN HAVANA NOW. WILL YOU SEE TO IT?

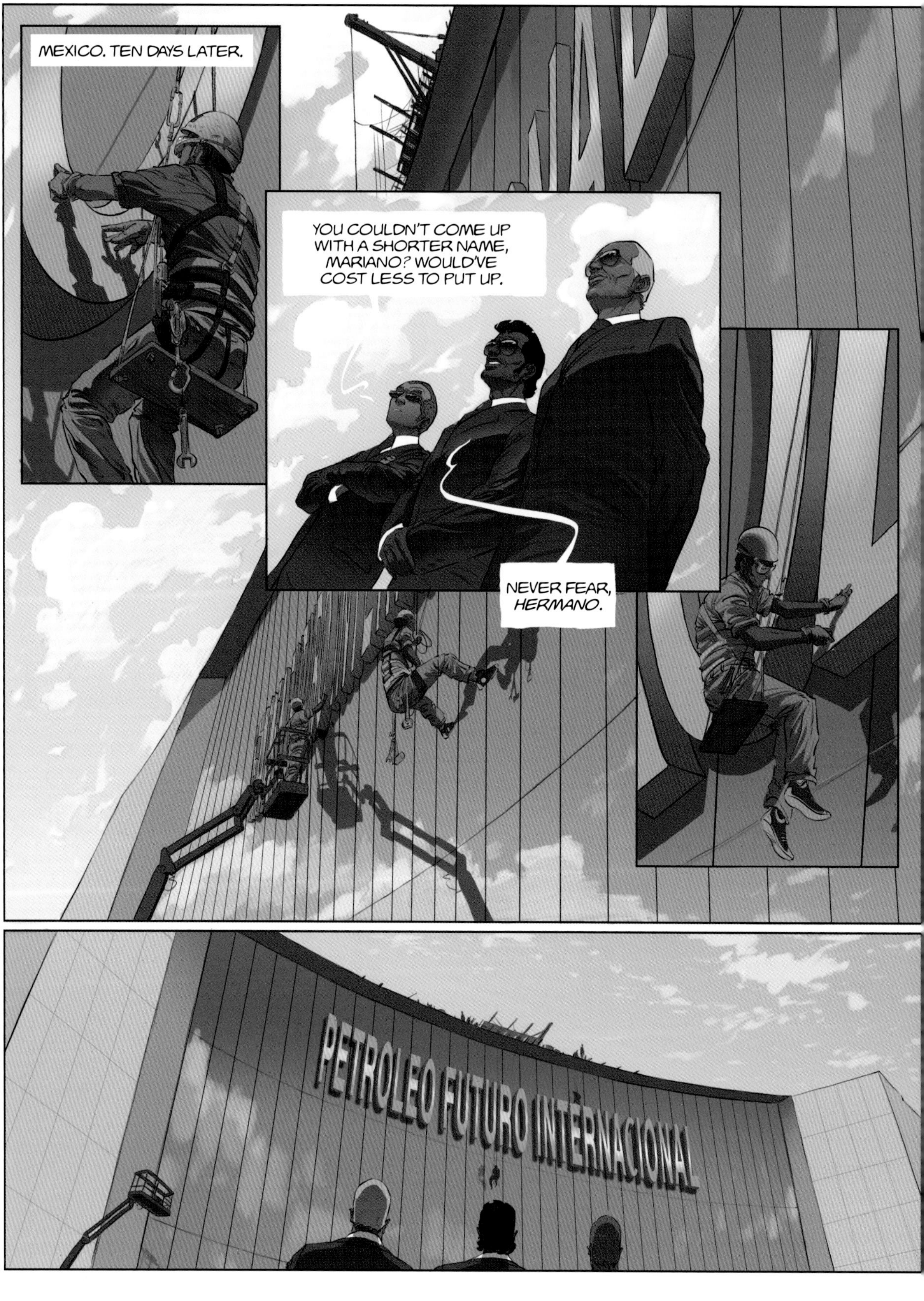
MEXICO. TEN DAYS LATER.
YOU COULDN'T COME UP WITH A SHORTER NAME, MARIANO? WOULD'VE COST LESS TO PUT UP.
NEVER FEAR, HERMANO.
PETROLEO FUTURO INTERNACIONAL

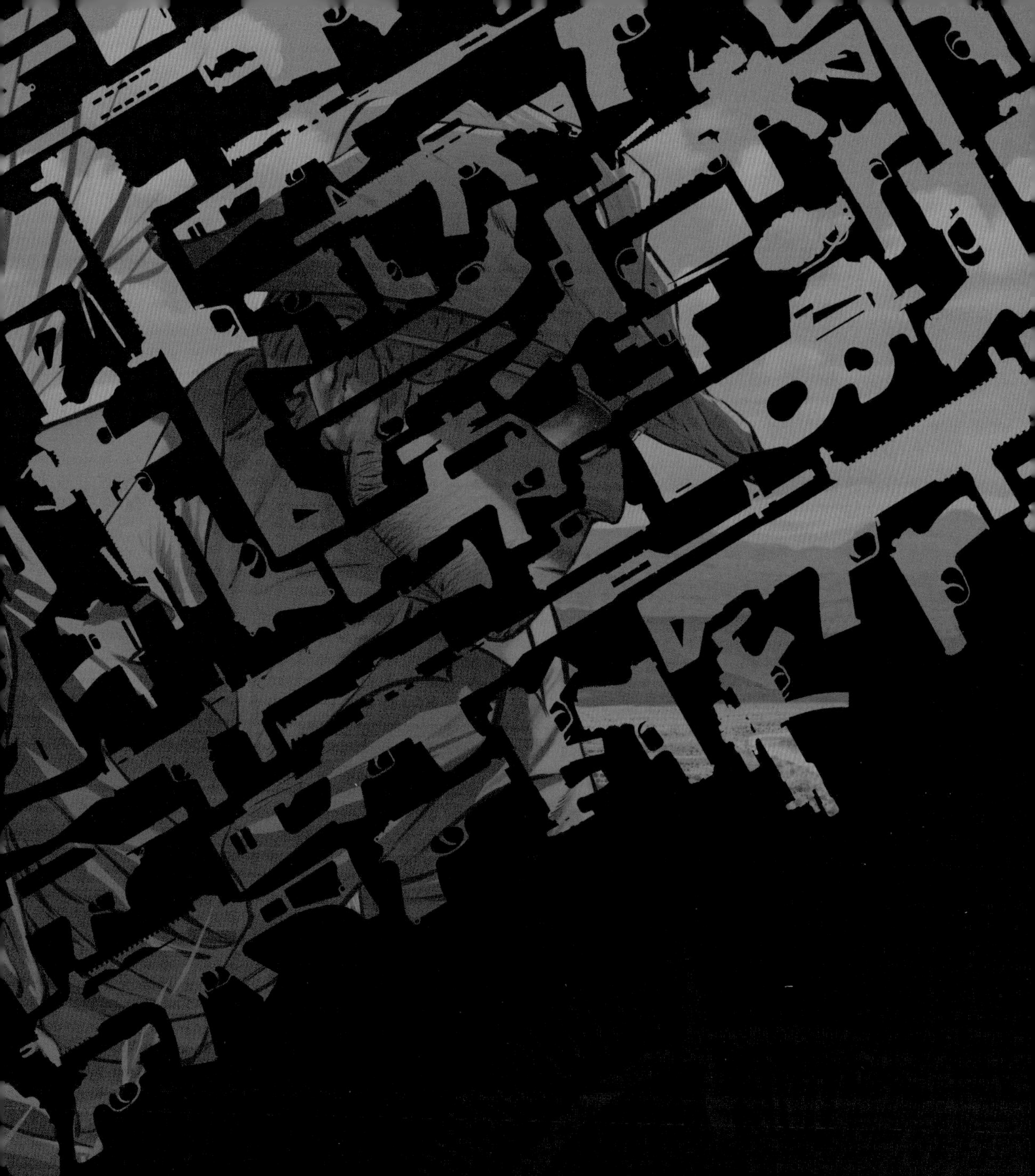

"... the older you get, the **shorter** life seems. The more you hope it lasts, the **harder** you hang on."

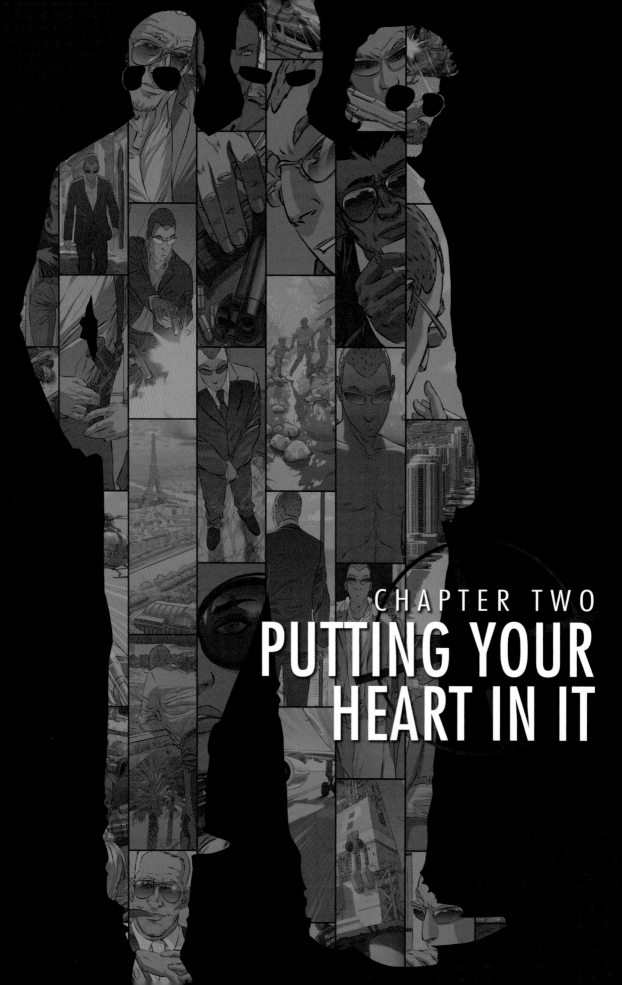

CHAPTER TWO

PUTTING YOUR HEART IN IT

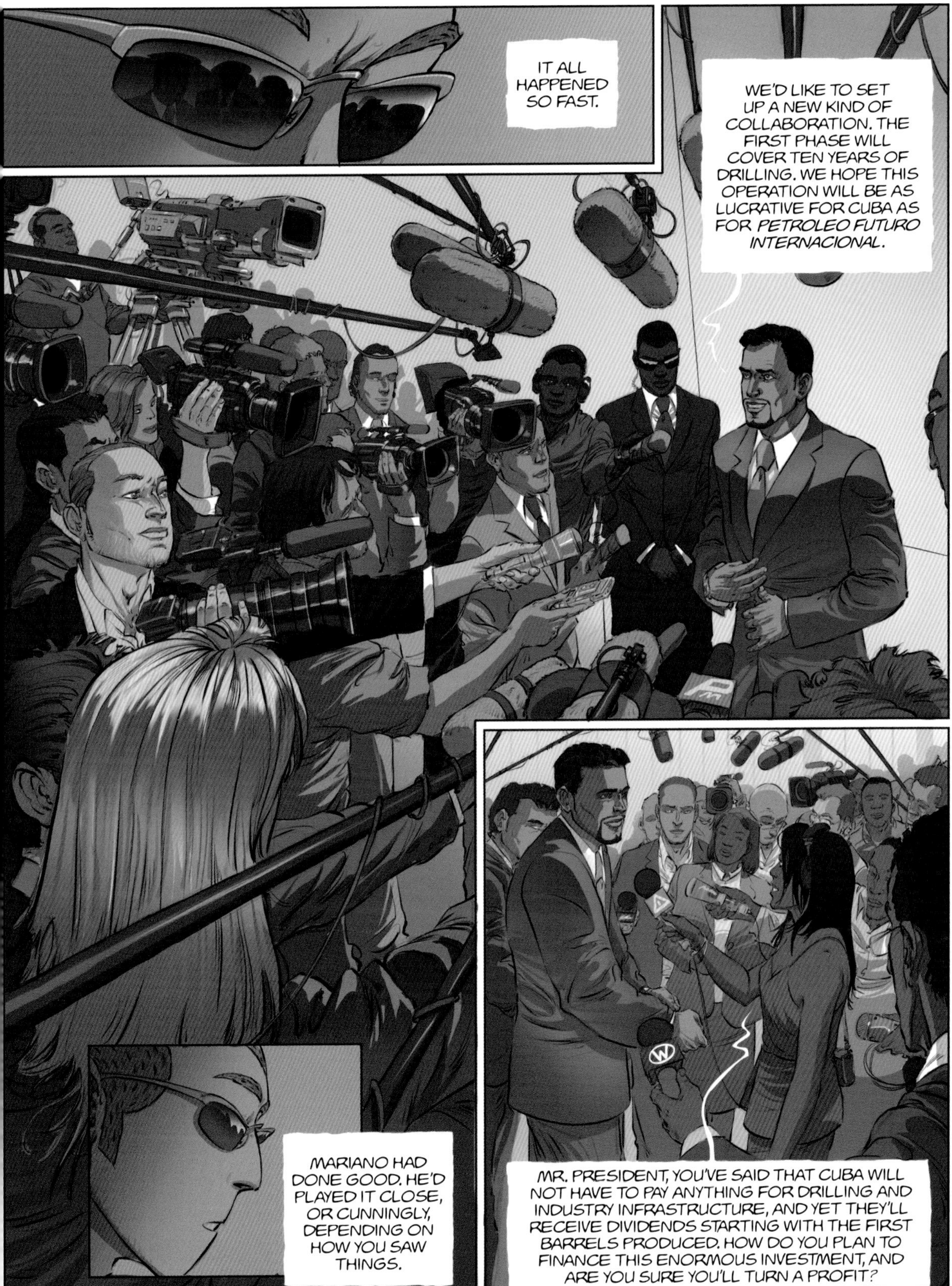
IT ALL HAPPENED SO FAST.
WE'D LIKE TO SET UP A NEW KIND OF COLLABORATION. THE FIRST PHASE WILL COVER TEN YEARS OF DRILLING. WE HOPE THIS OPERATION WILL BE AS LUCRATIVE FOR CUBA AS FOR *PETROLEO FUTURO INTERNACIONAL*.
MARIANO HAD DONE GOOD. HE'D PLAYED IT CLOSE, OR CUNNINGLY, DEPENDING ON HOW YOU SAW THINGS.
MR. PRESIDENT, YOU'VE SAID THAT CUBA WILL NOT HAVE TO PAY ANYTHING FOR DRILLING AND INDUSTRY INFRASTRUCTURE, AND YET THEY'LL RECEIVE DIVIDENDS STARTING WITH THE FIRST BARRELS PRODUCED. HOW DO YOU PLAN TO FINANCE THIS ENORMOUS INVESTMENT, AND ARE YOU SURE YOU'LL TURN A PROFIT?

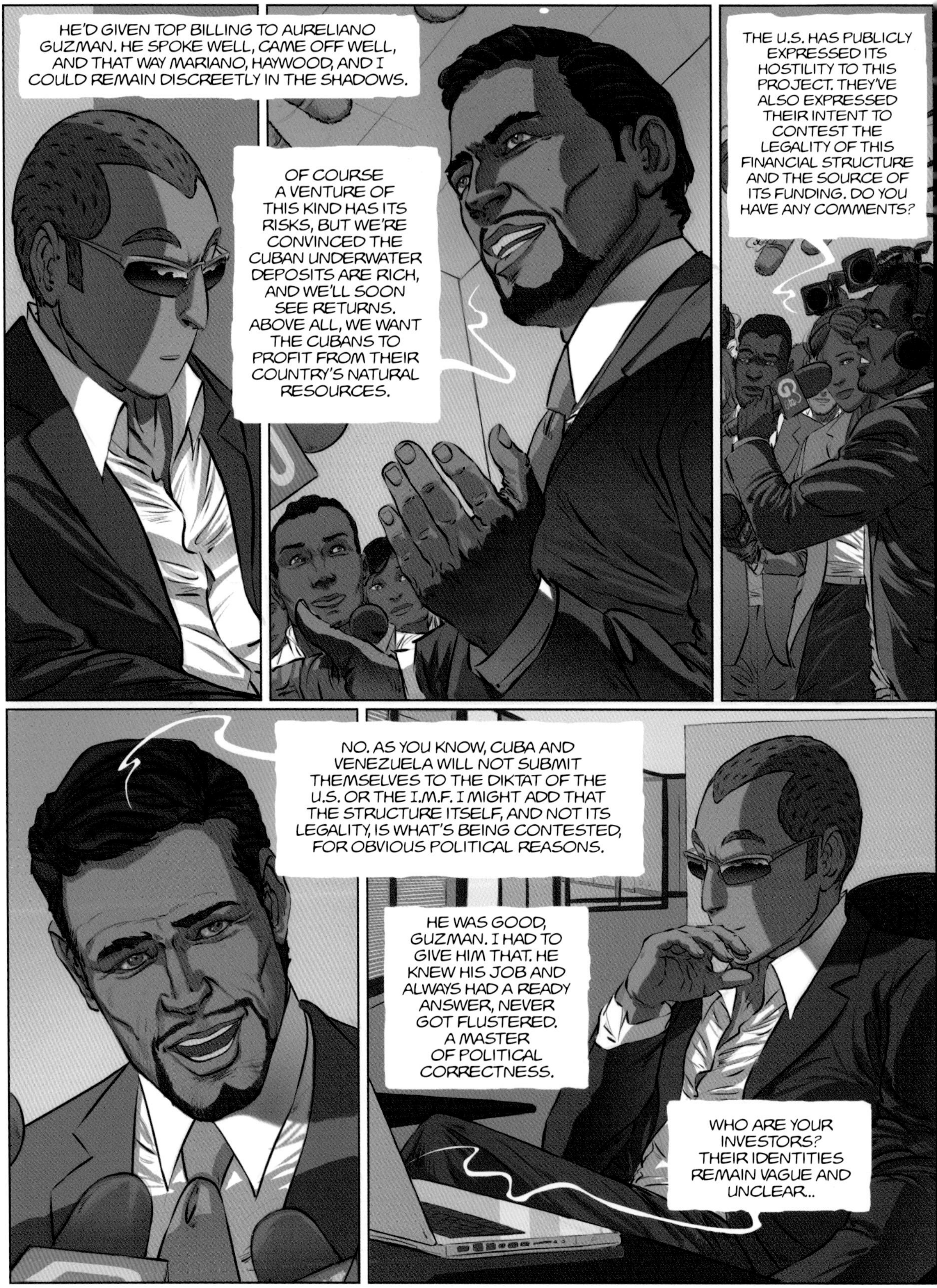
HE'D GIVEN TOP BILLING TO AURELIANO GUZMAN. HE SPOKE WELL, CAME OFF WELL, AND THAT WAY MARIANO, HAYWOOD, AND I COULD REMAIN DISCREETLY IN THE SHADOWS.
OF COURSE A VENTURE OF THIS KIND HAS ITS RISKS, BUT WE'RE CONVINCED THE CUBAN UNDERWATER DEPOSITS ARE RICH, AND WE'LL SOON SEE RETURNS. ABOVE ALL, WE WANT THE CUBANS TO PROFIT FROM THEIR COUNTRY'S NATURAL RESOURCES.
THE U.S. HAS PUBLICLY EXPRESSED ITS HOSTILITY TO THIS PROJECT. THEY'VE ALSO EXPRESSED THEIR INTENT TO CONTEST THE LEGALITY OF THIS FINANCIAL STRUCTURE AND THE SOURCE OF ITS FUNDING. DO YOU HAVE ANY COMMENTS?
NO. AS YOU KNOW, CUBA AND VENEZUELA WILL NOT SUBMIT THEMSELVES TO THE DIKTAT OF THE U.S. OR THE I.M.F. I MIGHT ADD THAT THE STRUCTURE ITSELF, AND NOT ITS LEGALITY, IS WHAT'S BEING CONTESTED, FOR OBVIOUS POLITICAL REASONS.
HE WAS GOOD, GUZMAN. I HAD TO GIVE HIM THAT. HE KNEW HIS JOB AND ALWAYS HAD A READY ANSWER, NEVER GOT FLUSTERED. A MASTER OF POLITICAL CORRECTNESS.
WHO ARE YOUR INVESTORS? THEIR IDENTITIES REMAIN VAGUE AND UNCLEAR...

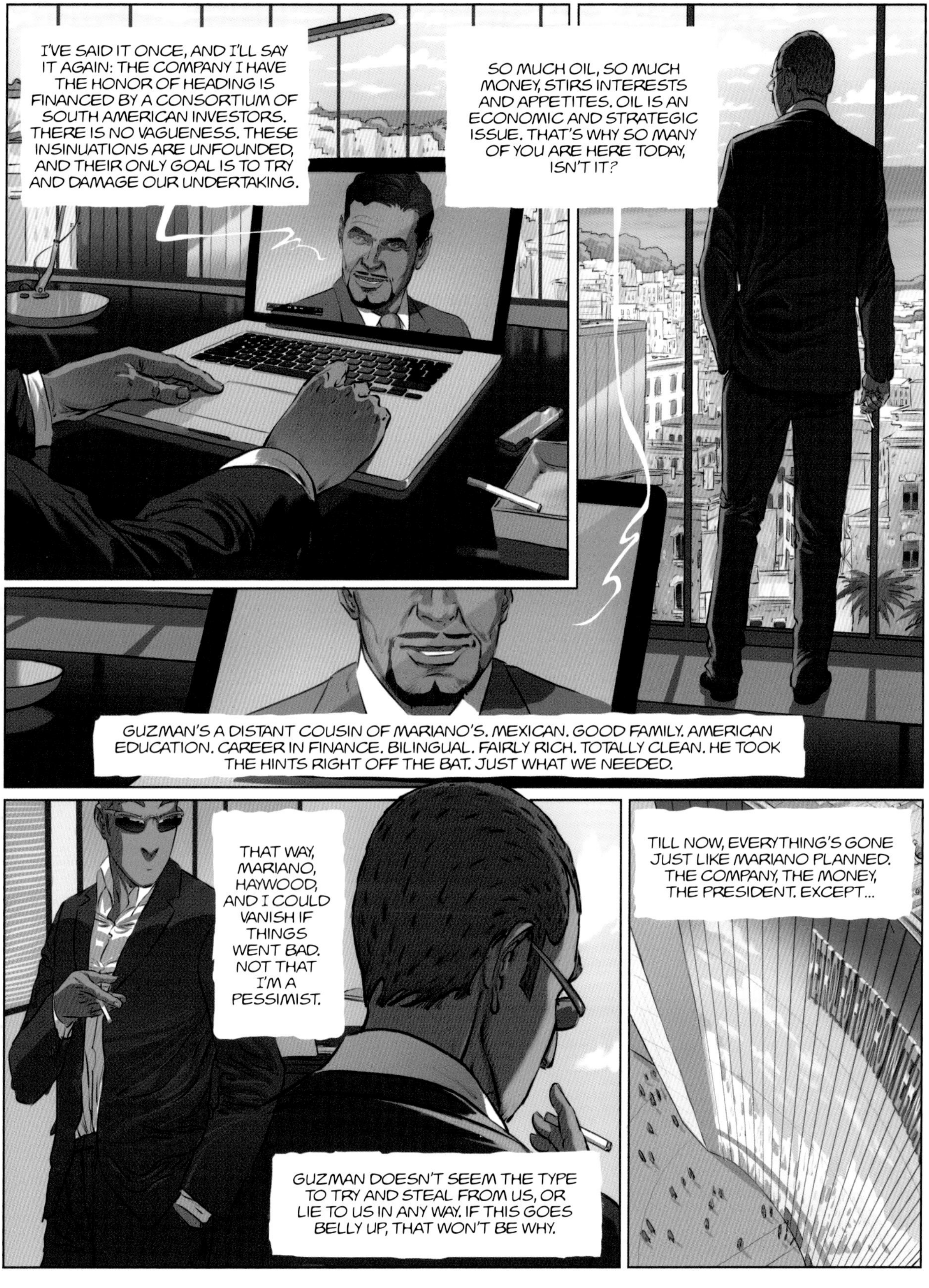
I'VE SAID IT ONCE, AND I'LL SAY IT AGAIN: THE COMPANY I HAVE THE HONOR OF HEADING IS FINANCED BY A CONSORTIUM OF SOUTH AMERICAN INVESTORS. THERE IS NO VAGUENESS. THESE INSINUATIONS ARE UNFOUNDED, AND THEIR ONLY GOAL IS TO TRY AND DAMAGE OUR UNDERTAKING.
SO MUCH OIL, SO MUCH MONEY, STIRS INTERESTS AND APPETITES. OIL IS AN ECONOMIC AND STRATEGIC ISSUE. THAT'S WHY SO MANY OF YOU ARE HERE TODAY, ISN'T IT?
GUZMAN'S A DISTANT COUSIN OF MARIANO'S. MEXICAN. GOOD FAMILY. AMERICAN EDUCATION. CAREER IN FINANCE. BILINGUAL. FAIRLY RICH. TOTALLY CLEAN. HE TOOK THE HINTS RIGHT OFF THE BAT. JUST WHAT WE NEEDED.
THAT WAY, MARIANO, HAYWOOD, AND I COULD VANISH IF THINGS WENT BAD. NOT THAT I'M A PESSIMIST.
GUZMAN DOESN'T SEEM THE TYPE TO TRY AND STEAL FROM US, OR LIE TO US IN ANY WAY. IF THIS GOES BELLY UP, THAT WON'T BE WHY.
TILL NOW, EVERYTHING'S GONE JUST LIKE MARIANO PLANNED. THE COMPANY, THE MONEY, THE PRESIDENT. EXCEPT...

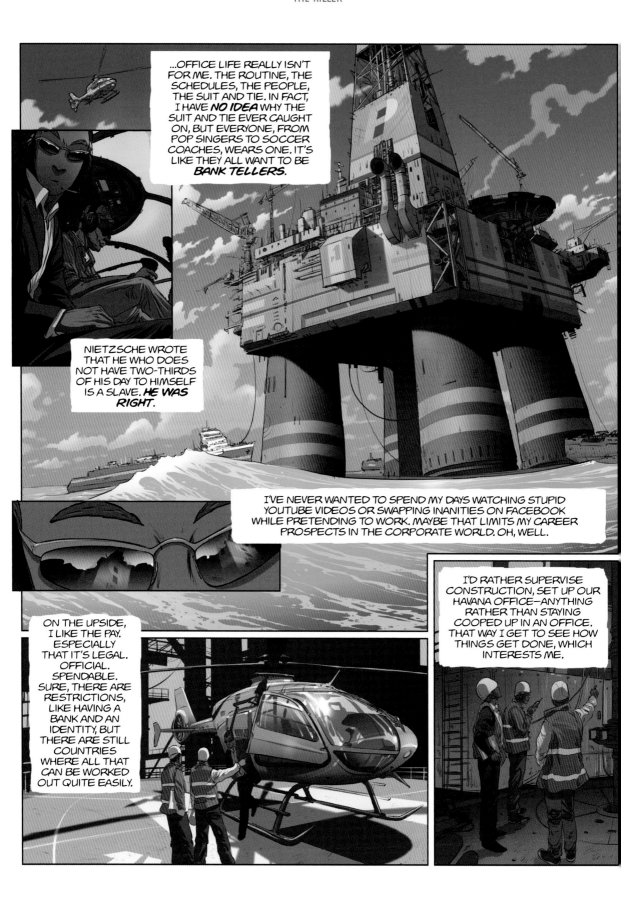

...OFFICE LIFE REALLY ISN'T FOR ME. THE ROUTINE, THE SCHEDULES, THE PEOPLE, THE SUIT AND TIE. IN FACT, I HAVE **NO IDEA** WHY THE SUIT AND TIE EVER CAUGHT ON, BUT EVERYONE, FROM POP SINGERS TO SOCCER COACHES, WEARS ONE. IT'S LIKE THEY ALL WANT TO BE *BANK TELLERS*.

NIETZSCHE WROTE THAT HE WHO DOES NOT HAVE TWO-THIRDS OF HIS DAY TO HIMSELF IS A SLAVE. *HE WAS RIGHT*.

I'VE NEVER WANTED TO SPEND MY DAYS WATCHING STUPID YOUTUBE VIDEOS OR SWAPPING INANITIES ON FACEBOOK WHILE PRETENDING TO WORK. MAYBE THAT LIMITS MY CAREER PROSPECTS IN THE CORPORATE WORLD. OH, WELL.

I'D RATHER SUPERVISE CONSTRUCTION, SET UP OUR HAVANA OFFICE—ANYTHING RATHER THAN STAYING COOPED UP IN AN OFFICE. THAT WAY I GET TO SEE HOW THINGS GET DONE, WHICH INTERESTS ME.

ON THE UPSIDE, I LIKE THE PAY. ESPECIALLY THAT IT'S LEGAL. OFFICIAL. SPENDABLE. SURE, THERE ARE RESTRICTIONS, LIKE HAVING A BANK AND AN IDENTITY, BUT THERE ARE STILL COUNTRIES WHERE ALL THAT CAN BE WORKED OUT QUITE EASILY.

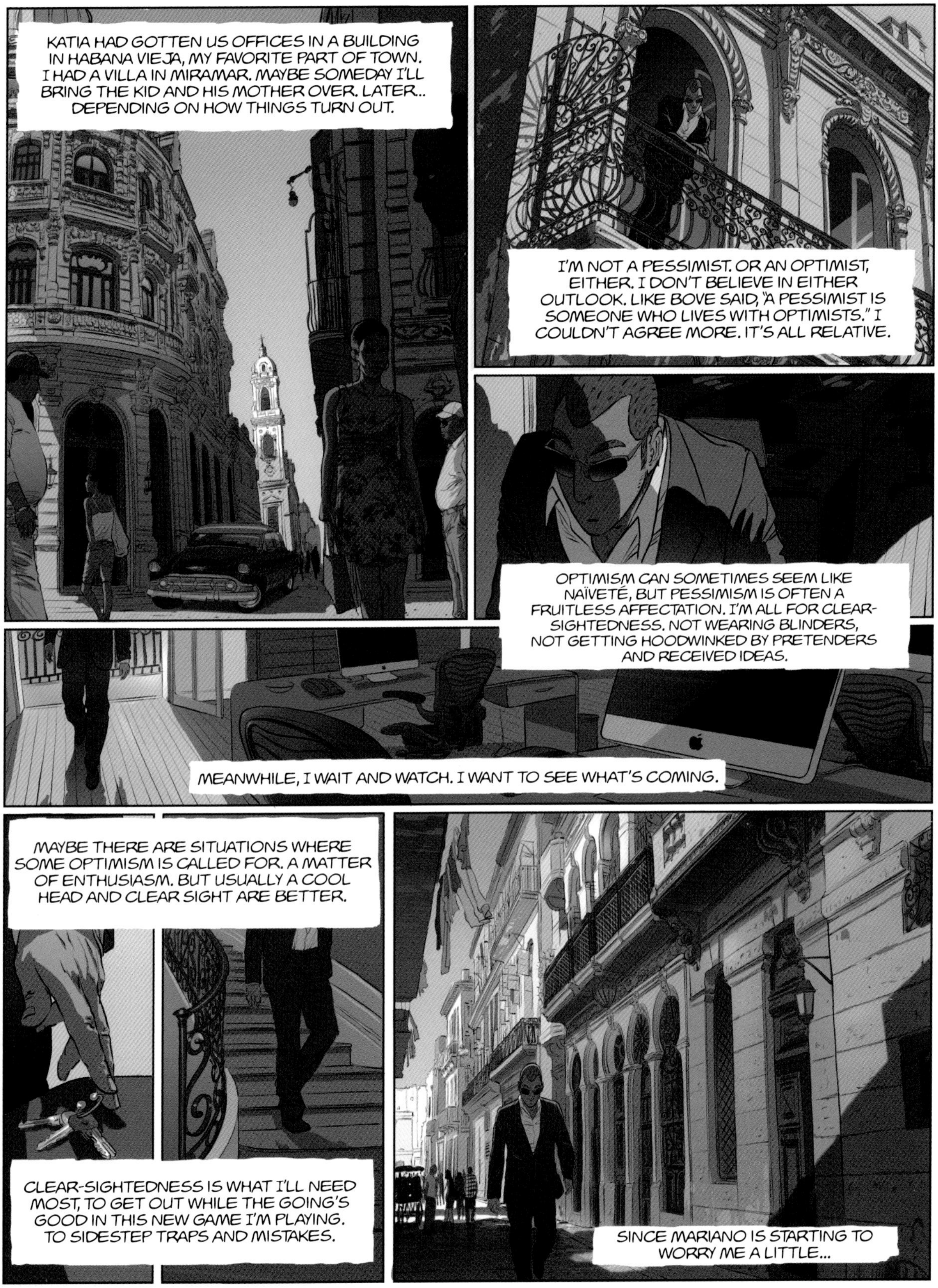
KATIA HAD GOTTEN US OFFICES IN A BUILDING IN HABANA VIEJA, MY FAVORITE PART OF TOWN. I HAD A VILLA IN MIRAMAR. MAYBE SOMEDAY I'LL BRING THE KID AND HIS MOTHER OVER. LATER.. DEPENDING ON HOW THINGS TURN OUT.
I'M NOT A PESSIMIST. OR AN OPTIMIST, EITHER. I DON'T BELIEVE IN EITHER OUTLOOK. LIKE BOVE SAID, "A PESSIMIST IS SOMEONE WHO LIVES WITH OPTIMISTS." I COULDN'T AGREE MORE. IT'S ALL RELATIVE.
OPTIMISM CAN SOMETIMES SEEM LIKE NAÏVETÉ, BUT PESSIMISM IS OFTEN A FRUITLESS AFFECTATION. I'M ALL FOR CLEAR-SIGHTEDNESS. NOT WEARING BLINDERS, NOT GETTING HOODWINKED BY PRETENDERS AND RECEIVED IDEAS.
MEANWHILE, I WAIT AND WATCH. I WANT TO SEE WHAT'S COMING.
MAYBE THERE ARE SITUATIONS WHERE SOME OPTIMISM IS CALLED FOR. A MATTER OF ENTHUSIASM. BUT USUALLY A COOL HEAD AND CLEAR SIGHT ARE BETTER.
CLEAR-SIGHTEDNESS IS WHAT I'LL NEED MOST, TO GET OUT WHILE THE GOING'S GOOD IN THIS NEW GAME I'M PLAYING. TO SIDESTEP TRAPS AND MISTAKES.
SINCE MARIANO IS STARTING TO WORRY ME A LITTLE...

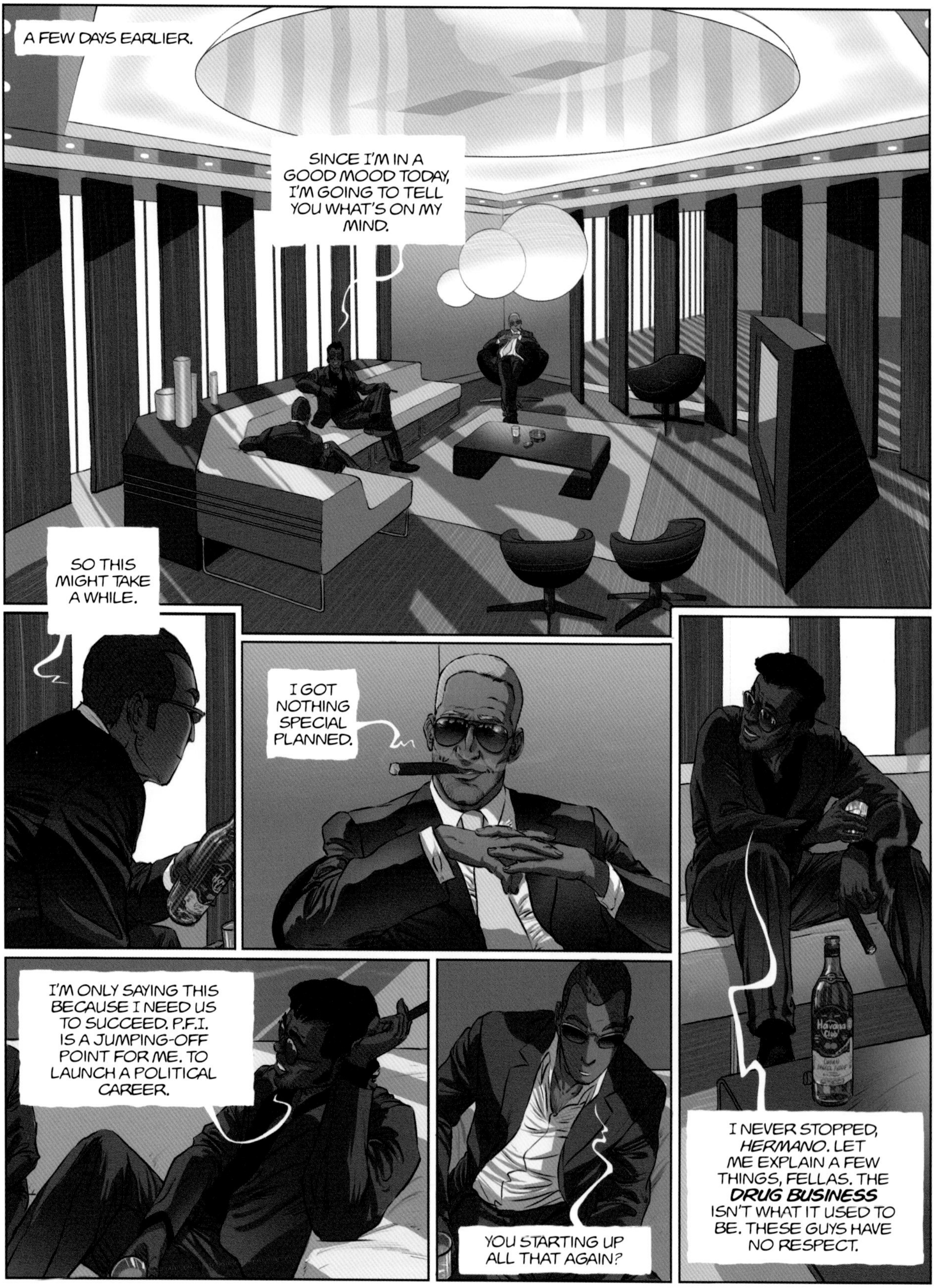
A FEW DAYS EARLIER.
SINCE I'M IN A GOOD MOOD TODAY, I'M GOING TO TELL YOU WHAT'S ON MY MIND.
SO THIS MIGHT TAKE A WHILE.
I GOT NOTHING SPECIAL PLANNED.
I'M ONLY SAYING THIS BECAUSE I NEED US TO SUCCEED. P.F.I. IS A JUMPING-OFF POINT FOR ME. TO LAUNCH A POLITICAL CAREER.
YOU STARTING UP ALL THAT AGAIN?
I NEVER STOPPED, *HERMANO*. LET ME EXPLAIN A FEW THINGS, FELLAS. THE ***DRUG BUSINESS*** ISN'T WHAT IT USED TO BE. THESE GUYS HAVE NO RESPECT.

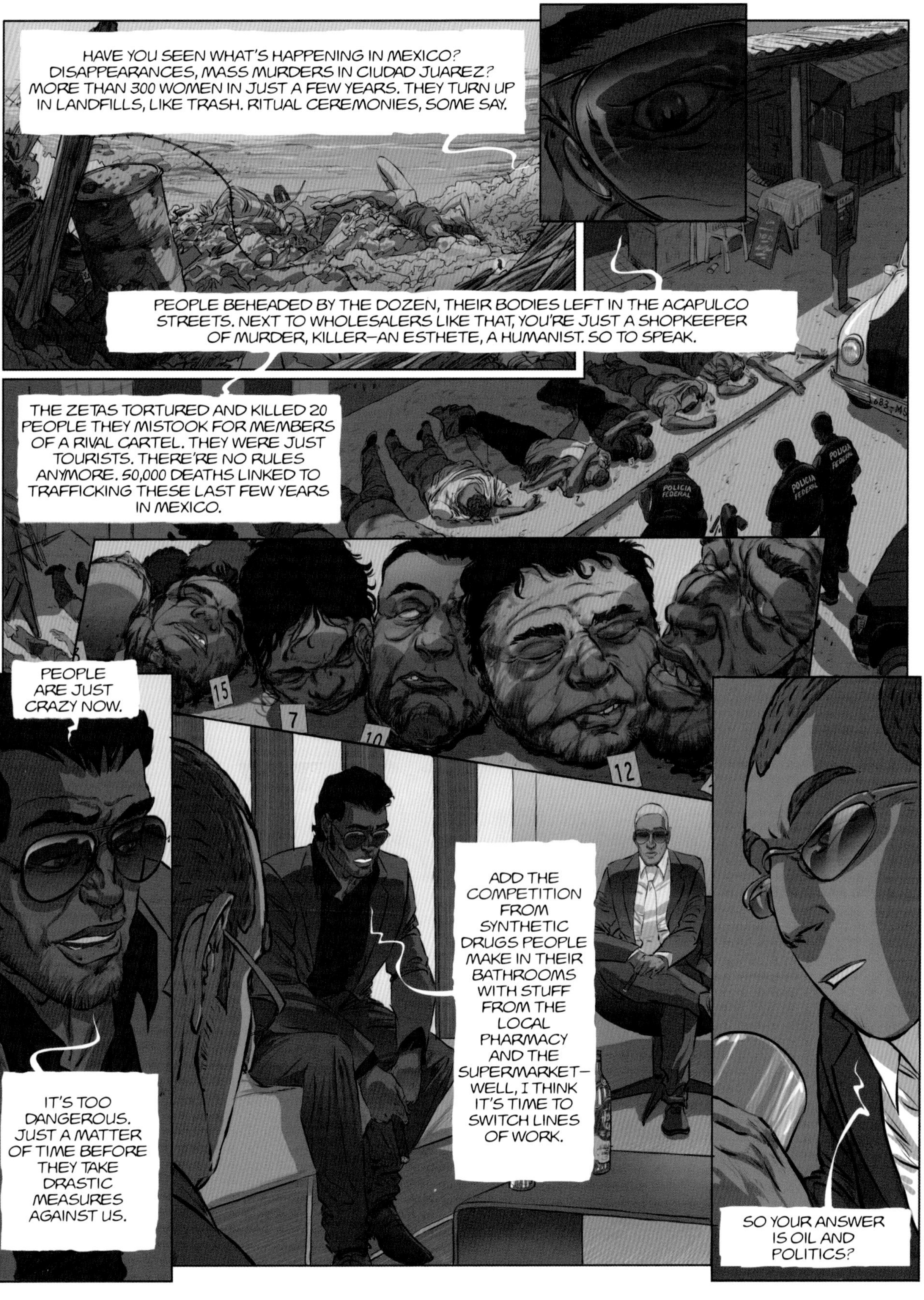
HAVE YOU SEEN WHAT'S HAPPENING IN MEXICO? DISAPPEARANCES, MASS MURDERS IN CIUDAD JUAREZ? MORE THAN 300 WOMEN IN JUST A FEW YEARS. THEY TURN UP IN LANDFILLS, LIKE TRASH. RITUAL CEREMONIES, SOME SAY.
PEOPLE BEHEADED BY THE DOZEN, THEIR BODIES LEFT IN THE ACAPULCO STREETS. NEXT TO WHOLESALERS LIKE THAT, YOU'RE JUST A SHOPKEEPER OF MURDER, KILLER—AN ESTHETE, A HUMANIST. SO TO SPEAK.
THE ZETAS TORTURED AND KILLED 20 PEOPLE THEY MISTOOK FOR MEMBERS OF A RIVAL CARTEL. THEY WERE JUST TOURISTS. THERE'RE NO RULES ANYMORE. 50,000 DEATHS LINKED TO TRAFFICKING THESE LAST FEW YEARS IN MEXICO.
POLICIA FEDERAL
15
7
10
12
PEOPLE ARE JUST CRAZY NOW.
IT'S TOO DANGEROUS. JUST A MATTER OF TIME BEFORE THEY TAKE DRASTIC MEASURES AGAINST US.
ADD THE COMPETITION FROM SYNTHETIC DRUGS PEOPLE MAKE IN THEIR BATHROOMS WITH STUFF FROM THE LOCAL PHARMACY AND THE SUPERMARKET—WELL, I THINK IT'S TIME TO SWITCH LINES OF WORK.
SO YOUR ANSWER IS OIL AND POLITICS?

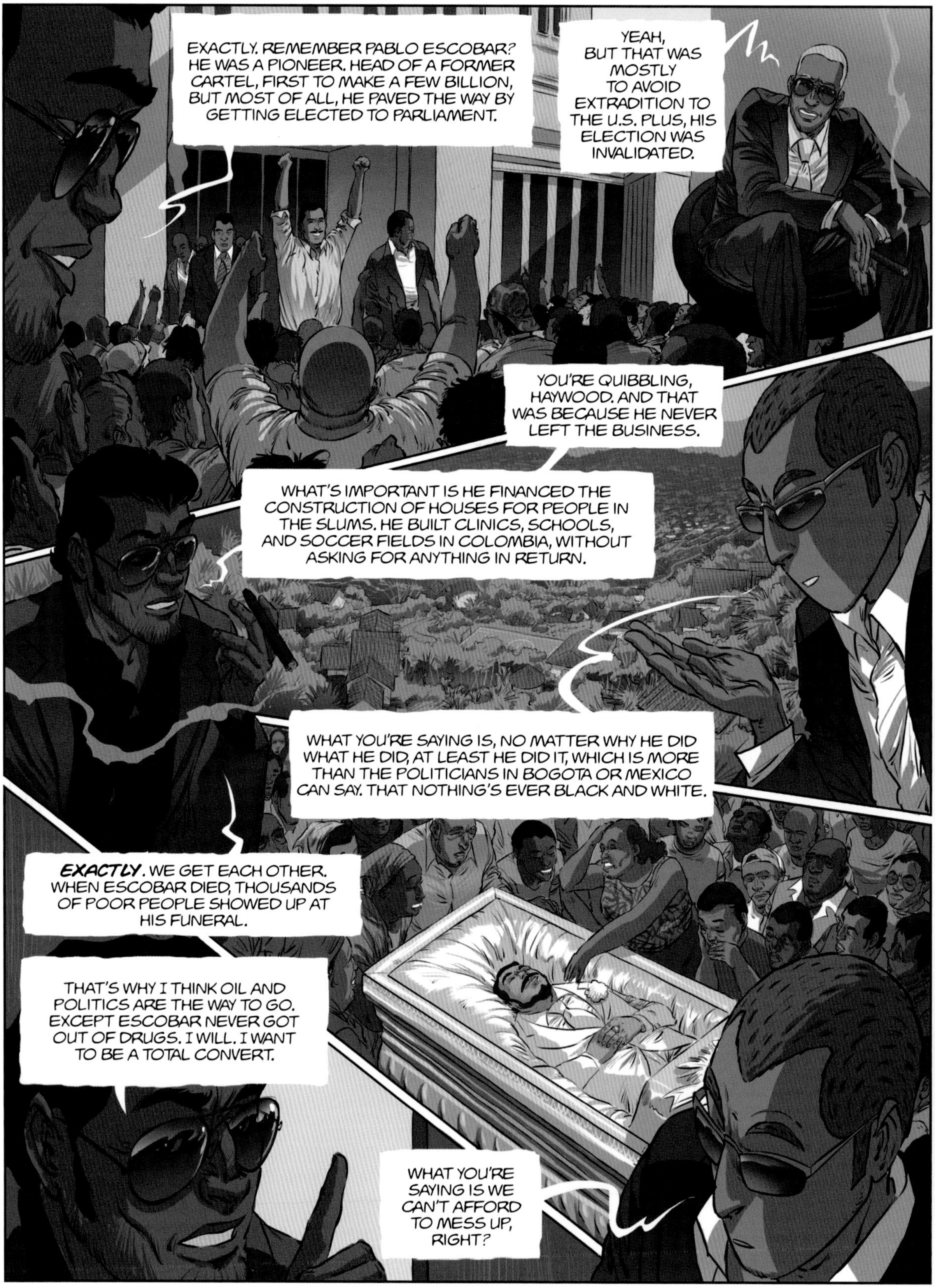
EXACTLY. REMEMBER PABLO ESCOBAR? HE WAS A PIONEER. HEAD OF A FORMER CARTEL, FIRST TO MAKE A FEW BILLION, BUT MOST OF ALL, HE PAVED THE WAY BY GETTING ELECTED TO PARLIAMENT.
YEAH, BUT THAT WAS MOSTLY TO AVOID EXTRADITION TO THE U.S. PLUS, HIS ELECTION WAS INVALIDATED.
YOU'RE QUIBBLING, HAYWOOD. AND THAT WAS BECAUSE HE NEVER LEFT THE BUSINESS.
WHAT'S IMPORTANT IS HE FINANCED THE CONSTRUCTION OF HOUSES FOR PEOPLE IN THE SLUMS. HE BUILT CLINICS, SCHOOLS, AND SOCCER FIELDS IN COLOMBIA, WITHOUT ASKING FOR ANYTHING IN RETURN.
WHAT YOU'RE SAYING IS, NO MATTER WHY HE DID WHAT HE DID, AT LEAST HE DID IT, WHICH IS MORE THAN THE POLITICIANS IN BOGOTA OR MEXICO CAN SAY. THAT NOTHING'S EVER BLACK AND WHITE.
EXACTLY. WE GET EACH OTHER. WHEN ESCOBAR DIED, THOUSANDS OF POOR PEOPLE SHOWED UP AT HIS FUNERAL.
THAT'S WHY I THINK OIL AND POLITICS ARE THE WAY TO GO. EXCEPT ESCOBAR NEVER GOT OUT OF DRUGS. I WILL. I WANT TO BE A TOTAL CONVERT.
WHAT YOU'RE SAYING IS WE CAN'T AFFORD TO MESS UP, RIGHT?

THIS IS MORE THAN JUST LAUNDERING OR A SIDELINE FOR ME. IT'S A SECOND CHANCE, A UNIQUE OPPORTUNITY. A NEW START. NOT MANY PEOPLE GET THAT IN LIFE, ESPECIALLY PEOPLE LIKE US.

SO YEAH, WE CAN'T MESS UP.

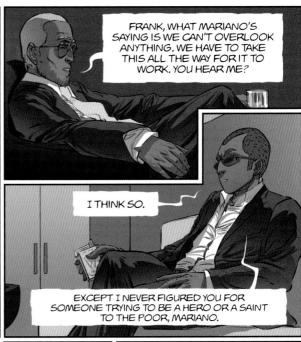

FRANK, WHAT MARIANO'S SAYING IS WE CAN'T OVERLOOK ANYTHING. WE HAVE TO TAKE THIS ALL THE WAY FOR IT TO WORK. YOU HEAR ME?

I THINK SO.

EXCEPT I NEVER FIGURED YOU FOR SOMEONE TRYING TO BE A HERO OR A SAINT TO THE POOR, MARIANO.

DON'T CHANGE THE SUBJECT. WHAT WE MEAN IS, IT'D BE A PITY NOT TO TAKE ADVANTAGE OF YOUR EXCEPTIONAL SKILLS IN YOUR AREA OF EXPERTISE.

A WELL-RUN COMPANY PUTS ITS BEST RESOURCES WHERE THEY'LL DO THE MOST GOOD.

YOU INTO HUMAN RESOURCES NOW, HAYWOOD?

WHY NOT? IT'S DEFINITELY LESS COMPLICATED AND LESS TIRING. I'LL PICK YOU OUT SOME ASSISTANT MYSELF, AND YOU CAN TELL ME HOW THEY WORK OUT.

SO WHAT HAVE YOU GOT PLANNED?

OR, TO USE BUSINESS PARLANCE, WHAT'S MY *NEW TITLE*?

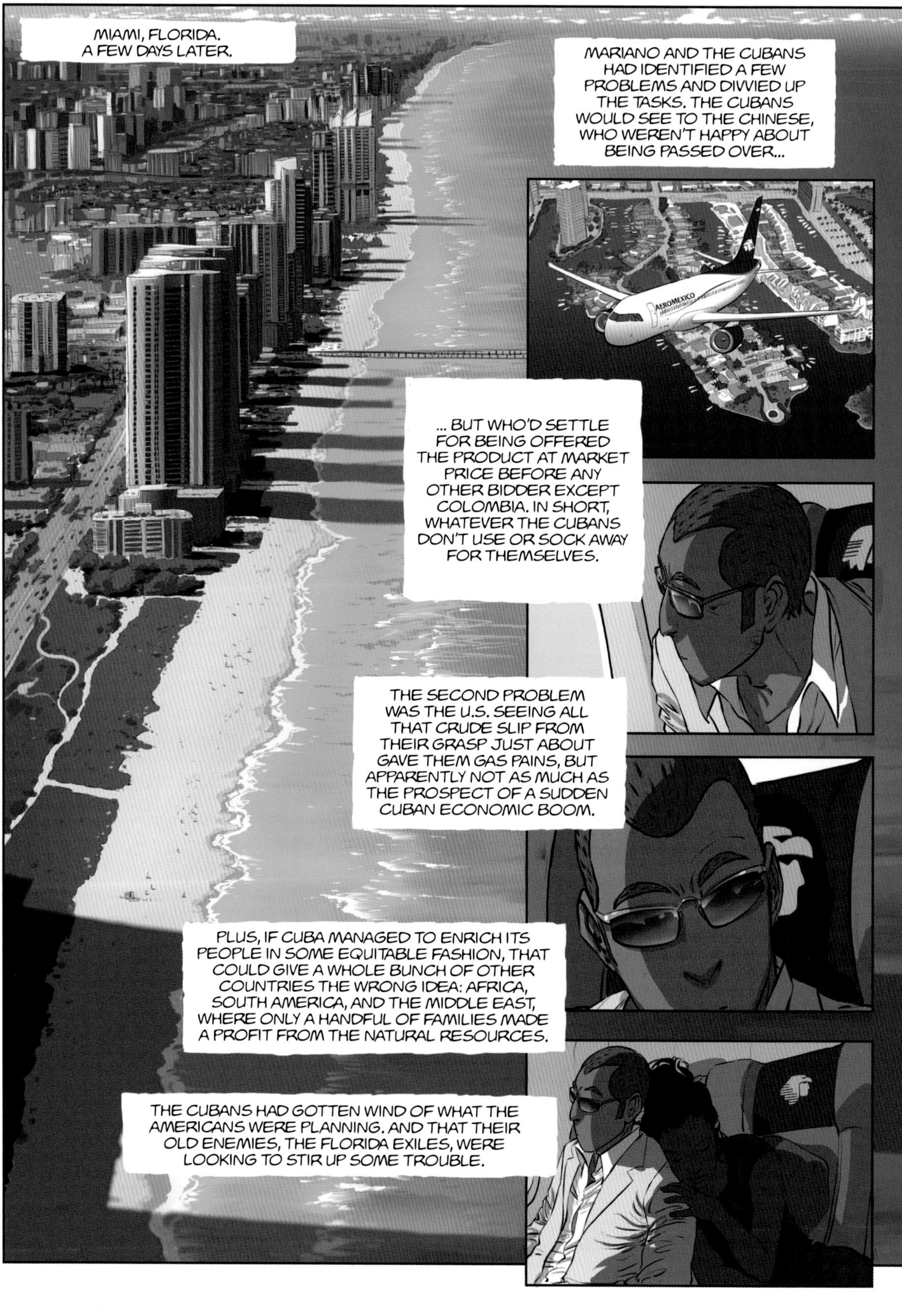
MIAMI, FLORIDA.
A FEW DAYS LATER.
MARIANO AND THE CUBANS HAD IDENTIFIED A FEW PROBLEMS AND DIVVIED UP THE TASKS. THE CUBANS WOULD SEE TO THE CHINESE, WHO WEREN'T HAPPY ABOUT BEING PASSED OVER...
AEROMEXICO
... BUT WHO'D SETTLE FOR BEING OFFERED THE PRODUCT AT MARKET PRICE BEFORE ANY OTHER BIDDER EXCEPT COLOMBIA. IN SHORT, WHATEVER THE CUBANS DON'T USE OR SOCK AWAY FOR THEMSELVES.
THE SECOND PROBLEM WAS THE U.S. SEEING ALL THAT CRUDE SLIP FROM THEIR GRASP JUST ABOUT GAVE THEM GAS PAINS, BUT APPARENTLY NOT AS MUCH AS THE PROSPECT OF A SUDDEN CUBAN ECONOMIC BOOM.
PLUS, IF CUBA MANAGED TO ENRICH ITS PEOPLE IN SOME EQUITABLE FASHION, THAT COULD GIVE A WHOLE BUNCH OF OTHER COUNTRIES THE WRONG IDEA: AFRICA, SOUTH AMERICA, AND THE MIDDLE EAST, WHERE ONLY A HANDFUL OF FAMILIES MADE A PROFIT FROM THE NATURAL RESOURCES.
THE CUBANS HAD GOTTEN WIND OF WHAT THE AMERICANS WERE PLANNING. AND THAT THEIR OLD ENEMIES, THE FLORIDA EXILES, WERE LOOKING TO STIR UP SOME TROUBLE.

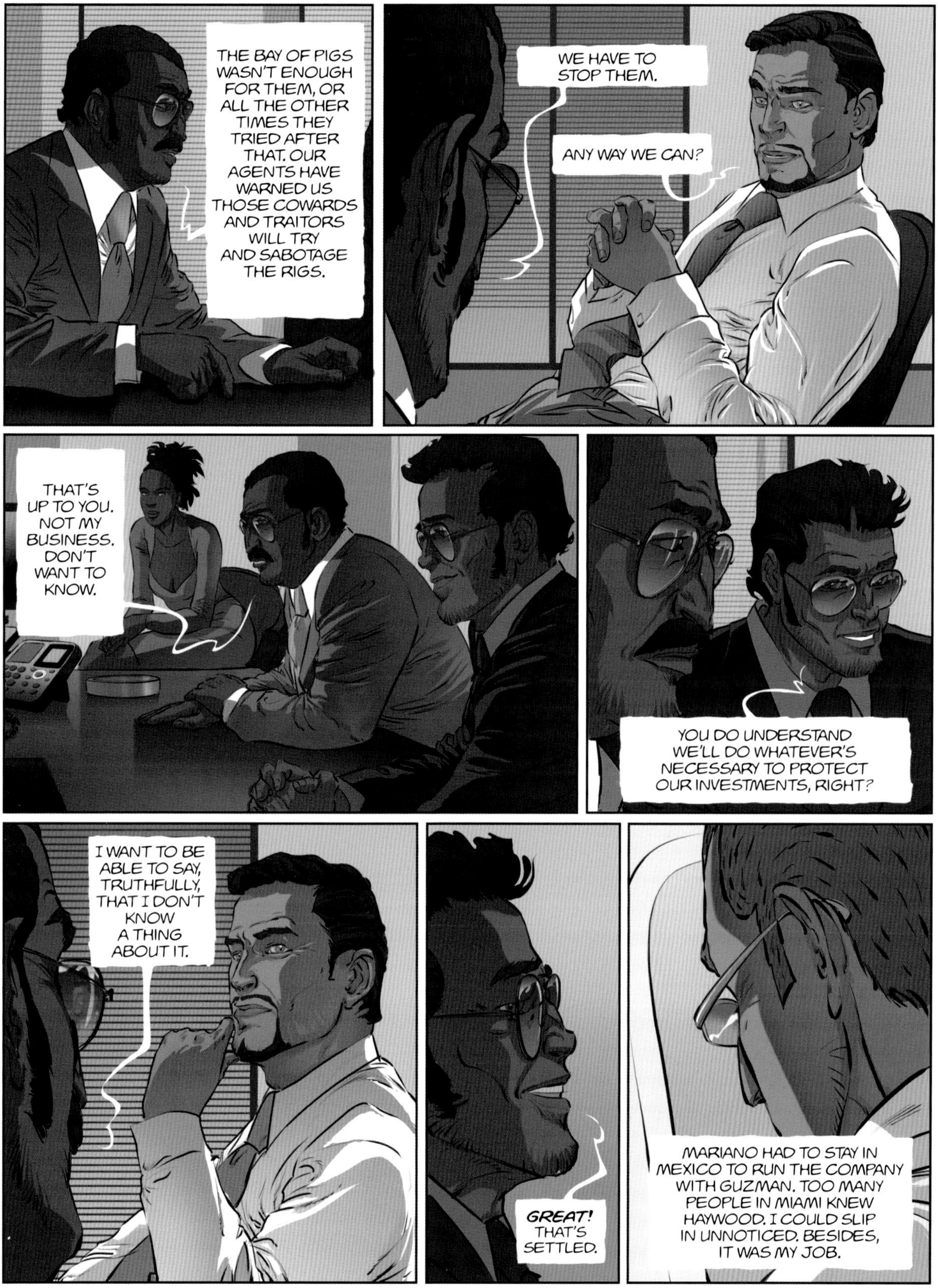
THE BAY OF PIGS WASN'T ENOUGH FOR THEM, OR ALL THE OTHER TIMES THEY TRIED AFTER THAT. OUR AGENTS HAVE WARNED US THOSE COWARDS AND TRAITORS WILL TRY AND SABOTAGE THE RIGS.
WE HAVE TO STOP THEM.
ANY WAY WE CAN?
THAT'S UP TO YOU. NOT MY BUSINESS. DON'T WANT TO KNOW.
YOU DO UNDERSTAND WE'LL DO WHATEVER'S NECESSARY TO PROTECT OUR INVESTMENTS, RIGHT?
I WANT TO BE ABLE TO SAY, TRUTHFULLY, THAT I DON'T KNOW A THING ABOUT IT.
GREAT! THAT'S SETTLED.
MARIANO HAD TO STAY IN MEXICO TO RUN THE COMPANY WITH GUZMAN. TOO MANY PEOPLE IN MIAMI KNEW HAYWOOD. I COULD SLIP IN UNNOTICED. BESIDES, IT WAS MY JOB.

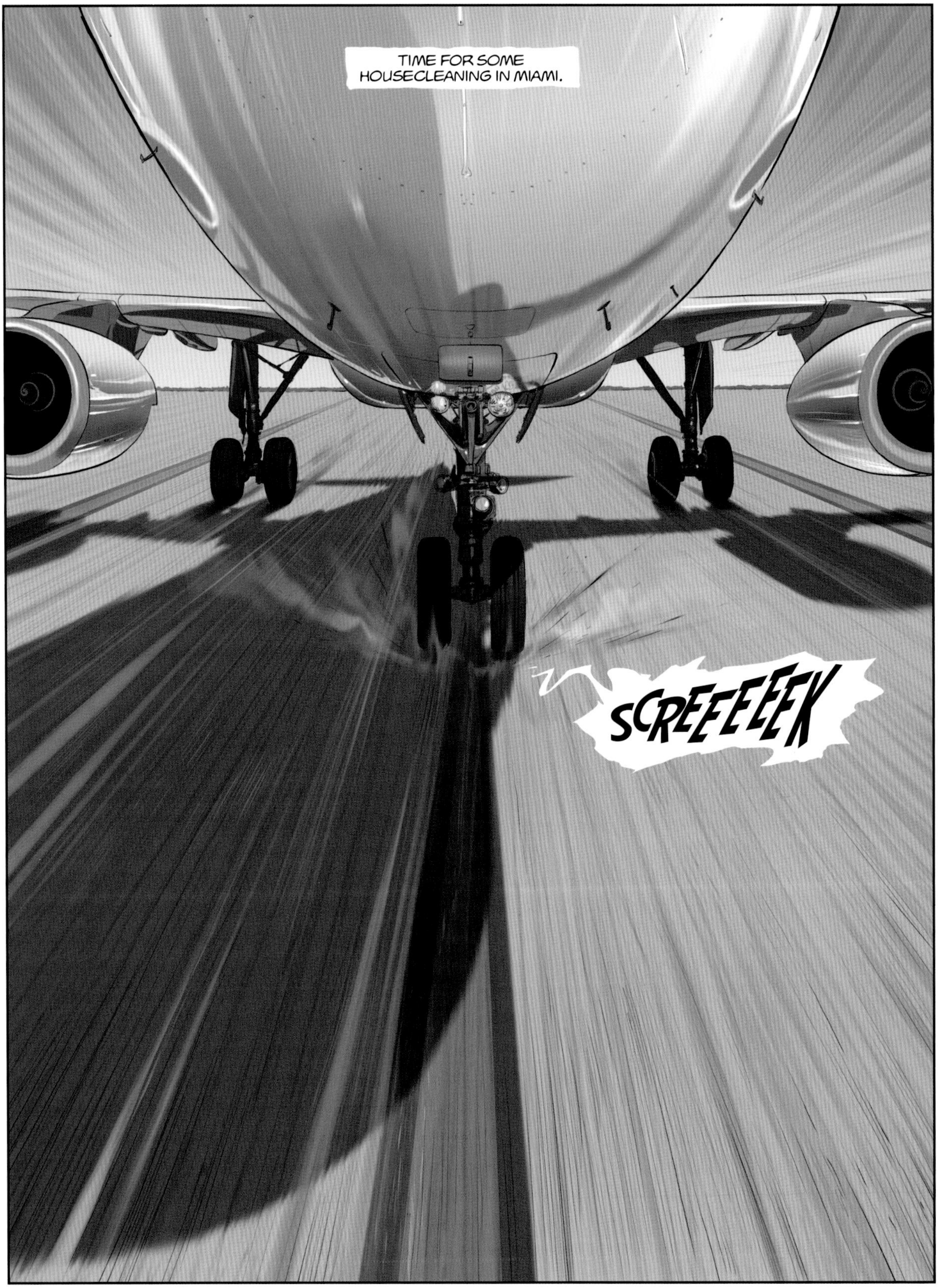
TIME FOR SOME
HOUSECLEANING IN MIAMI.
SCREEEEEK

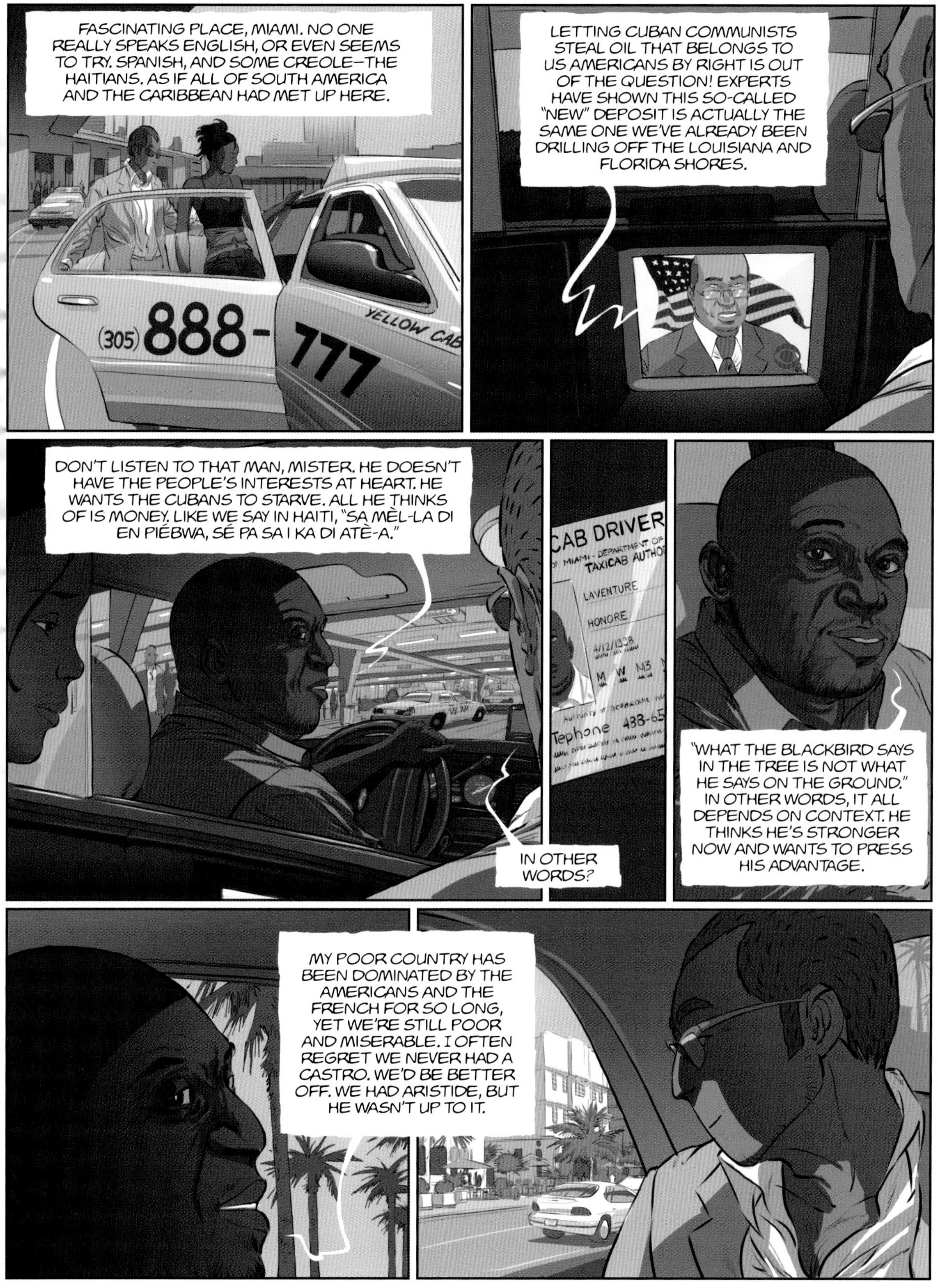
FASCINATING PLACE, MIAMI. NO ONE REALLY SPEAKS ENGLISH, OR EVEN SEEMS TO TRY. SPANISH, AND SOME CREOLE—THE HAITIANS. AS IF ALL OF SOUTH AMERICA AND THE CARIBBEAN HAD MET UP HERE.
(305) 888-777
YELLOW CAB
LETTING CUBAN COMMUNISTS STEAL OIL THAT BELONGS TO US AMERICANS BY RIGHT IS OUT OF THE QUESTION! EXPERTS HAVE SHOWN THIS SO-CALLED "NEW" DEPOSIT IS ACTUALLY THE SAME ONE WE'VE ALREADY BEEN DRILLING OFF THE LOUISIANA AND FLORIDA SHORES.
DON'T LISTEN TO THAT MAN, MISTER. HE DOESN'T HAVE THE PEOPLE'S INTERESTS AT HEART. HE WANTS THE CUBANS TO STARVE. ALL HE THINKS OF IS MONEY. LIKE WE SAY IN HAITI, "SA MÈL-LA DI EN PIÉBWA, SÉ PA SA I KA DI ATÈ-A."
IN OTHER WORDS?
CAB DRIVER
LAVENTURE
HONORE
"WHAT THE BLACKBIRD SAYS IN THE TREE IS NOT WHAT HE SAYS ON THE GROUND." IN OTHER WORDS, IT ALL DEPENDS ON CONTEXT. HE THINKS HE'S STRONGER NOW AND WANTS TO PRESS HIS ADVANTAGE.
MY POOR COUNTRY HAS BEEN DOMINATED BY THE AMERICANS AND THE FRENCH FOR SO LONG, YET WE'RE STILL POOR AND MISERABLE. I OFTEN REGRET WE NEVER HAD A CASTRO. WE'D BE BETTER OFF. WE HAD ARISTIDE, BUT HE WASN'T UP TO IT.

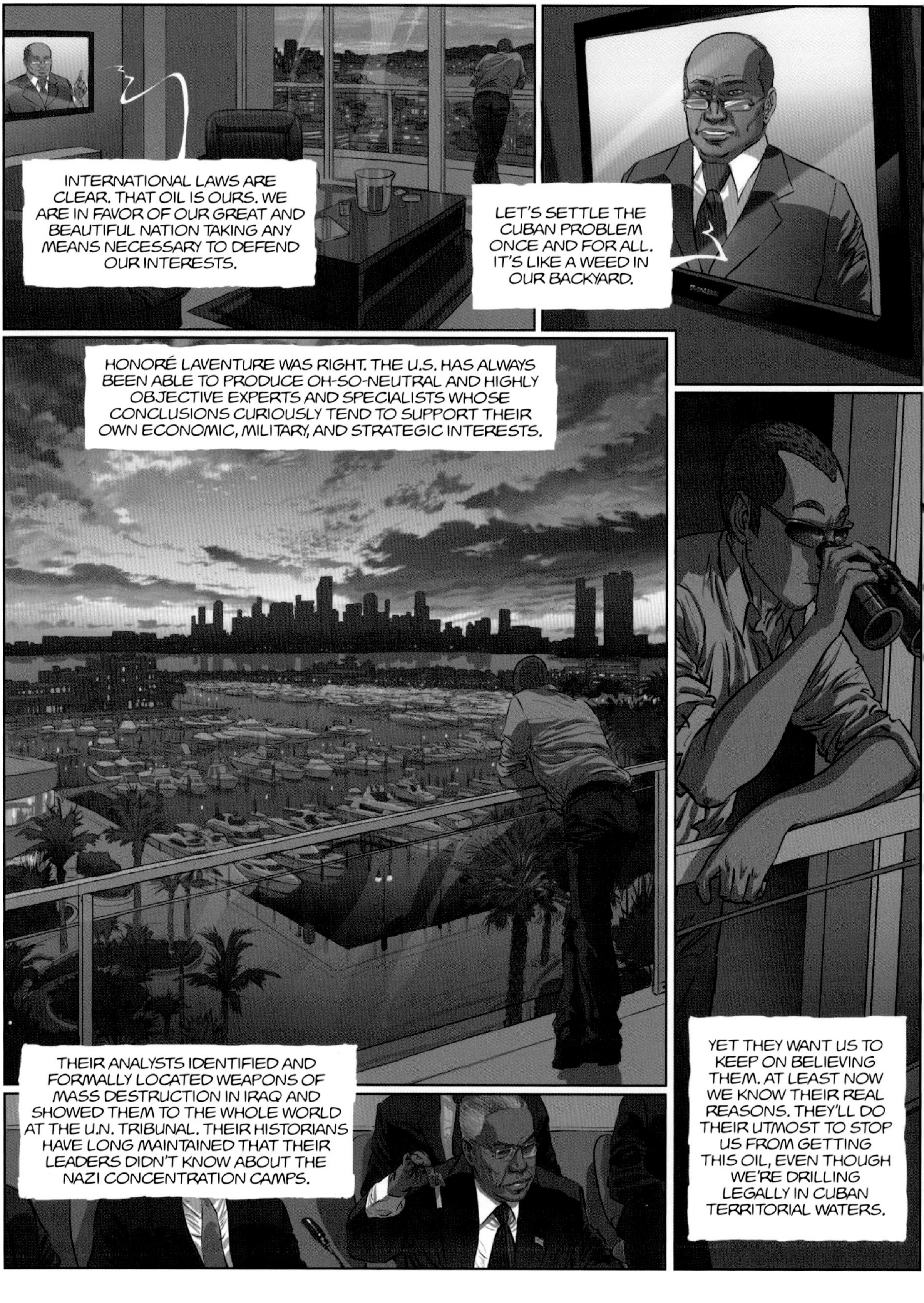
INTERNATIONAL LAWS ARE CLEAR. THAT OIL IS OURS. WE ARE IN FAVOR OF OUR GREAT AND BEAUTIFUL NATION TAKING ANY MEANS NECESSARY TO DEFEND OUR INTERESTS.
LET'S SETTLE THE CUBAN PROBLEM ONCE AND FOR ALL. IT'S LIKE A WEED IN OUR BACKYARD.
HONORÉ LAVENTURE WAS RIGHT. THE U.S. HAS ALWAYS BEEN ABLE TO PRODUCE OH-SO-NEUTRAL AND HIGHLY OBJECTIVE EXPERTS AND SPECIALISTS WHOSE CONCLUSIONS CURIOUSLY TEND TO SUPPORT THEIR OWN ECONOMIC, MILITARY, AND STRATEGIC INTERESTS.
THEIR ANALYSTS IDENTIFIED AND FORMALLY LOCATED WEAPONS OF MASS DESTRUCTION IN IRAQ AND SHOWED THEM TO THE WHOLE WORLD AT THE U.N. TRIBUNAL. THEIR HISTORIANS HAVE LONG MAINTAINED THAT THEIR LEADERS DIDN'T KNOW ABOUT THE NAZI CONCENTRATION CAMPS.
YET THEY WANT US TO KEEP ON BELIEVING THEM. AT LEAST NOW WE KNOW THEIR REAL REASONS. THEY'LL DO THEIR UTMOST TO STOP US FROM GETTING THIS OIL, EVEN THOUGH WE'RE DRILLING LEGALLY IN CUBAN TERRITORIAL WATERS.

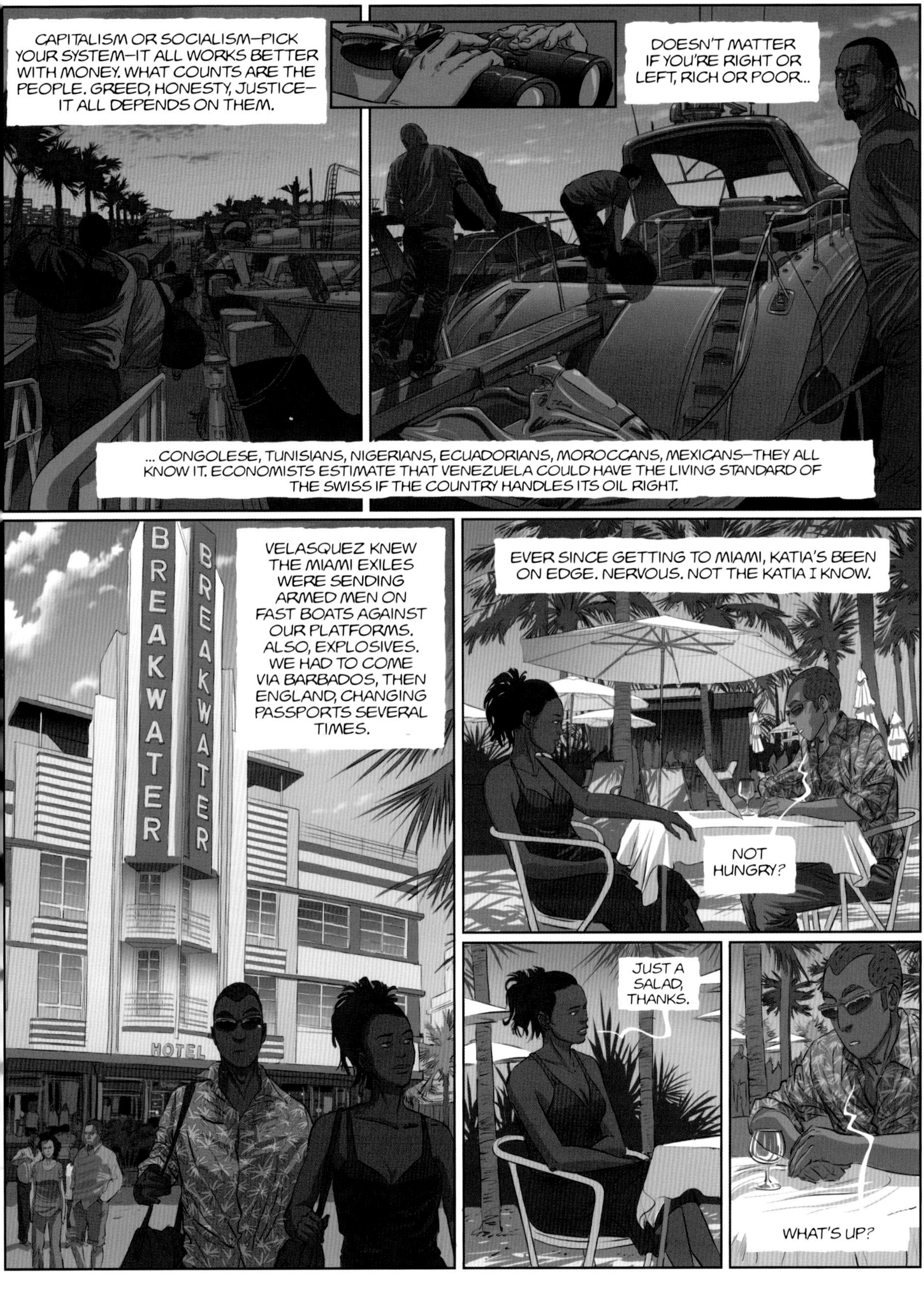
CAPITALISM OR SOCIALISM—PICK YOUR SYSTEM—IT ALL WORKS BETTER WITH MONEY. WHAT COUNTS ARE THE PEOPLE. GREED, HONESTY, JUSTICE—IT ALL DEPENDS ON THEM.
DOESN'T MATTER IF YOU'RE RIGHT OR LEFT, RICH OR POOR...
... CONGOLESE, TUNISIANS, NIGERIANS, ECUADORIANS, MOROCCANS, MEXICANS—THEY ALL KNOW IT. ECONOMISTS ESTIMATE THAT VENEZUELA COULD HAVE THE LIVING STANDARD OF THE SWISS IF THE COUNTRY HANDLES ITS OIL RIGHT.
BREAKWATER
BREAKWATER
HOTEL
VELASQUEZ KNEW THE MIAMI EXILES WERE SENDING ARMED MEN ON FAST BOATS AGAINST OUR PLATFORMS. ALSO, EXPLOSIVES. WE HAD TO COME VIA BARBADOS, THEN ENGLAND, CHANGING PASSPORTS SEVERAL TIMES.
EVER SINCE GETTING TO MIAMI, KATIA'S BEEN ON EDGE. NERVOUS. NOT THE KATIA I KNOW.
NOT HUNGRY?
JUST A SALAD, THANKS.
WHAT'S UP?

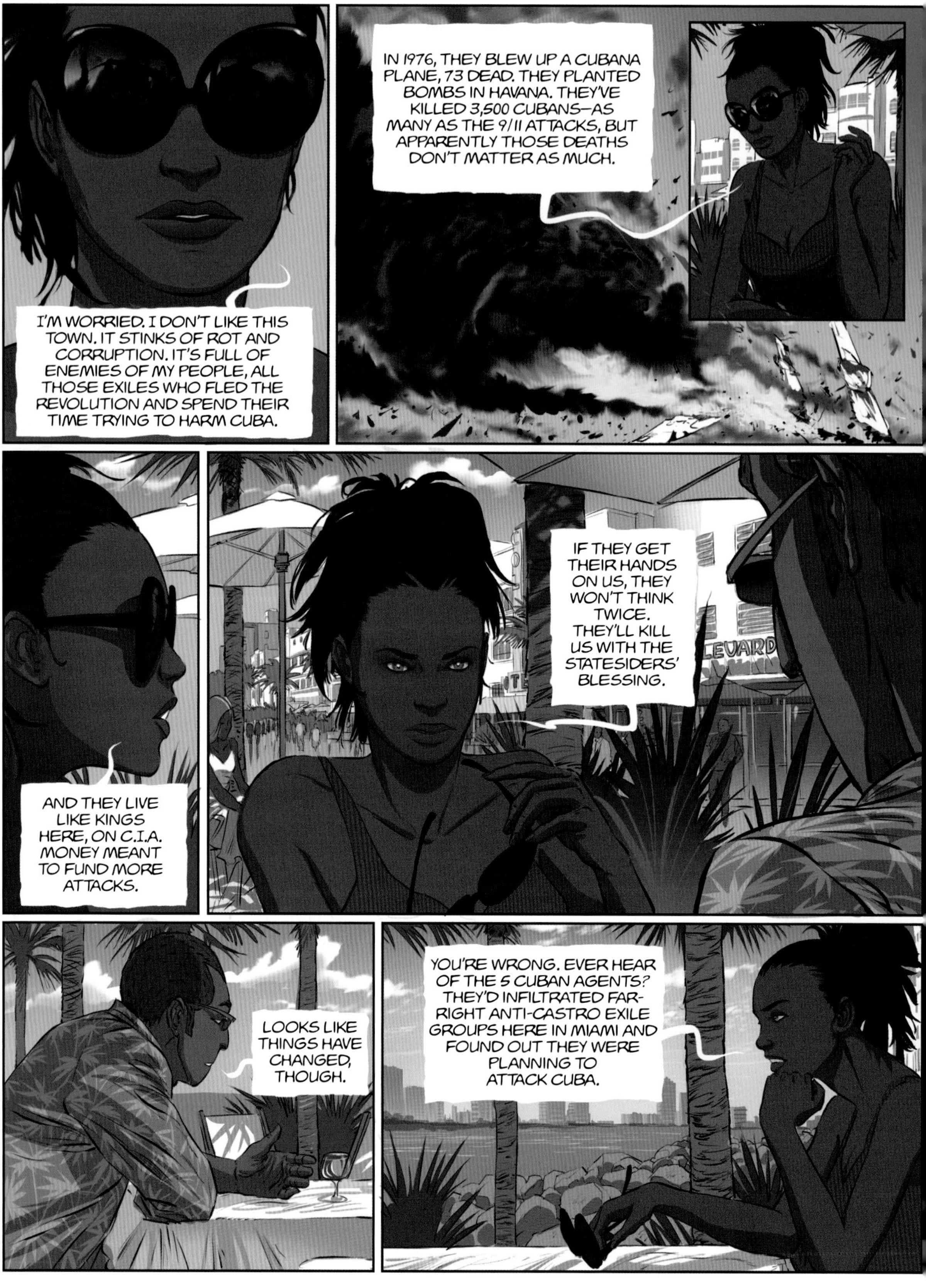
I'M WORRIED. I DON'T LIKE THIS TOWN. IT STINKS OF ROT AND CORRUPTION. IT'S FULL OF ENEMIES OF MY PEOPLE, ALL THOSE EXILES WHO FLED THE REVOLUTION AND SPEND THEIR TIME TRYING TO HARM CUBA.
IN 1976, THEY BLEW UP A CUBANA PLANE, 73 DEAD. THEY PLANTED BOMBS IN HAVANA. THEY'VE KILLED 3,500 CUBANS—AS MANY AS THE 9/11 ATTACKS, BUT APPARENTLY THOSE DEATHS DON'T MATTER AS MUCH.
AND THEY LIVE LIKE KINGS HERE, ON C.I.A. MONEY MEANT TO FUND MORE ATTACKS.
IF THEY GET THEIR HANDS ON US, THEY WON'T THINK TWICE. THEY'LL KILL US WITH THE STATESIDERS' BLESSING.
LOOKS LIKE THINGS HAVE CHANGED, THOUGH.
YOU'RE WRONG. EVER HEAR OF THE 5 CUBAN AGENTS? THEY'D INFILTRATED FAR-RIGHT ANTI-CASTRO EXILE GROUPS HERE IN MIAMI AND FOUND OUT THEY WERE PLANNING TO ATTACK CUBA.

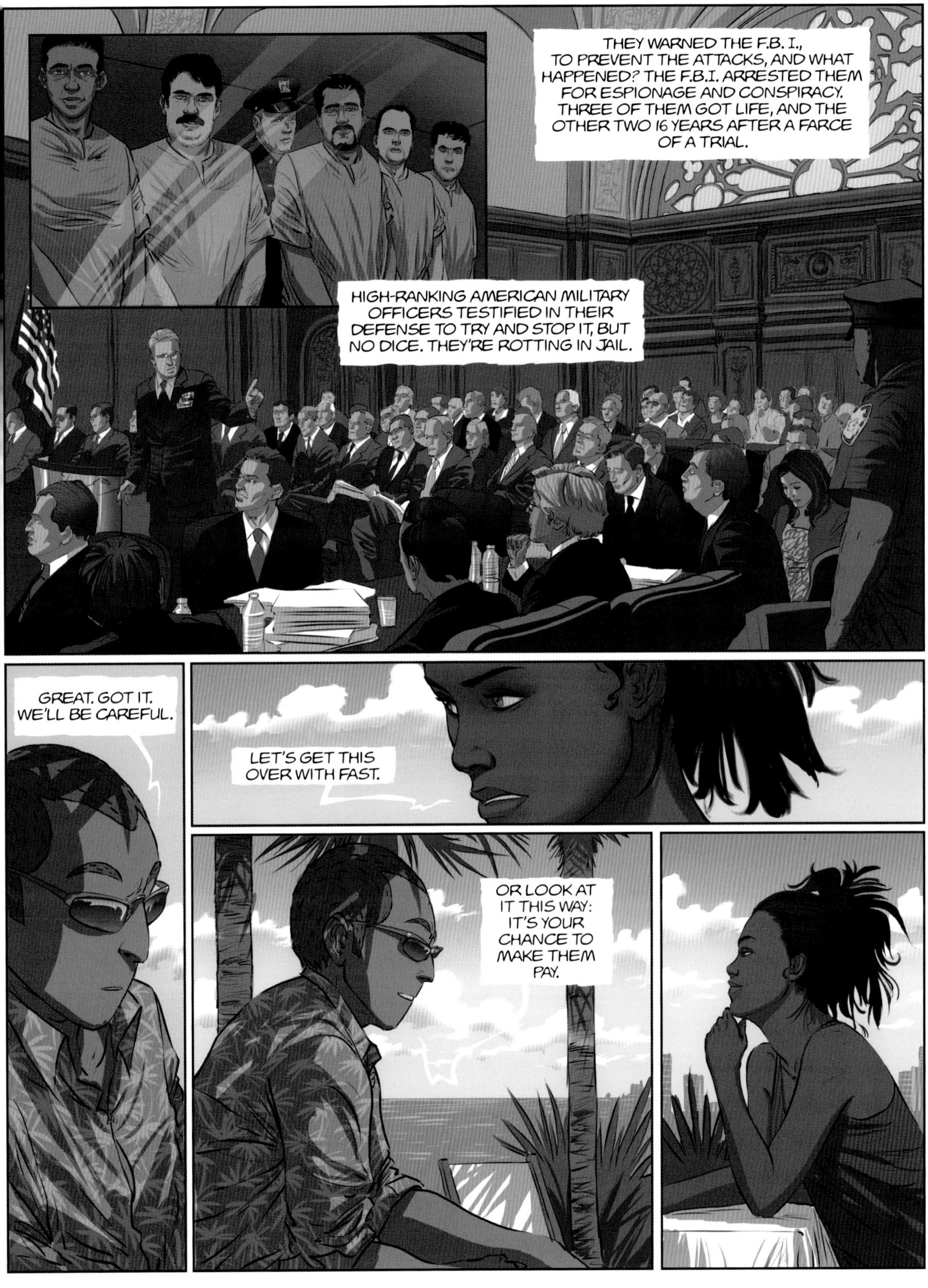
THEY WARNED THE F.B. I., TO PREVENT THE ATTACKS, AND WHAT HAPPENED? THE F.B.I. ARRESTED THEM FOR ESPIONAGE AND CONSPIRACY. THREE OF THEM GOT LIFE, AND THE OTHER TWO 16 YEARS AFTER A FARCE OF A TRIAL.
HIGH-RANKING AMERICAN MILITARY OFFICERS TESTIFIED IN THEIR DEFENSE TO TRY AND STOP IT, BUT NO DICE. THEY'RE ROTTING IN JAIL.
GREAT. GOT IT. WE'LL BE CAREFUL.
LET'S GET THIS OVER WITH FAST.
OR LOOK AT IT THIS WAY: IT'S YOUR CHANCE TO MAKE THEM PAY.

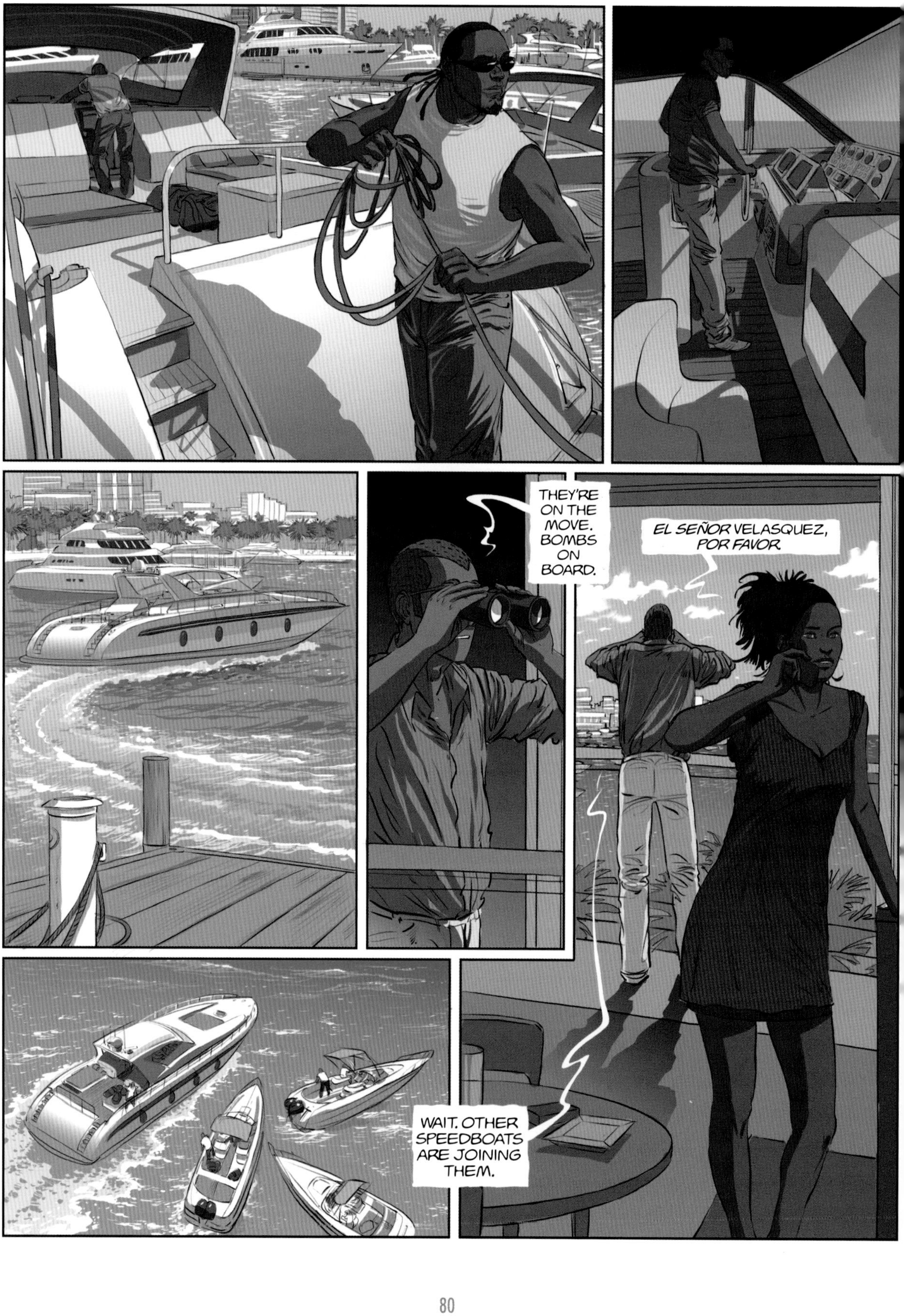
THEY'RE ON THE MOVE. BOMBS ON BOARD.
EL SEÑOR VELASQUEZ, POR FAVOR.
WAIT. OTHER SPEEDBOATS ARE JOINING THEM.

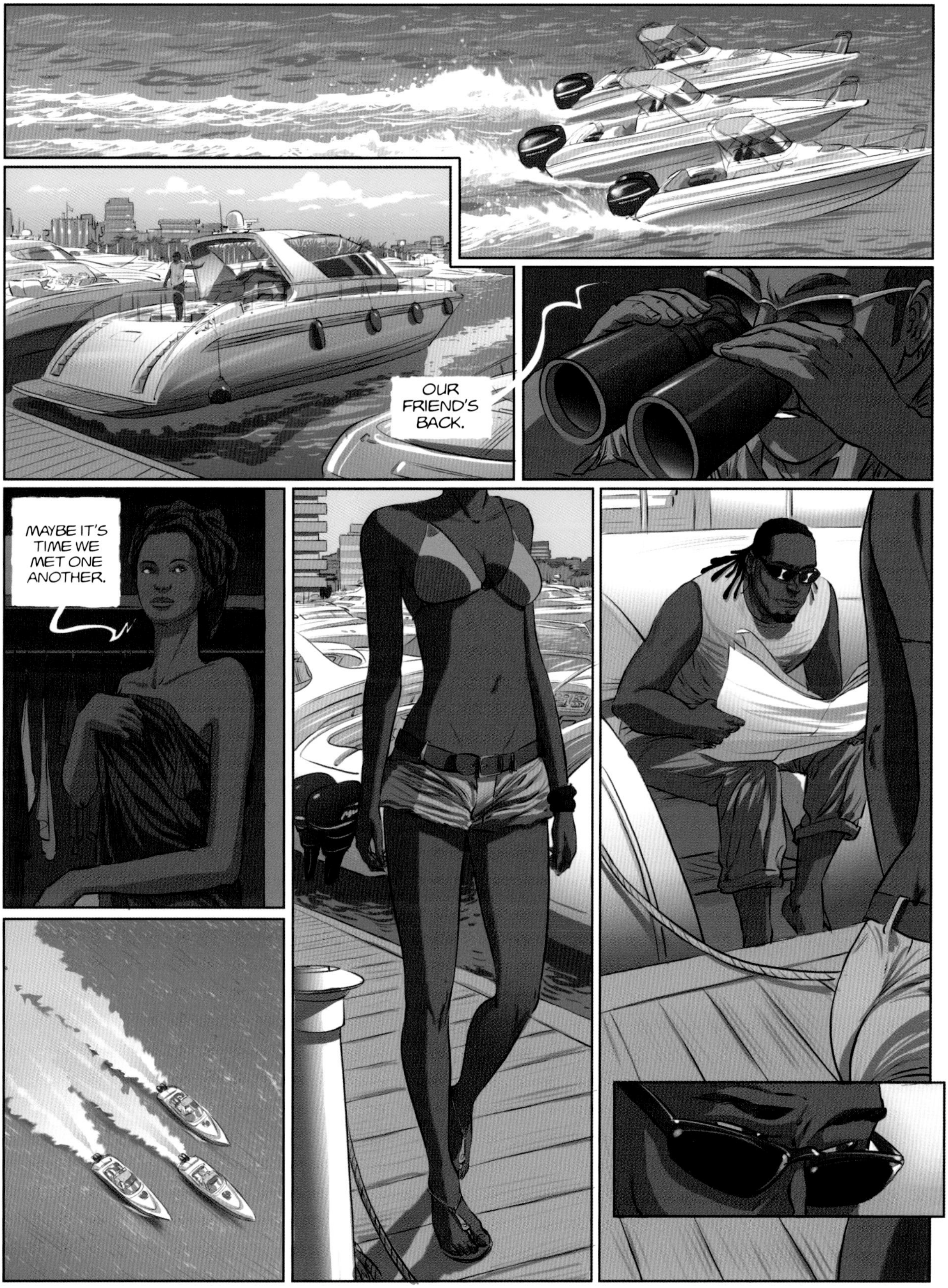
OUR FRIEND'S BACK.
MAYBE IT'S TIME WE MET ONE ANOTHER.

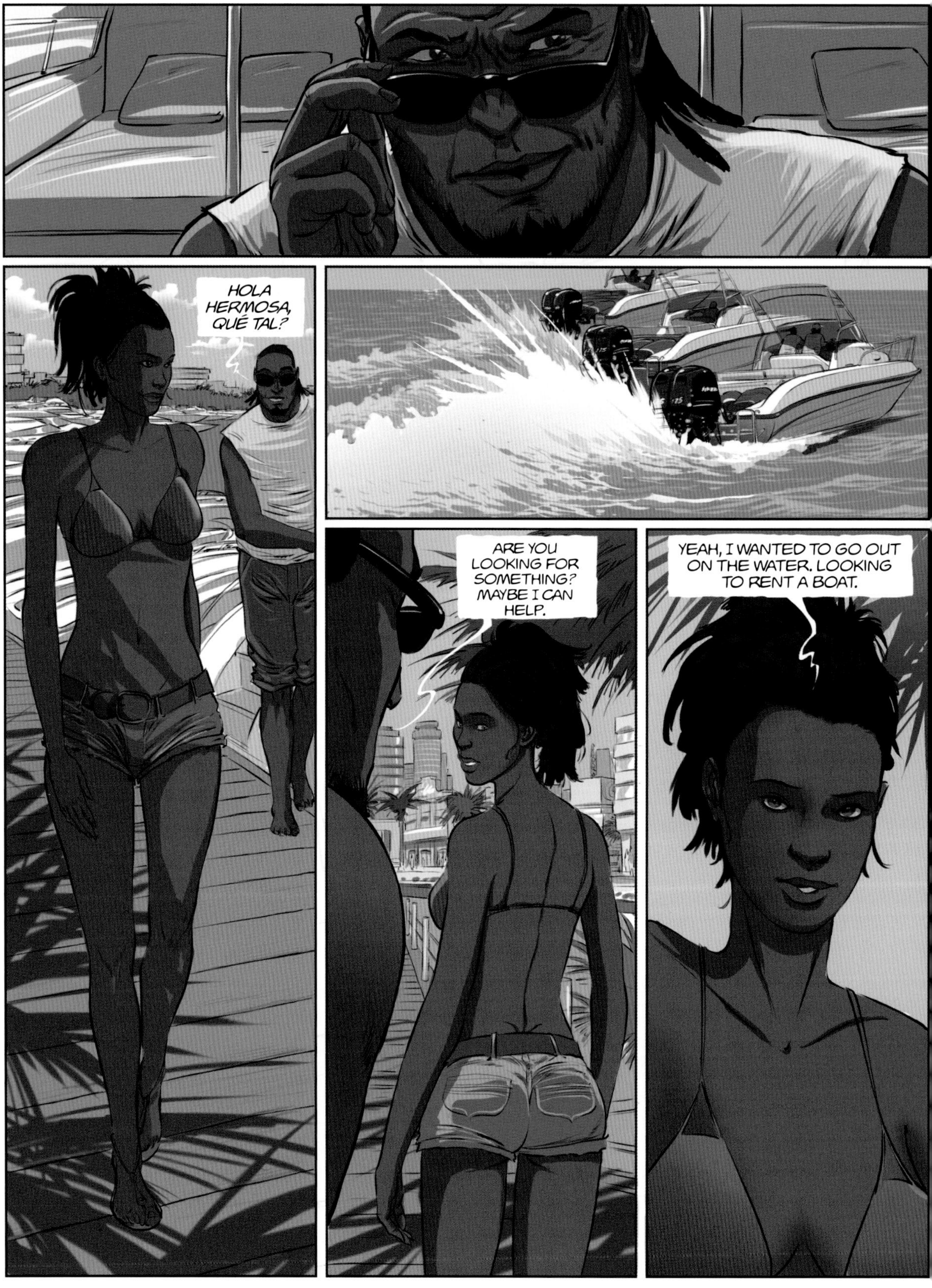
HOLA HERMOSA, QUÉ TAL?
ARE YOU LOOKING FOR SOMETHING? MAYBE I CAN HELP.
YEAH, I WANTED TO GO OUT ON THE WATER. LOOKING TO RENT A BOAT.

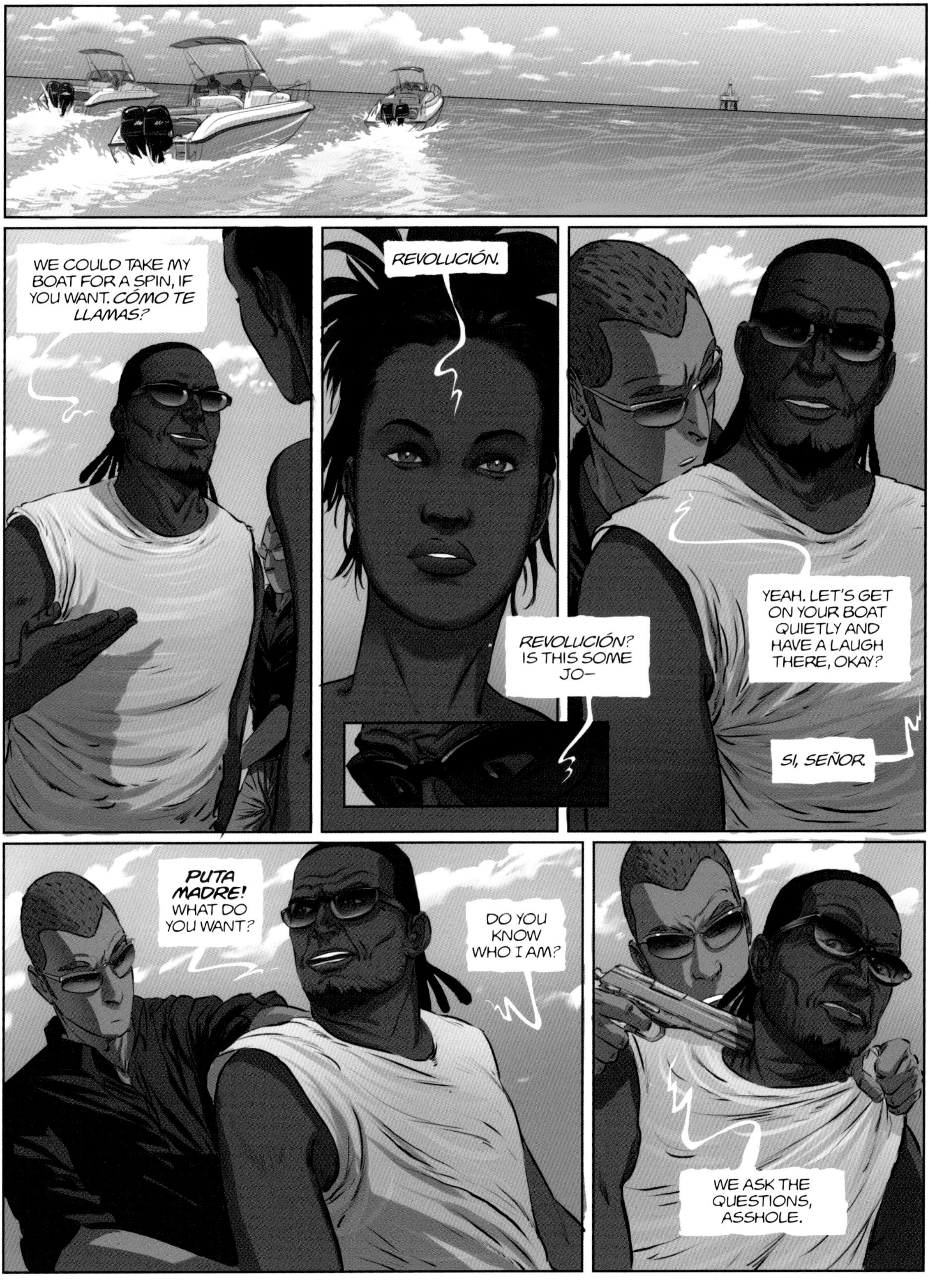
WE COULD TAKE MY BOAT FOR A SPIN, IF YOU WANT. CÓMO TE LLAMAS?
REVOLUCIÓN.
REVOLUCIÓN? IS THIS SOME JO—
YEAH. LET'S GET ON YOUR BOAT QUIETLY AND HAVE A LAUGH THERE, OKAY?
SI, SEÑOR.
PUTA MADRE! WHAT DO YOU WANT?
DO YOU KNOW WHO I AM?
WE ASK THE QUESTIONS, ASSHOLE.

NICE FISHING EQUIPMENT, THERE. BETTER TALK, FRIEND. FAST.

GREAT. THANKS, SEÑOR VELASQUEZ. WE'RE READY.

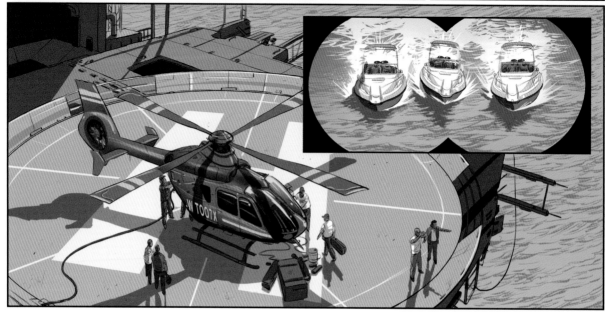

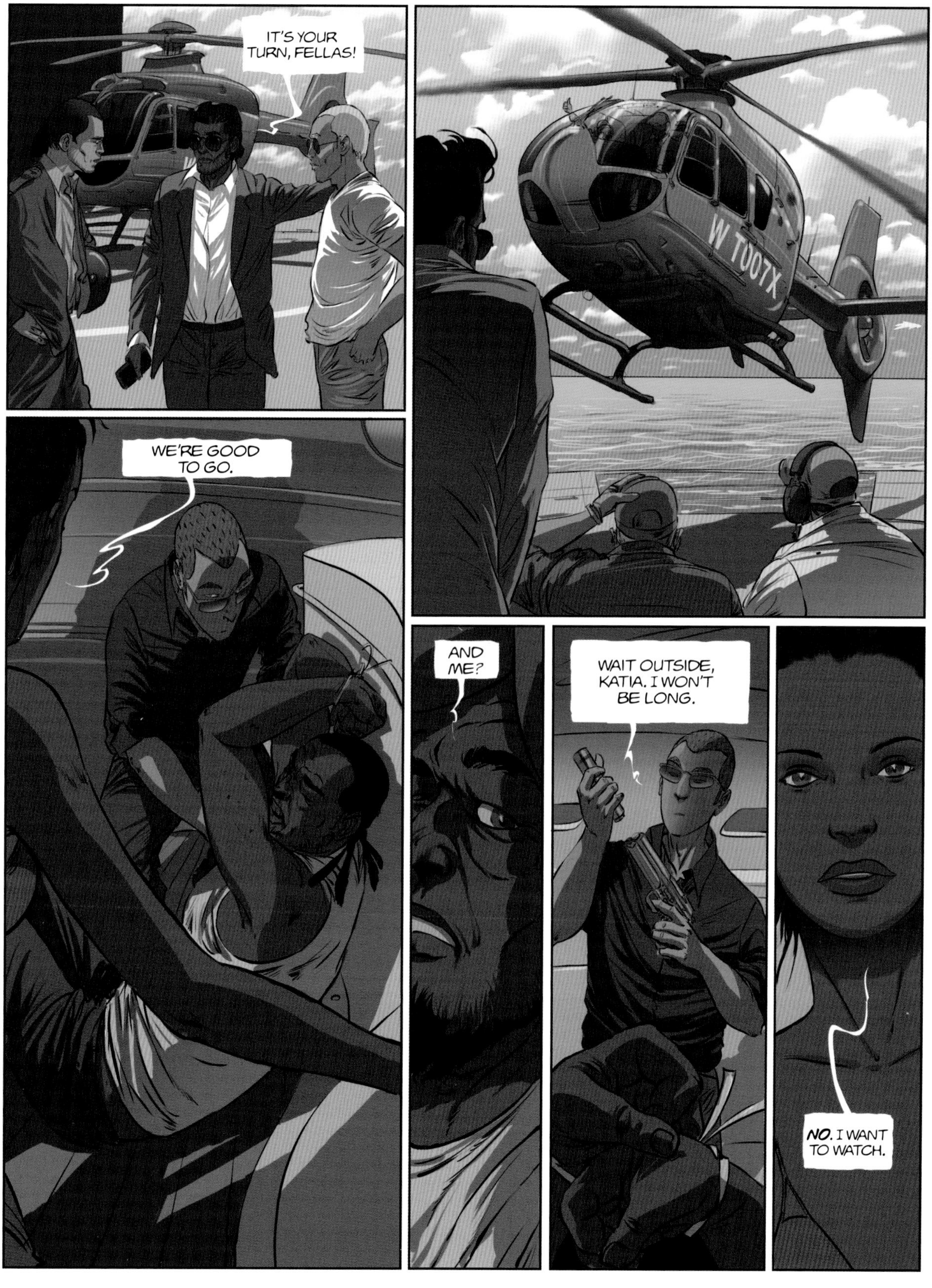
IT'S YOUR TURN, FELLAS!
W T007X
WE'RE GOOD TO GO.
AND ME?
WAIT OUTSIDE, KATIA. I WON'T BE LONG.
NO. I WANT TO WATCH.

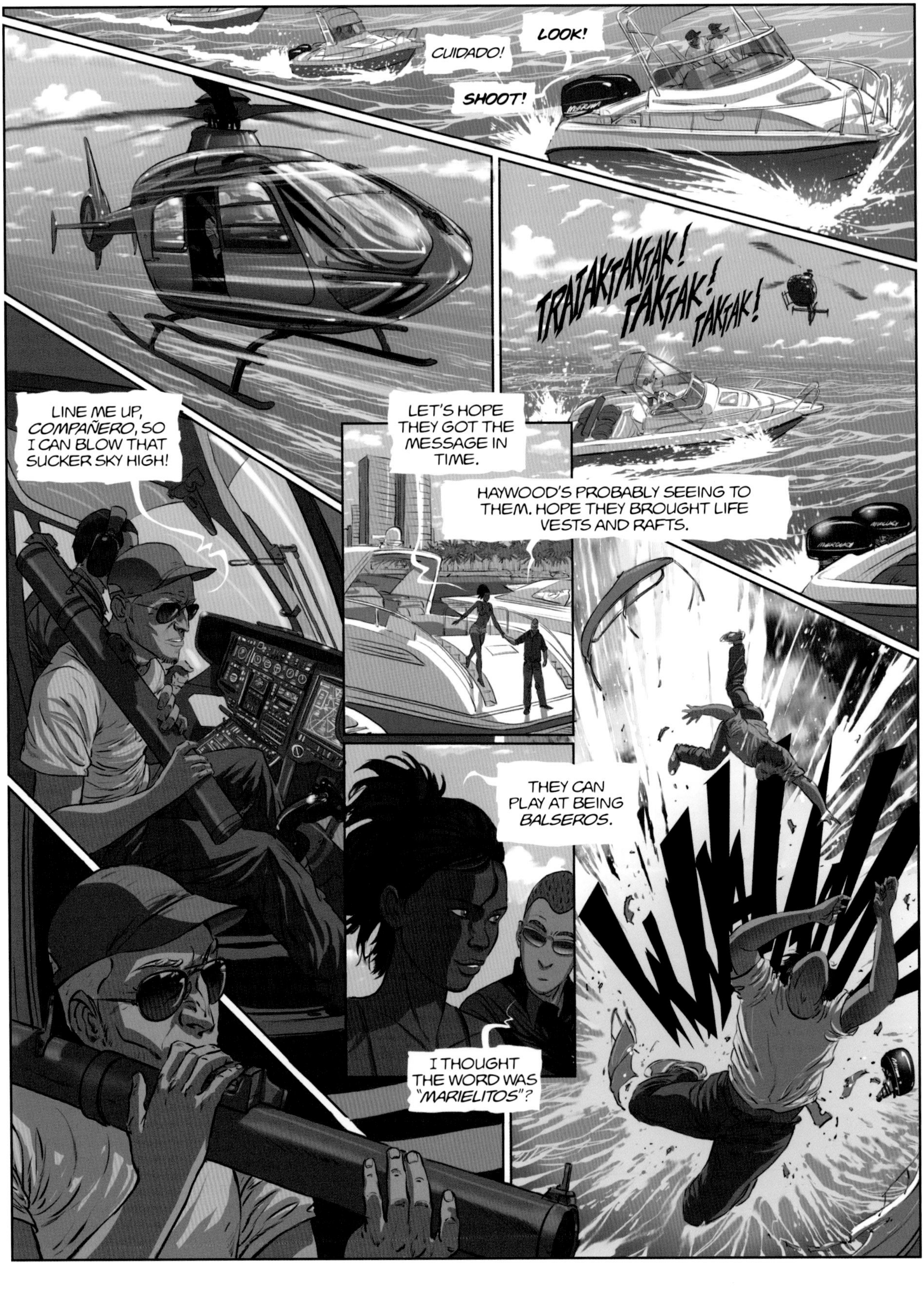
CUIDADO!
LOOK!
SHOOT!
TRATATAKTAKTAK! TAKTAK! TAKTAK!
LINE ME UP, COMPAÑERO, SO I CAN BLOW THAT SUCKER SKY HIGH!
LET'S HOPE THEY GOT THE MESSAGE IN TIME.
HAYWOOD'S PROBABLY SEEING TO THEM. HOPE THEY BROUGHT LIFE VESTS AND RAFTS.
THEY CAN PLAY AT BEING BALSEROS.
I THOUGHT THE WORD WAS "MARIELITOS"?

STAY ON'EM!

HOVER TEN SECS. I GOT'EM.

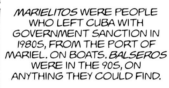

MARIELITOS WERE PEOPLE WHO LEFT CUBA WITH GOVERNMENT SANCTION IN 1980S, FROM THE PORT OF MARIEL. ON BOATS. BALSEROS WERE IN THE 90S, ON ANYTHING THEY COULD FIND.

WOSH!!

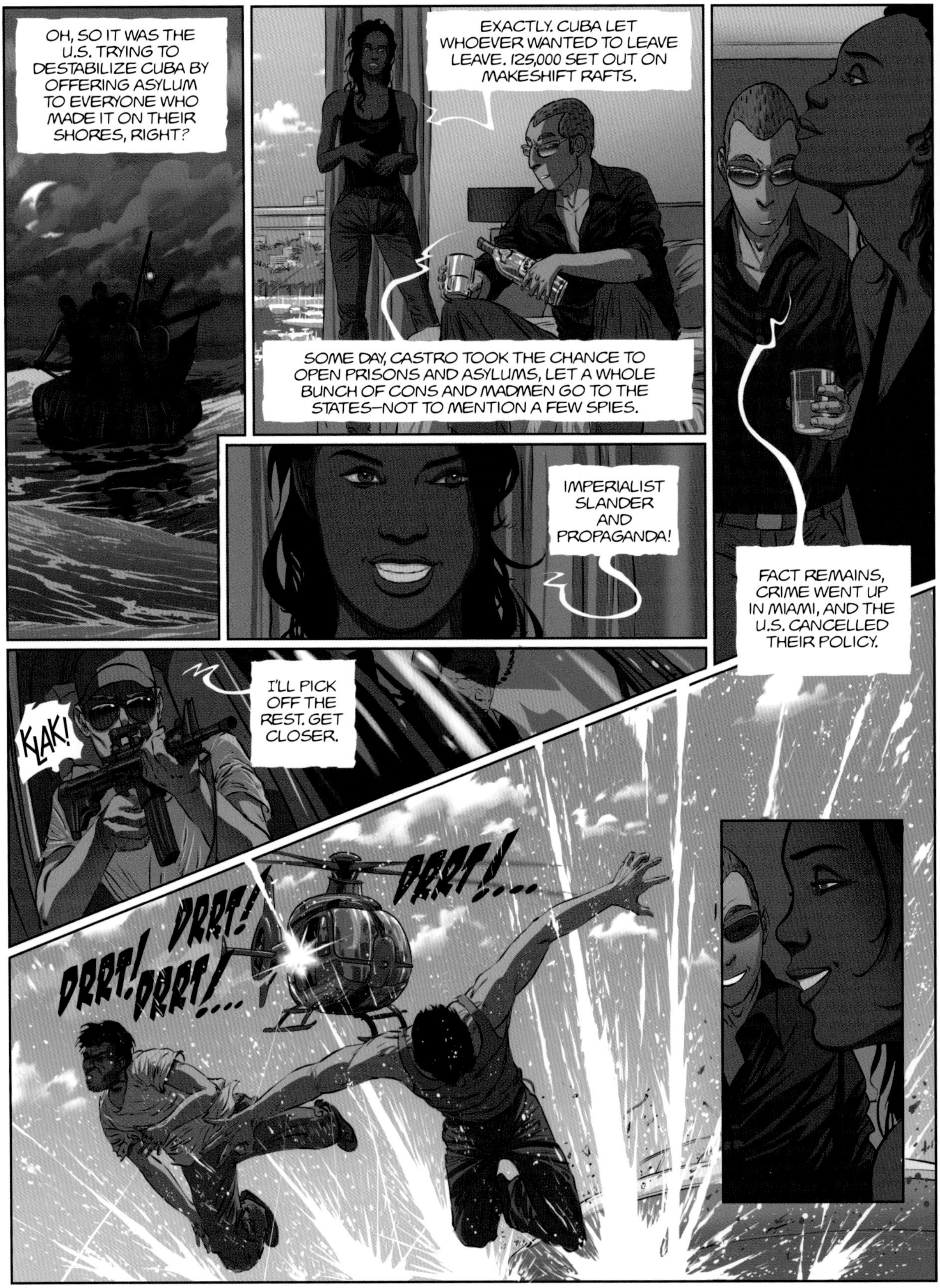
OH, SO IT WAS THE U.S. TRYING TO DESTABILIZE CUBA BY OFFERING ASYLUM TO EVERYONE WHO MADE IT ON THEIR SHORES, RIGHT?
EXACTLY. CUBA LET WHOEVER WANTED TO LEAVE LEAVE. 125,000 SET OUT ON MAKESHIFT RAFTS.
SOME DAY, CASTRO TOOK THE CHANCE TO OPEN PRISONS AND ASYLUMS, LET A WHOLE BUNCH OF CONS AND MADMEN GO TO THE STATES—NOT TO MENTION A FEW SPIES.
IMPERIALIST SLANDER AND PROPAGANDA!
FACT REMAINS, CRIME WENT UP IN MIAMI, AND THE U.S. CANCELLED THEIR POLICY.
KLAK!
I'LL PICK OFF THE REST. GET CLOSER.
DRRT!...
DRRT! DRRT! DRRT!...

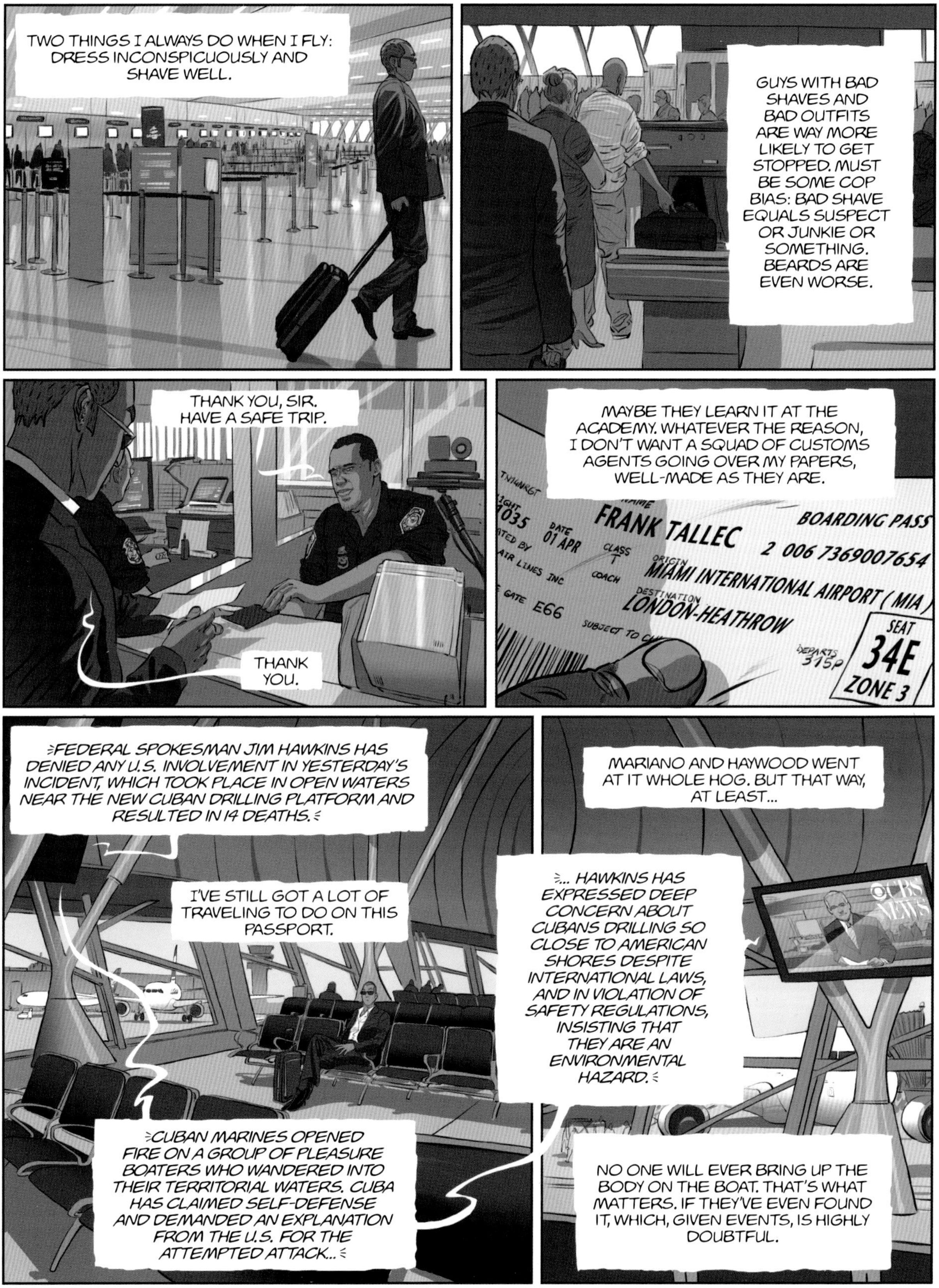
TWO THINGS I ALWAYS DO WHEN I FLY: DRESS INCONSPICUOUSLY AND SHAVE WELL.
GUYS WITH BAD SHAVES AND BAD OUTFITS ARE WAY MORE LIKELY TO GET STOPPED. MUST BE SOME COP BIAS: BAD SHAVE EQUALS SUSPECT OR JUNKIE OR SOMETHING. BEARDS ARE EVEN WORSE.
THANK YOU, SIR. HAVE A SAFE TRIP.
THANK YOU.
MAYBE THEY LEARN IT AT THE ACADEMY. WHATEVER THE REASON, I DON'T WANT A SQUAD OF CUSTOMS AGENTS GOING OVER MY PAPERS, WELL-MADE AS THEY ARE.
FRANK TALLEC
BOARDING PASS
2 006 7369007654
1035
01 APR
CLASS T COACH
MIAMI INTERNATIONAL AIRPORT (MIA)
DESTINATION LONDON-HEATHROW
GATE E66
DEPARTS 315P
SEAT 34E
ZONE 3
FEDERAL SPOKESMAN JIM HAWKINS HAS DENIED ANY U.S. INVOLVEMENT IN YESTERDAY'S INCIDENT, WHICH TOOK PLACE IN OPEN WATERS NEAR THE NEW CUBAN DRILLING PLATFORM AND RESULTED IN 14 DEATHS.
I'VE STILL GOT A LOT OF TRAVELING TO DO ON THIS PASSPORT.
CUBAN MARINES OPENED FIRE ON A GROUP OF PLEASURE BOATERS WHO WANDERED INTO THEIR TERRITORIAL WATERS. CUBA HAS CLAIMED SELF-DEFENSE AND DEMANDED AN EXPLANATION FROM THE U.S. FOR THE ATTEMPTED ATTACK...
MARIANO AND HAYWOOD WENT AT IT WHOLE HOG. BUT THAT WAY, AT LEAST...
... HAWKINS HAS EXPRESSED DEEP CONCERN ABOUT CUBANS DRILLING SO CLOSE TO AMERICAN SHORES DESPITE INTERNATIONAL LAWS, AND IN VIOLATION OF SAFETY REGULATIONS, INSISTING THAT THEY ARE AN ENVIRONMENTAL HAZARD.
CBS NEWS
NO ONE WILL EVER BRING UP THE BODY ON THE BOAT. THAT'S WHAT MATTERS. IF THEY'VE EVEN FOUND IT, WHICH, GIVEN EVENTS, IS HIGHLY DOUBTFUL.

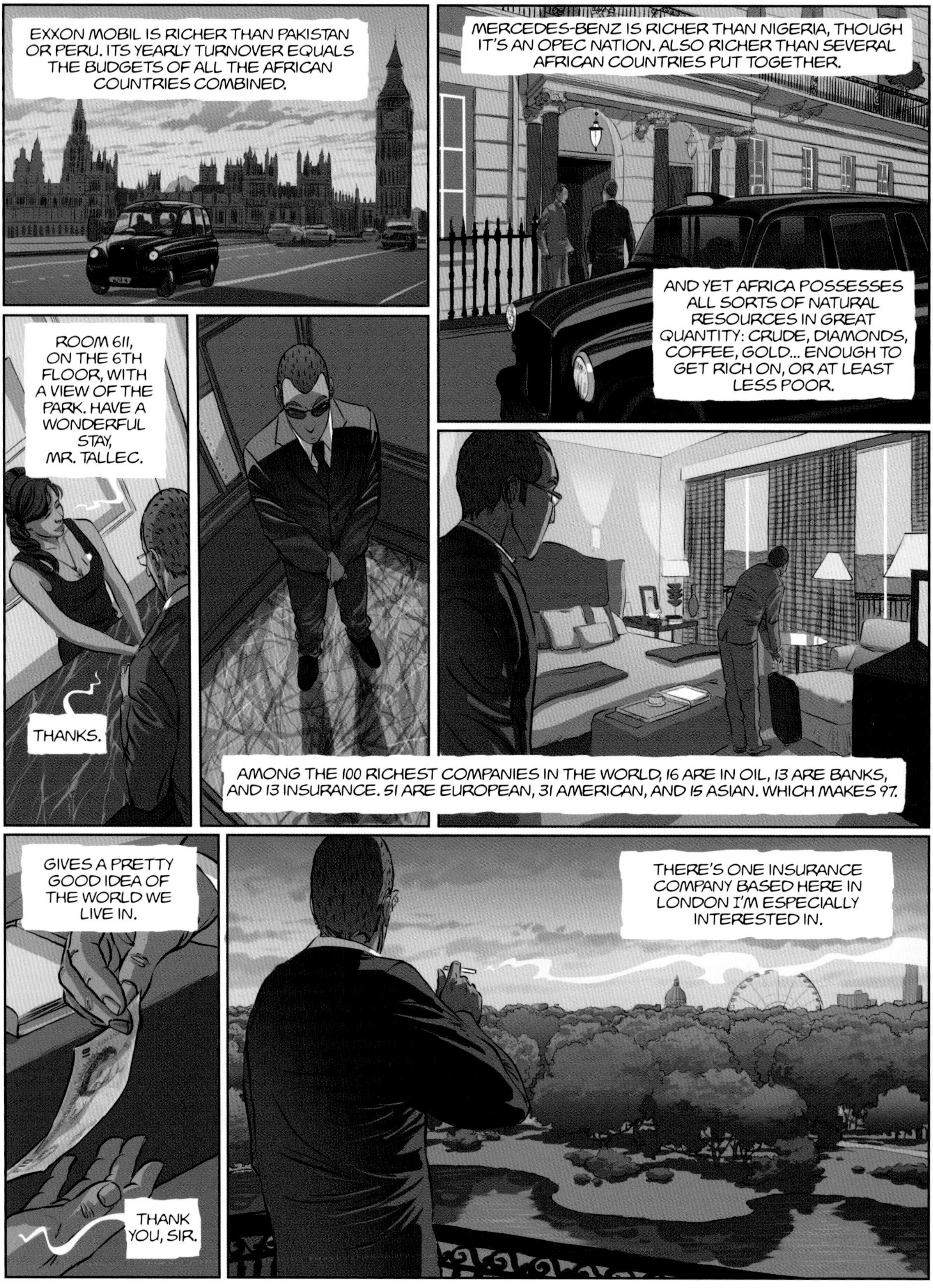
EXXON MOBIL IS RICHER THAN PAKISTAN OR PERU. ITS YEARLY TURNOVER EQUALS THE BUDGETS OF ALL THE AFRICAN COUNTRIES COMBINED.
MERCEDES-BENZ IS RICHER THAN NIGERIA, THOUGH IT'S AN OPEC NATION. ALSO RICHER THAN SEVERAL AFRICAN COUNTRIES PUT TOGETHER.
AND YET AFRICA POSSESSES ALL SORTS OF NATURAL RESOURCES IN GREAT QUANTITY: CRUDE, DIAMONDS, COFFEE, GOLD... ENOUGH TO GET RICH ON, OR AT LEAST LESS POOR.
ROOM 611, ON THE 6TH FLOOR, WITH A VIEW OF THE PARK. HAVE A WONDERFUL STAY, MR. TALLEC.
THANKS.
AMONG THE 100 RICHEST COMPANIES IN THE WORLD, 16 ARE IN OIL, 13 ARE BANKS, AND 13 INSURANCE. 51 ARE EUROPEAN, 31 AMERICAN, AND 15 ASIAN. WHICH MAKES 97.
GIVES A PRETTY GOOD IDEA OF THE WORLD WE LIVE IN.
THANK YOU, SIR.
THERE'S ONE INSURANCE COMPANY BASED HERE IN LONDON I'M ESPECIALLY INTERESTED IN.

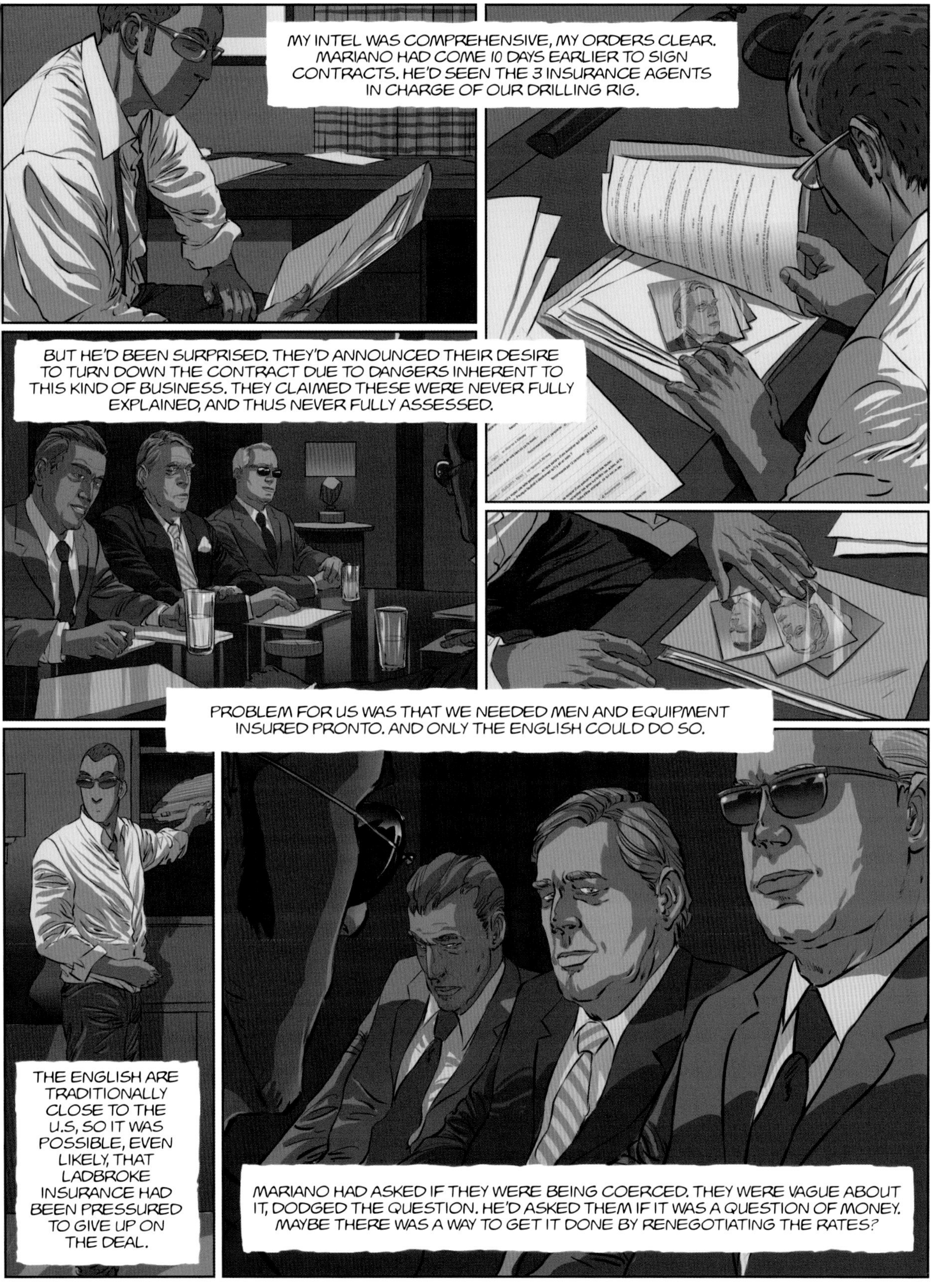
MY INTEL WAS COMPREHENSIVE, MY ORDERS CLEAR. MARIANO HAD COME 10 DAYS EARLIER TO SIGN CONTRACTS. HE'D SEEN THE 3 INSURANCE AGENTS IN CHARGE OF OUR DRILLING RIG.
BUT HE'D BEEN SURPRISED. THEY'D ANNOUNCED THEIR DESIRE TO TURN DOWN THE CONTRACT DUE TO DANGERS INHERENT TO THIS KIND OF BUSINESS. THEY CLAIMED THESE WERE NEVER FULLY EXPLAINED, AND THUS NEVER FULLY ASSESSED.
PROBLEM FOR US WAS THAT WE NEEDED MEN AND EQUIPMENT INSURED PRONTO. AND ONLY THE ENGLISH COULD DO SO.
THE ENGLISH ARE TRADITIONALLY CLOSE TO THE U.S, SO IT WAS POSSIBLE, EVEN LIKELY, THAT LADBROKE INSURANCE HAD BEEN PRESSURED TO GIVE UP ON THE DEAL.
MARIANO HAD ASKED IF THEY WERE BEING COERCED. THEY WERE VAGUE ABOUT IT, DODGED THE QUESTION. HE'D ASKED THEM IF IT WAS A QUESTION OF MONEY. MAYBE THERE WAS A WAY TO GET IT DONE BY RENEGOTIATING THE RATES?

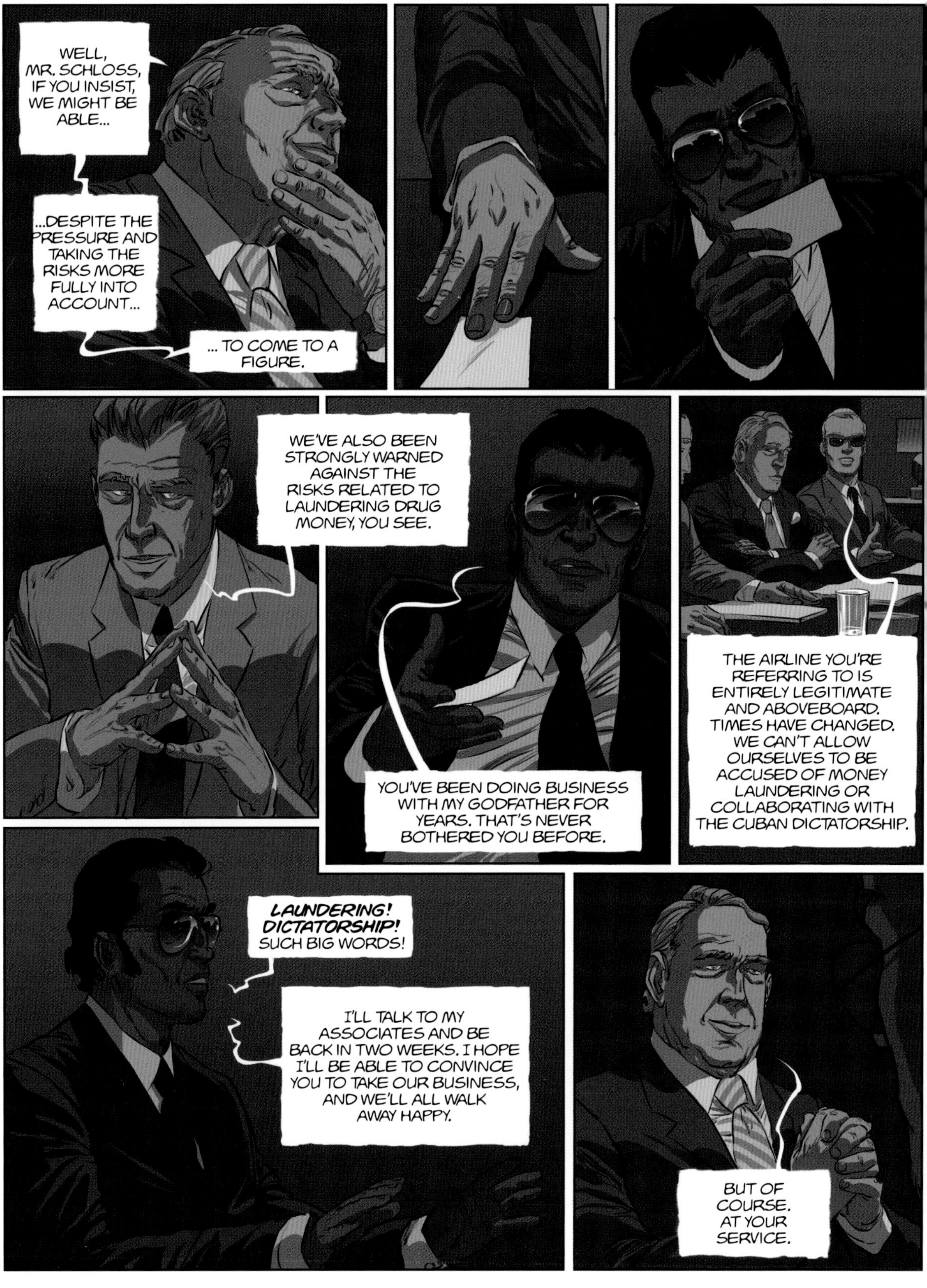
WELL, MR. SCHLOSS, IF YOU INSIST, WE MIGHT BE ABLE...
...DESPITE THE PRESSURE AND TAKING THE RISKS MORE FULLY INTO ACCOUNT...
... TO COME TO A FIGURE.
WE'VE ALSO BEEN STRONGLY WARNED AGAINST THE RISKS RELATED TO LAUNDERING DRUG MONEY, YOU SEE.
YOU'VE BEEN DOING BUSINESS WITH MY GODFATHER FOR YEARS. THAT'S NEVER BOTHERED YOU BEFORE.
THE AIRLINE YOU'RE REFERRING TO IS ENTIRELY LEGITIMATE AND ABOVEBOARD. TIMES HAVE CHANGED. WE CAN'T ALLOW OURSELVES TO BE ACCUSED OF MONEY LAUNDERING OR COLLABORATING WITH THE CUBAN DICTATORSHIP.
LAUNDERING! DICTATORSHIP! SUCH BIG WORDS!
I'LL TALK TO MY ASSOCIATES AND BE BACK IN TWO WEEKS. I HOPE I'LL BE ABLE TO CONVINCE YOU TO TAKE OUR BUSINESS, AND WE'LL ALL WALK AWAY HAPPY.
BUT OF COURSE. AT YOUR SERVICE.

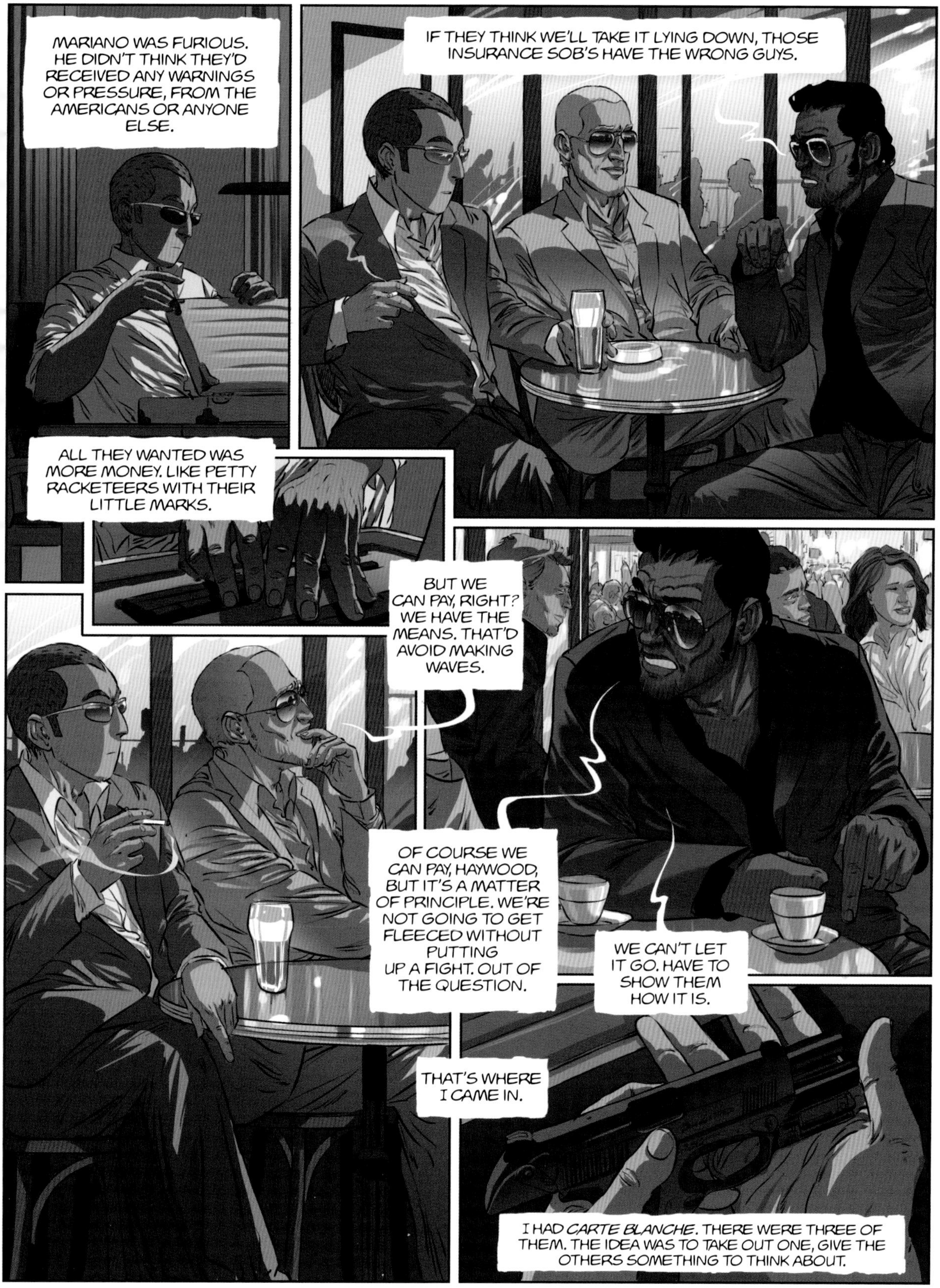
MARIANO WAS FURIOUS. HE DIDN'T THINK THEY'D RECEIVED ANY WARNINGS OR PRESSURE, FROM THE AMERICANS OR ANYONE ELSE.
IF THEY THINK WE'LL TAKE IT LYING DOWN, THOSE INSURANCE SOB'S HAVE THE WRONG GUYS.
ALL THEY WANTED WAS MORE MONEY. LIKE PETTY RACKETEERS WITH THEIR LITTLE MARKS.
BUT WE CAN PAY, RIGHT? WE HAVE THE MEANS. THAT'D AVOID MAKING WAVES.
OF COURSE WE CAN PAY, HAYWOOD, BUT IT'S A MATTER OF PRINCIPLE. WE'RE NOT GOING TO GET FLEECED WITHOUT PUTTING UP A FIGHT. OUT OF THE QUESTION.
WE CAN'T LET IT GO. HAVE TO SHOW THEM HOW IT IS.
THAT'S WHERE I CAME IN.
I HAD *CARTE BLANCHE*. THERE WERE THREE OF THEM. THE IDEA WAS TO TAKE OUT ONE, GIVE THE OTHERS SOMETHING TO THINK ABOUT.

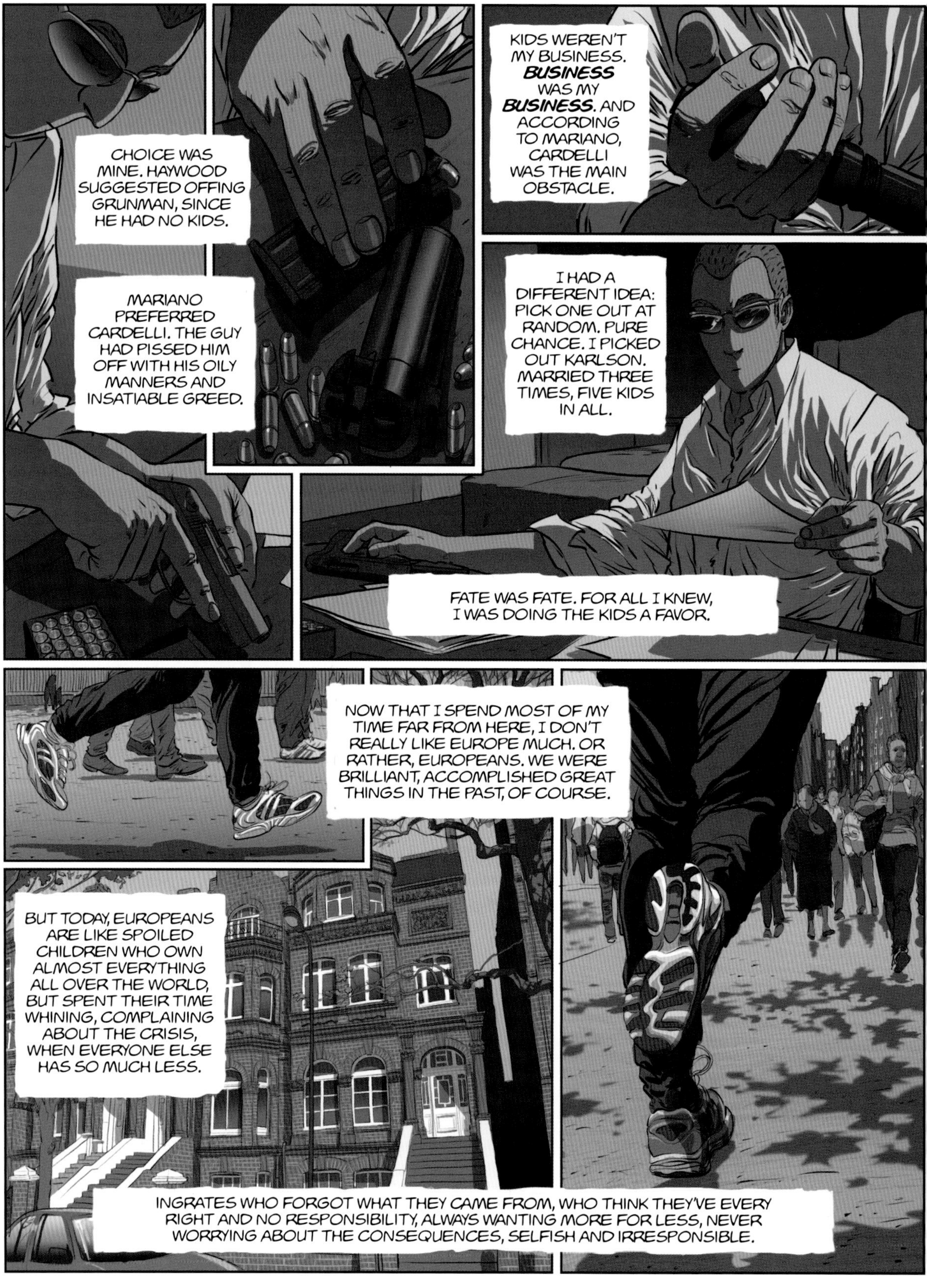
CHOICE WAS MINE. HAYWOOD SUGGESTED OFFING GRUNMAN, SINCE HE HAD NO KIDS.
MARIANO PREFERRED CARDELLI. THE GUY HAD PISSED HIM OFF WITH HIS OILY MANNERS AND INSATIABLE GREED.
KIDS WEREN'T MY BUSINESS. BUSINESS WAS MY BUSINESS. AND ACCORDING TO MARIANO, CARDELLI WAS THE MAIN OBSTACLE.
I HAD A DIFFERENT IDEA: PICK ONE OUT AT RANDOM. PURE CHANCE. I PICKED OUT KARLSON. MARRIED THREE TIMES, FIVE KIDS IN ALL.
FATE WAS FATE. FOR ALL I KNEW, I WAS DOING THE KIDS A FAVOR.
NOW THAT I SPEND MOST OF MY TIME FAR FROM HERE, I DON'T REALLY LIKE EUROPE MUCH. OR RATHER, EUROPEANS. WE WERE BRILLIANT, ACCOMPLISHED GREAT THINGS IN THE PAST, OF COURSE.
BUT TODAY, EUROPEANS ARE LIKE SPOILED CHILDREN WHO OWN ALMOST EVERYTHING ALL OVER THE WORLD, BUT SPENT THEIR TIME WHINING, COMPLAINING ABOUT THE CRISIS, WHEN EVERYONE ELSE HAS SO MUCH LESS.
INGRATES WHO FORGOT WHAT THEY CAME FROM, WHO THINK THEY'VE EVERY RIGHT AND NO RESPONSIBILITY, ALWAYS WANTING MORE FOR LESS, NEVER WORRYING ABOUT THE CONSEQUENCES, SELFISH AND IRRESPONSIBLE.

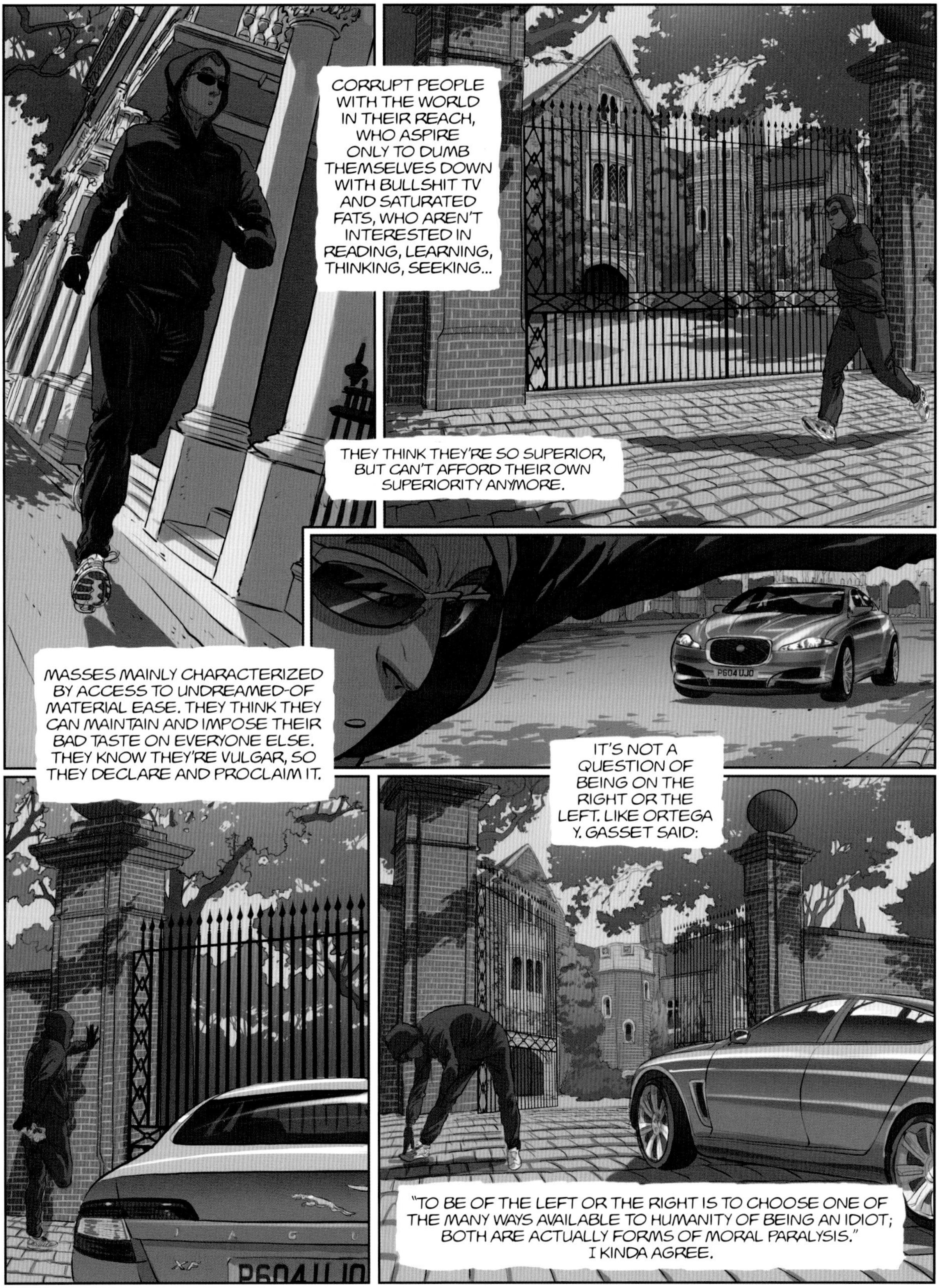
CORRUPT PEOPLE WITH THE WORLD IN THEIR REACH, WHO ASPIRE ONLY TO DUMB THEMSELVES DOWN WITH BULLSHIT TV AND SATURATED FATS, WHO AREN'T INTERESTED IN READING, LEARNING, THINKING, SEEKING...
THEY THINK THEY'RE SO SUPERIOR, BUT CAN'T AFFORD THEIR OWN SUPERIORITY ANYMORE.
MASSES MAINLY CHARACTERIZED BY ACCESS TO UNDREAMED-OF MATERIAL EASE. THEY THINK THEY CAN MAINTAIN AND IMPOSE THEIR BAD TASTE ON EVERYONE ELSE. THEY KNOW THEY'RE VULGAR, SO THEY DECLARE AND PROCLAIM IT.
IT'S NOT A QUESTION OF BEING ON THE RIGHT OR THE LEFT. LIKE ORTEGA Y. GASSET SAID:
"TO BE OF THE LEFT OR THE RIGHT IS TO CHOOSE ONE OF THE MANY WAYS AVAILABLE TO HUMANITY OF BEING AN IDIOT; BOTH ARE ACTUALLY FORMS OF MORAL PARALYSIS." I KINDA AGREE.

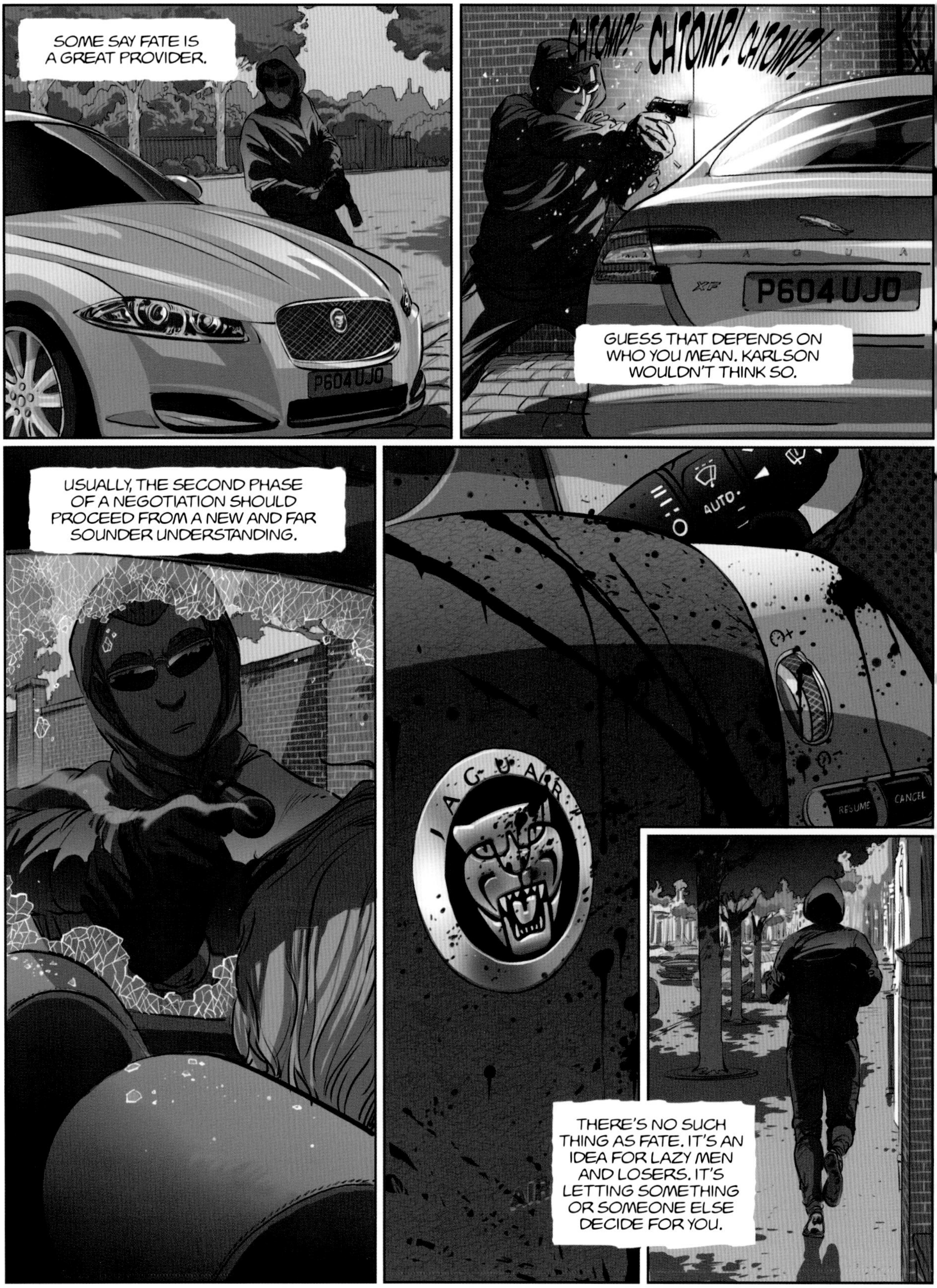
SOME SAY FATE IS A GREAT PROVIDER.
CHTOMP! CHTOMP! CHTOMP!
P604 UJO
GUESS THAT DEPENDS ON WHO YOU MEAN. KARLSON WOULDN'T THINK SO.
USUALLY, THE SECOND PHASE OF A NEGOTIATION SHOULD PROCEED FROM A NEW AND FAR SOUNDER UNDERSTANDING.
AUTO
JAGUAR
RESUME
CANCEL
THERE'S NO SUCH THING AS FATE. IT'S AN IDEA FOR LAZY MEN AND LOSERS. IT'S LETTING SOMETHING OR SOMEONE ELSE DECIDE FOR YOU.

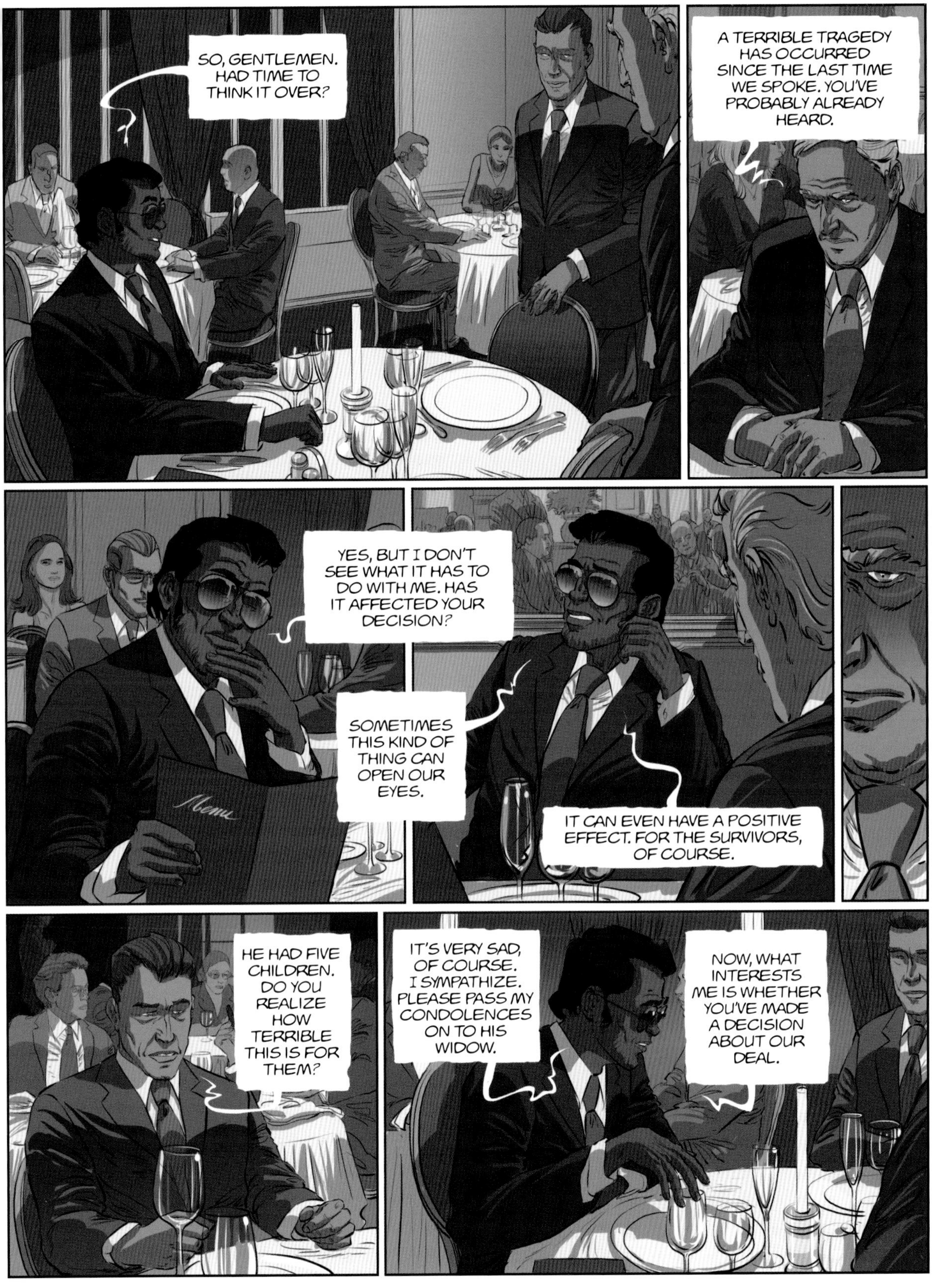
SO, GENTLEMEN. HAD TIME TO THINK IT OVER?
A TERRIBLE TRAGEDY HAS OCCURRED SINCE THE LAST TIME WE SPOKE. YOU'VE PROBABLY ALREADY HEARD.
YES, BUT I DON'T SEE WHAT IT HAS TO DO WITH ME. HAS IT AFFECTED YOUR DECISION?
Menu
SOMETIMES THIS KIND OF THING CAN OPEN OUR EYES.
IT CAN EVEN HAVE A POSITIVE EFFECT. FOR THE SURVIVORS, OF COURSE.
HE HAD FIVE CHILDREN. DO YOU REALIZE HOW TERRIBLE THIS IS FOR THEM?
IT'S VERY SAD, OF COURSE. I SYMPATHIZE. PLEASE PASS MY CONDOLENCES ON TO HIS WIDOW.
NOW, WHAT INTERESTS ME IS WHETHER YOU'VE MADE A DECISION ABOUT OUR DEAL.

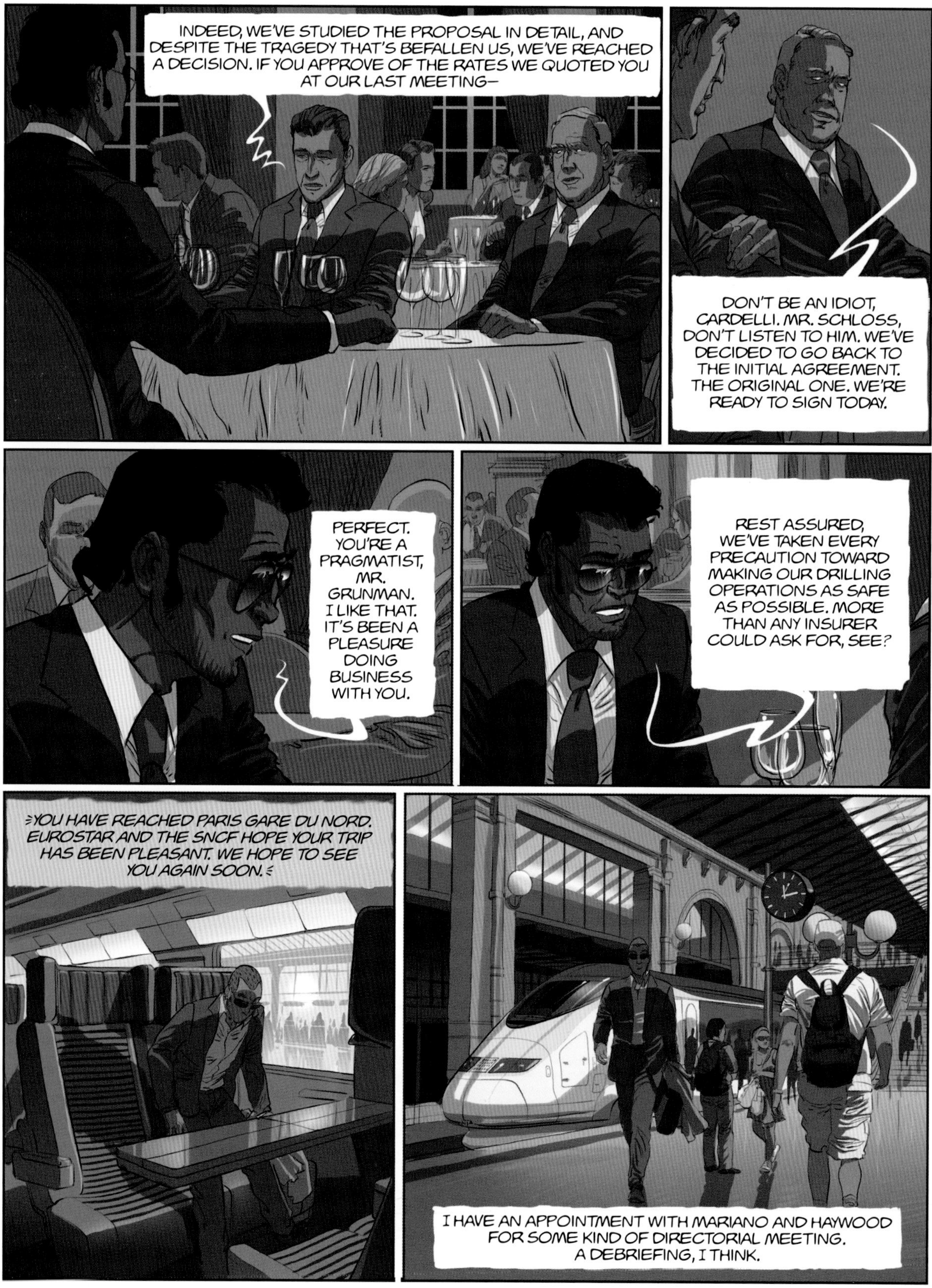
INDEED, WE'VE STUDIED THE PROPOSAL IN DETAIL, AND DESPITE THE TRAGEDY THAT'S BEFALLEN US, WE'VE REACHED A DECISION. IF YOU APPROVE OF THE RATES WE QUOTED YOU AT OUR LAST MEETING–
DON'T BE AN IDIOT, CARDELLI. MR. SCHLOSS, DON'T LISTEN TO HIM. WE'VE DECIDED TO GO BACK TO THE INITIAL AGREEMENT. THE ORIGINAL ONE. WE'RE READY TO SIGN TODAY.
PERFECT. YOU'RE A PRAGMATIST, MR. GRUNMAN. I LIKE THAT. IT'S BEEN A PLEASURE DOING BUSINESS WITH YOU.
REST ASSURED, WE'VE TAKEN EVERY PRECAUTION TOWARD MAKING OUR DRILLING OPERATIONS AS SAFE AS POSSIBLE. MORE THAN ANY INSURER COULD ASK FOR, SEE?
YOU HAVE REACHED PARIS GARE DU NORD. EUROSTAR AND THE SNCF HOPE YOUR TRIP HAS BEEN PLEASANT. WE HOPE TO SEE YOU AGAIN SOON.
I HAVE AN APPOINTMENT WITH MARIANO AND HAYWOOD FOR SOME KIND OF DIRECTORIAL MEETING. A DEBRIEFING, I THINK.

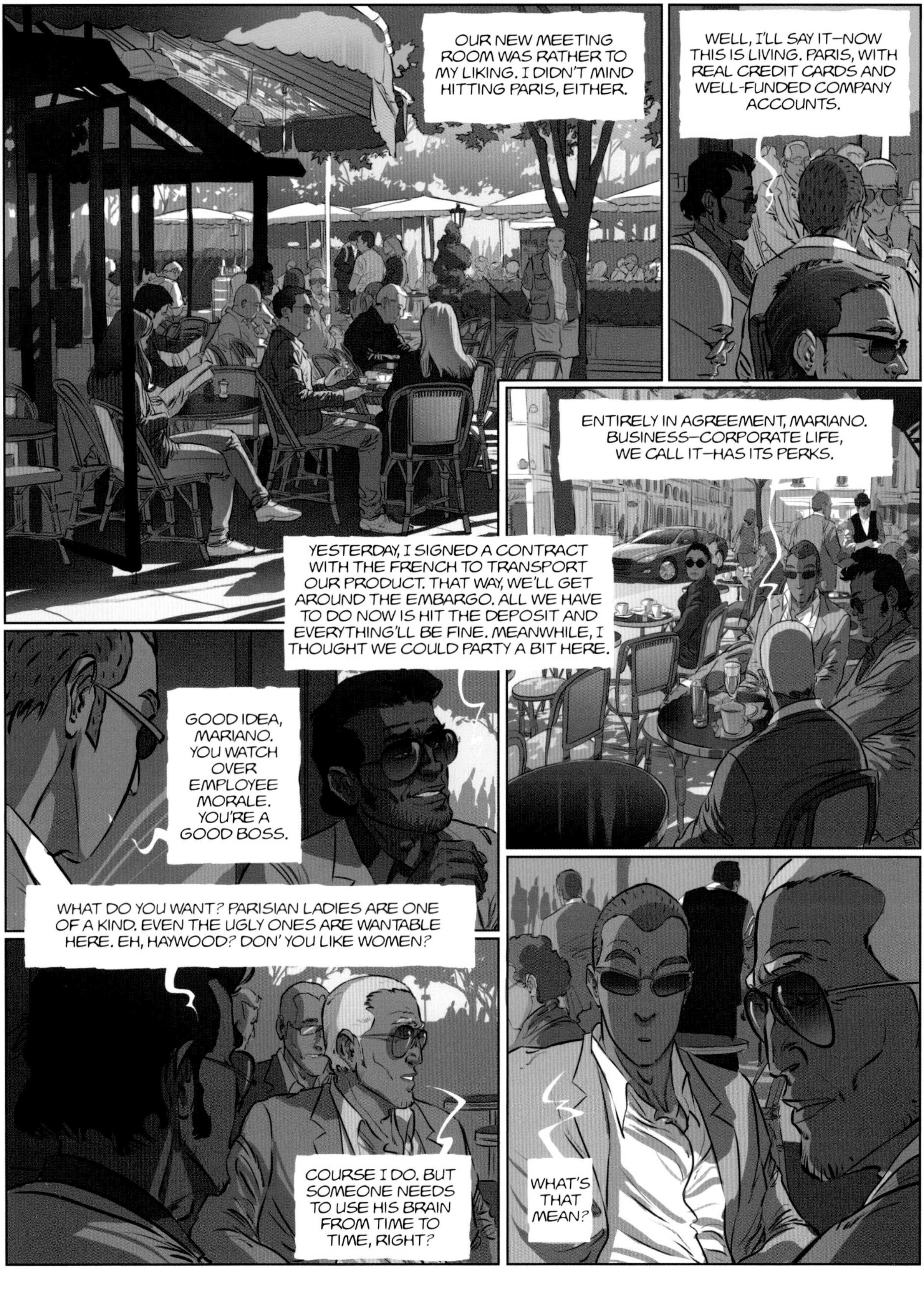
OUR NEW MEETING ROOM WAS RATHER TO MY LIKING. I DIDN'T MIND HITTING PARIS, EITHER.
WELL, I'LL SAY IT—NOW THIS IS LIVING. PARIS, WITH REAL CREDIT CARDS AND WELL-FUNDED COMPANY ACCOUNTS.
ENTIRELY IN AGREEMENT, MARIANO. BUSINESS—CORPORATE LIFE, WE CALL IT—HAS ITS PERKS.
YESTERDAY, I SIGNED A CONTRACT WITH THE FRENCH TO TRANSPORT OUR PRODUCT. THAT WAY, WE'LL GET AROUND THE EMBARGO. ALL WE HAVE TO DO NOW IS HIT THE DEPOSIT AND EVERYTHING'LL BE FINE. MEANWHILE, I THOUGHT WE COULD PARTY A BIT HERE.
GOOD IDEA, MARIANO. YOU WATCH OVER EMPLOYEE MORALE. YOU'RE A GOOD BOSS.
WHAT DO YOU WANT? PARISIAN LADIES ARE ONE OF A KIND. EVEN THE UGLY ONES ARE WANTABLE HERE. EH, HAYWOOD? DON' YOU LIKE WOMEN?
COURSE I DO. BUT SOMEONE NEEDS TO USE HIS BRAIN FROM TIME TO TIME, RIGHT?
WHAT'S THAT MEAN?

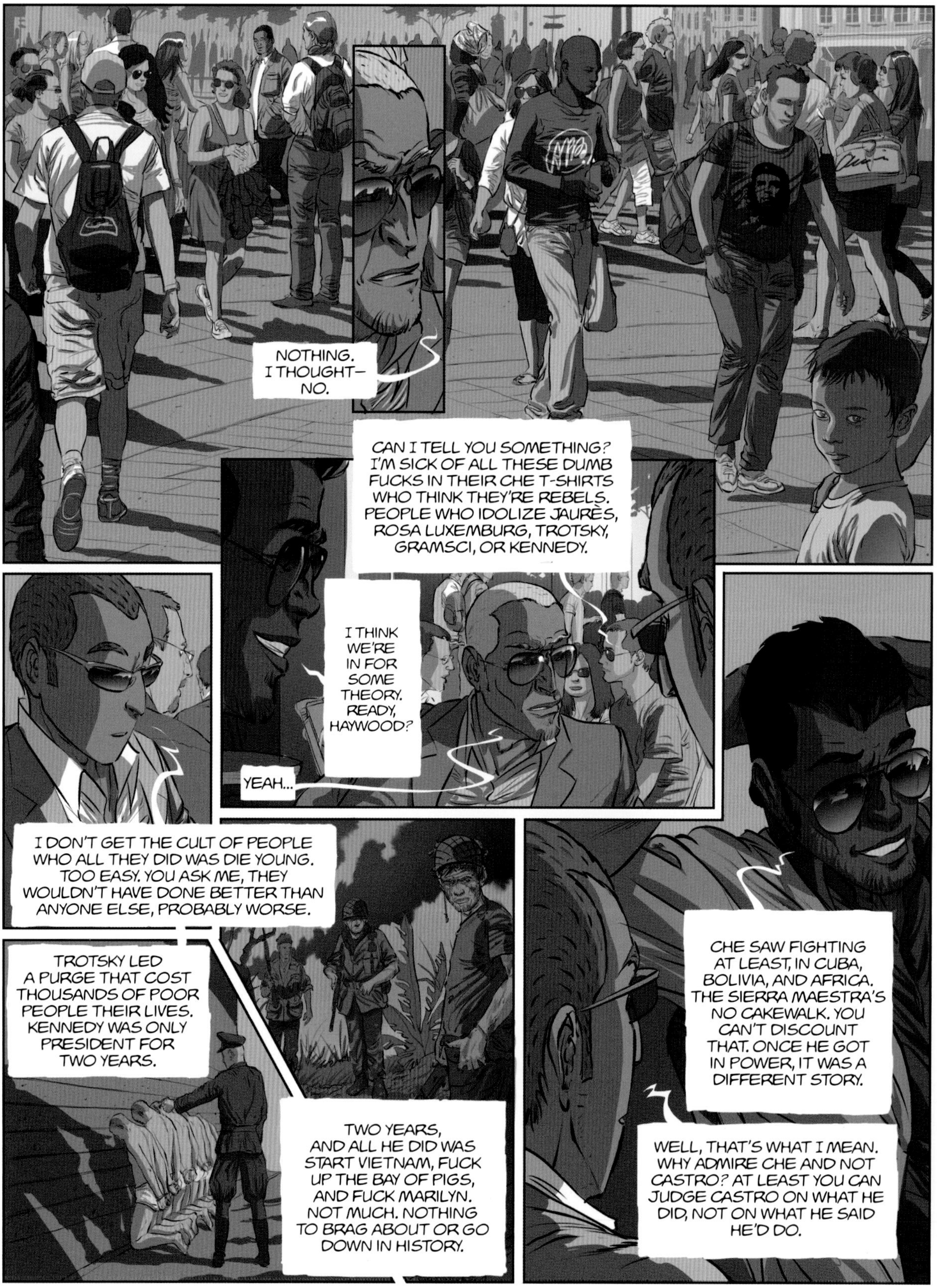
NOTHING. I THOUGHT— NO.
CAN I TELL YOU SOMETHING? I'M SICK OF ALL THESE DUMB FUCKS IN THEIR CHE T-SHIRTS WHO THINK THEY'RE REBELS. PEOPLE WHO IDOLIZE JAURÈS, ROSA LUXEMBURG, TROTSKY, GRAMSCI, OR KENNEDY.
I THINK WE'RE IN FOR SOME THEORY. READY, HAYWOOD?
YEAH...
I DON'T GET THE CULT OF PEOPLE WHO ALL THEY DID WAS DIE YOUNG. TOO EASY. YOU ASK ME, THEY WOULDN'T HAVE DONE BETTER THAN ANYONE ELSE, PROBABLY WORSE.
TROTSKY LED A PURGE THAT COST THOUSANDS OF POOR PEOPLE THEIR LIVES. KENNEDY WAS ONLY PRESIDENT FOR TWO YEARS.
TWO YEARS, AND ALL HE DID WAS START VIETNAM, FUCK UP THE BAY OF PIGS, AND FUCK MARILYN. NOT MUCH. NOTHING TO BRAG ABOUT OR GO DOWN IN HISTORY.
CHE SAW FIGHTING AT LEAST, IN CUBA, BOLIVIA, AND AFRICA. THE SIERRA MAESTRA'S NO CAKEWALK. YOU CAN'T DISCOUNT THAT. ONCE HE GOT IN POWER, IT WAS A DIFFERENT STORY.
WELL, THAT'S WHAT I MEAN. WHY ADMIRE CHE AND NOT CASTRO? AT LEAST YOU CAN JUDGE CASTRO ON WHAT HE DID, NOT ON WHAT HE SAID HE'D DO.

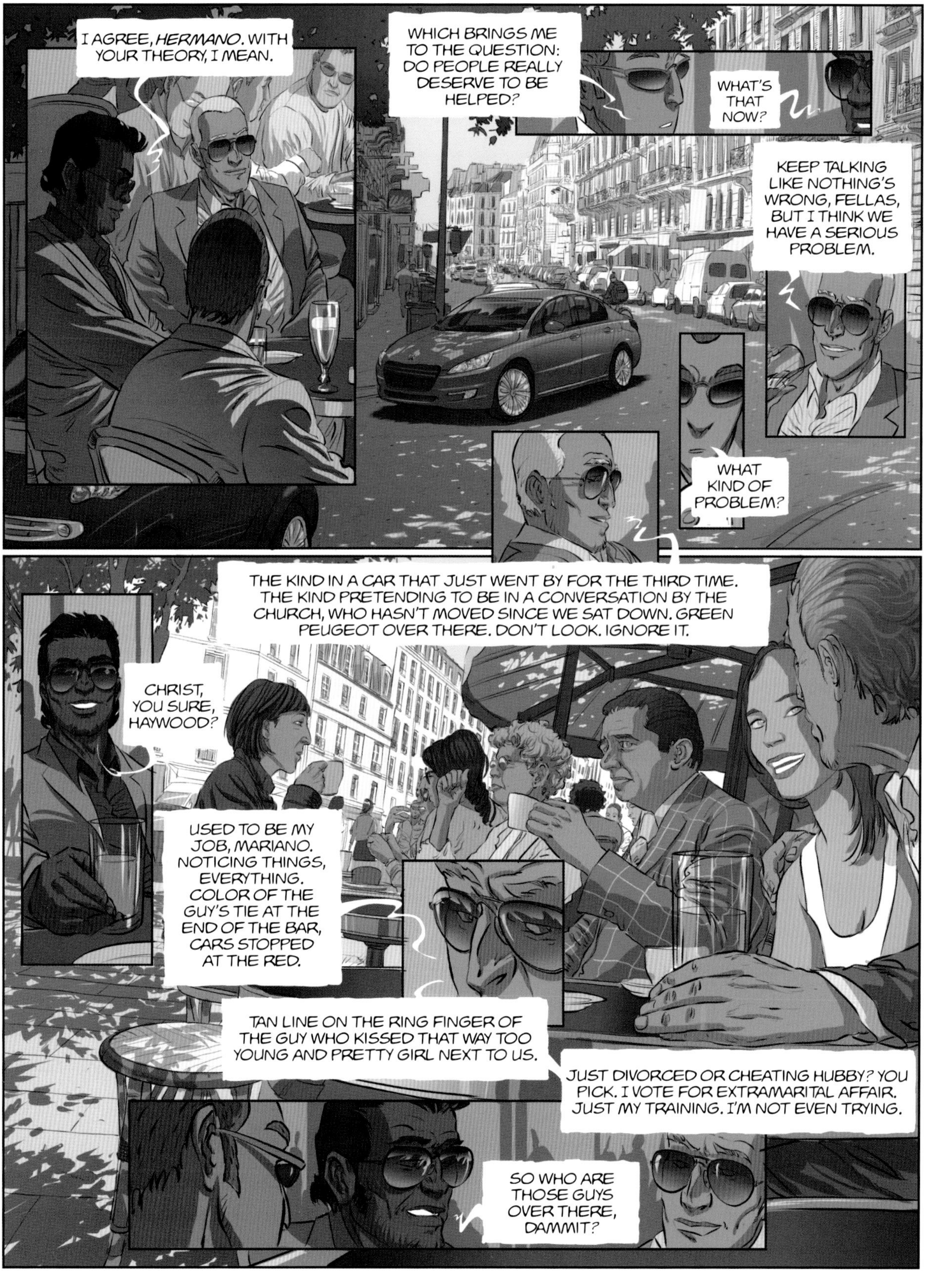
I AGREE, *HERMANO*. WITH YOUR THEORY, I MEAN.
WHICH BRINGS ME TO THE QUESTION: DO PEOPLE REALLY DESERVE TO BE HELPED?
WHAT'S THAT NOW?
KEEP TALKING LIKE NOTHING'S WRONG, FELLAS, BUT I THINK WE HAVE A SERIOUS PROBLEM.
WHAT KIND OF PROBLEM?
THE KIND IN A CAR THAT JUST WENT BY FOR THE THIRD TIME. THE KIND PRETENDING TO BE IN A CONVERSATION BY THE CHURCH, WHO HASN'T MOVED SINCE WE SAT DOWN. GREEN PEUGEOT OVER THERE. DON'T LOOK. IGNORE IT.
CHRIST, YOU SURE, HAYWOOD?
USED TO BE MY JOB, MARIANO. NOTICING THINGS, EVERYTHING. COLOR OF THE GUY'S TIE AT THE END OF THE BAR, CARS STOPPED AT THE RED.
TAN LINE ON THE RING FINGER OF THE GUY WHO KISSED THAT WAY TOO YOUNG AND PRETTY GIRL NEXT TO US.
JUST DIVORCED OR CHEATING HUBBY? YOU PICK. I VOTE FOR EXTRAMARITAL AFFAIR. JUST MY TRAINING. I'M NOT EVEN TRYING.
SO WHO ARE THOSE GUYS OVER THERE, DAMMIT?

WHY NOT GO ASK THEM, MARIANO? I BET THEY'RE AMERICANS. BUT THEY COULD BE ANYONE—CHINESE, RUSSIAN...

YOU KEEP WALKING AND TALKING AS NATURALLY AS YOU CAN. WE'LL MEET AT THE HOTEL. I'LL CHECK IF THEY'RE FOLLOWING US AND HOW MANY THERE ARE. DON'T CALL. WE'LL GET RID OF OUR CELLS.

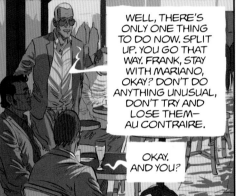

WELL, THERE'S ONLY ONE THING TO DO NOW. SPLIT UP. YOU GO THAT WAY. FRANK, STAY WITH MARIANO, OKAY? DON'T DO ANYTHING UNUSUAL, DON'T TRY AND LOSE THEM— AU CONTRAIRE.

OKAY. AND YOU?

WELL? WHAT WERE YOU GOING TO SAY? SEEMED INTERESTING.

LOOK AT ALL THESE PEOPLE: ALL THEY WANT IS MORE MONEY, AND AS SOON AS THEY GET SOME, THEY GO BUY LUXURY CARS AND BRAND NAME CLOTHES, VEG OUT BY THE TV AND SURF THE WEB FOR PORN OR GORE.

THEY WALLOW IN WEAKNESS LIKE IT'S THE FINAL STAGE OF EVOLUTION AND COMPLAIN ALL THE TIME. WHAT CAN YOU HOPE FOR FROM PEOPLE WHO ALL THEY CAN THINK OF IS SATISFYING THEIR PETTY NEEDS AND BASEST INSTINCTS?

WHY ASK THEM TO VOTE WHEN THEY CAN'T UNDERSTAND POLITICS, MUCH LESS ECONOMICS, AND DON'T EVEN WANT TO THINK ABOUT IT OR LEARN ANYTHING AT ALL?

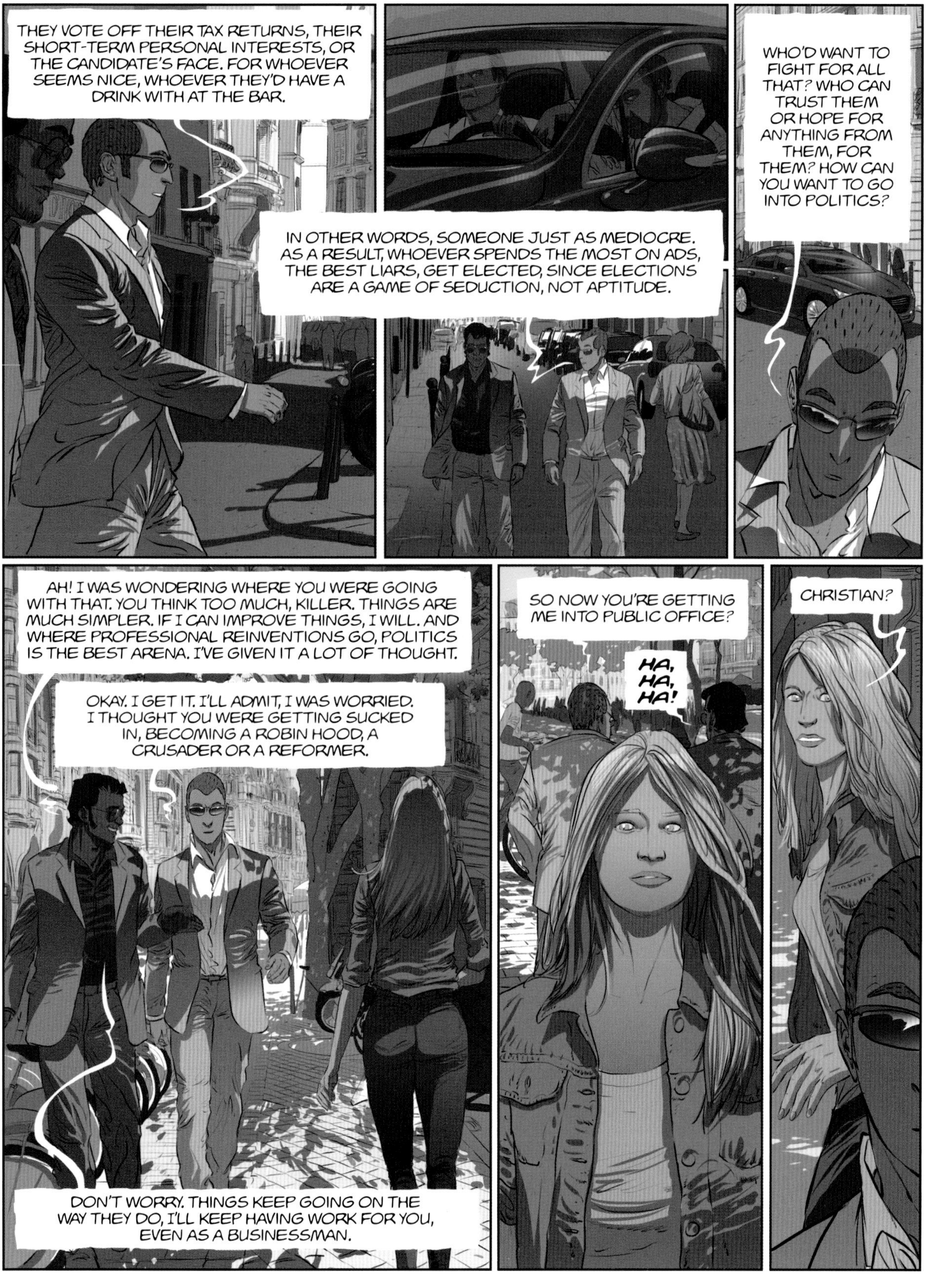
THEY VOTE OFF THEIR TAX RETURNS, THEIR SHORT-TERM PERSONAL INTERESTS, OR THE CANDIDATE'S FACE. FOR WHOEVER SEEMS NICE, WHOEVER THEY'D HAVE A DRINK WITH AT THE BAR.
IN OTHER WORDS, SOMEONE JUST AS MEDIOCRE. AS A RESULT, WHOEVER SPENDS THE MOST ON ADS, THE BEST LIARS, GET ELECTED, SINCE ELECTIONS ARE A GAME OF SEDUCTION, NOT APTITUDE.
WHO'D WANT TO FIGHT FOR ALL THAT? WHO CAN TRUST THEM OR HOPE FOR ANYTHING FROM THEM, FOR THEM? HOW CAN YOU WANT TO GO INTO POLITICS?
AH! I WAS WONDERING WHERE YOU WERE GOING WITH THAT. YOU THINK TOO MUCH, KILLER. THINGS ARE MUCH SIMPLER. IF I CAN IMPROVE THINGS, I WILL. AND WHERE PROFESSIONAL REINVENTIONS GO, POLITICS IS THE BEST ARENA. I'VE GIVEN IT A LOT OF THOUGHT.
OKAY. I GET IT. I'LL ADMIT, I WAS WORRIED. I THOUGHT YOU WERE GETTING SUCKED IN, BECOMING A ROBIN HOOD, A CRUSADER OR A REFORMER.
DON'T WORRY. THINGS KEEP GOING ON THE WAY THEY DO, I'LL KEEP HAVING WORK FOR YOU, EVEN AS A BUSINESSMAN.
SO NOW YOU'RE GETTING ME INTO PUBLIC OFFICE?
HA, HA, HA!
CHRISTIAN?

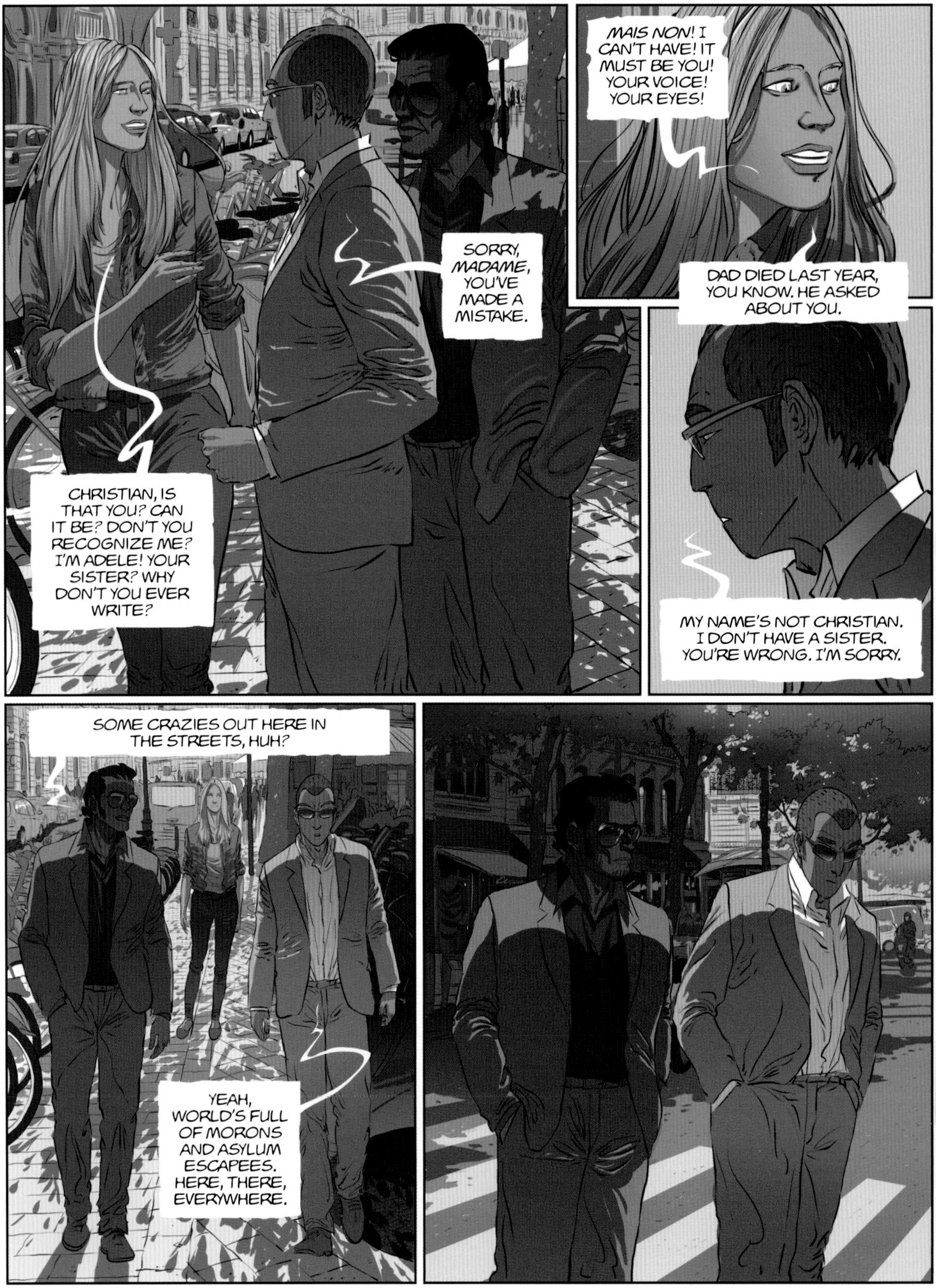
CHRISTIAN, IS THAT YOU? CAN IT BE? DON'T YOU RECOGNIZE ME? I'M ADELE! YOUR SISTER? WHY DON'T YOU EVER WRITE?
SORRY, *MADAME*, YOU'VE MADE A MISTAKE.
MAIS NON! I CAN'T HAVE! IT MUST BE YOU! YOUR VOICE! YOUR EYES!
DAD DIED LAST YEAR, YOU KNOW. HE ASKED ABOUT YOU.
MY NAME'S NOT CHRISTIAN. I DON'T HAVE A SISTER. YOU'RE WRONG. I'M SORRY.
SOME CRAZIES OUT HERE IN THE STREETS, HUH?
YEAH, WORLD'S FULL OF MORONS AND ASYLUM ESCAPEES. HERE, THERE, EVERYWHERE.

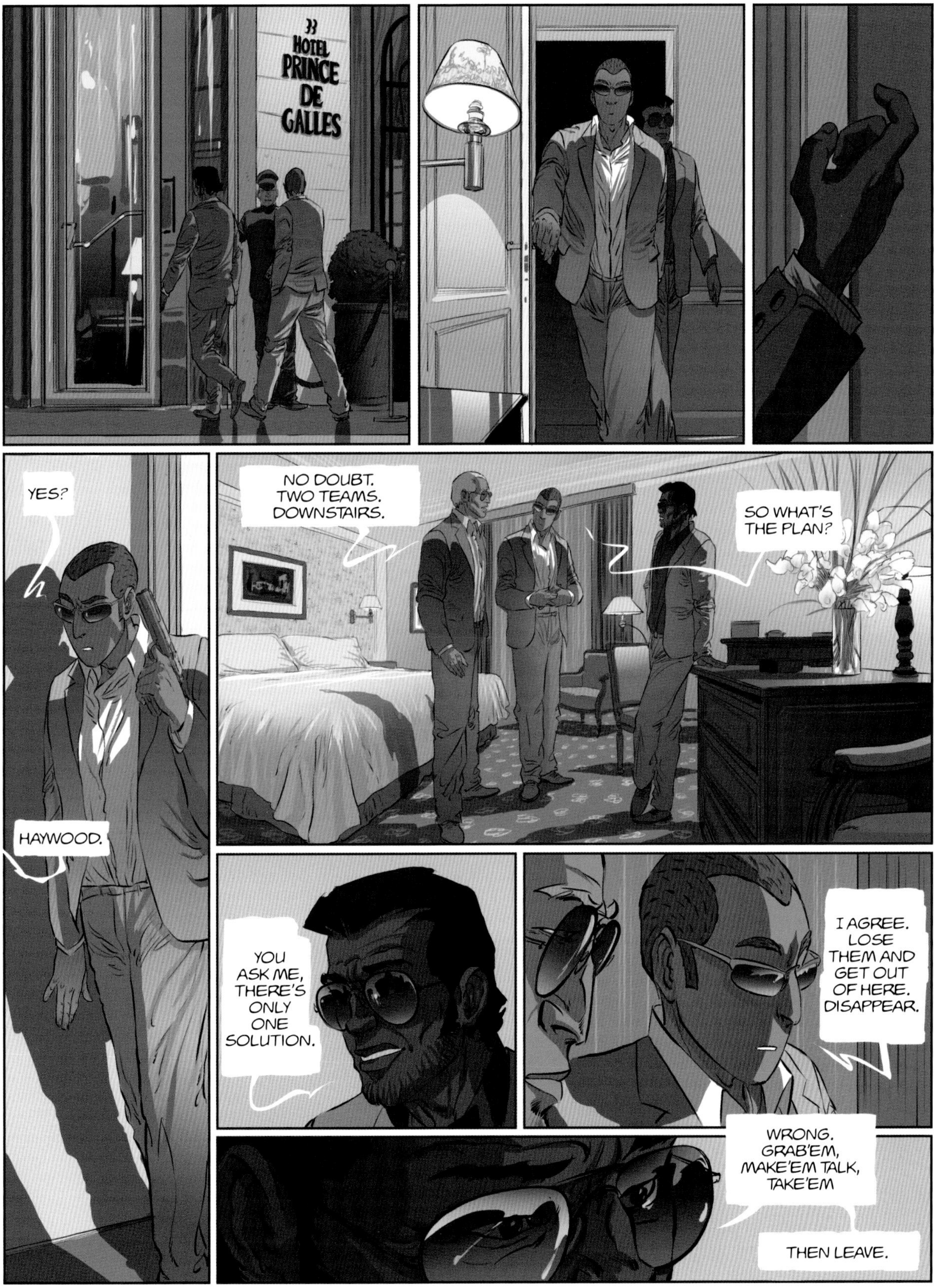
33
HOTEL
PRINCE
DE
GALLES
YES?
HAYWOOD.
NO DOUBT. TWO TEAMS. DOWNSTAIRS.
SO WHAT'S THE PLAN?
YOU ASK ME, THERE'S ONLY ONE SOLUTION.
I AGREE. LOSE THEM AND GET OUT OF HERE. DISAPPEAR.
WRONG. GRAB'EM, MAKE'EM TALK, TAKE'EM
THEN LEAVE.

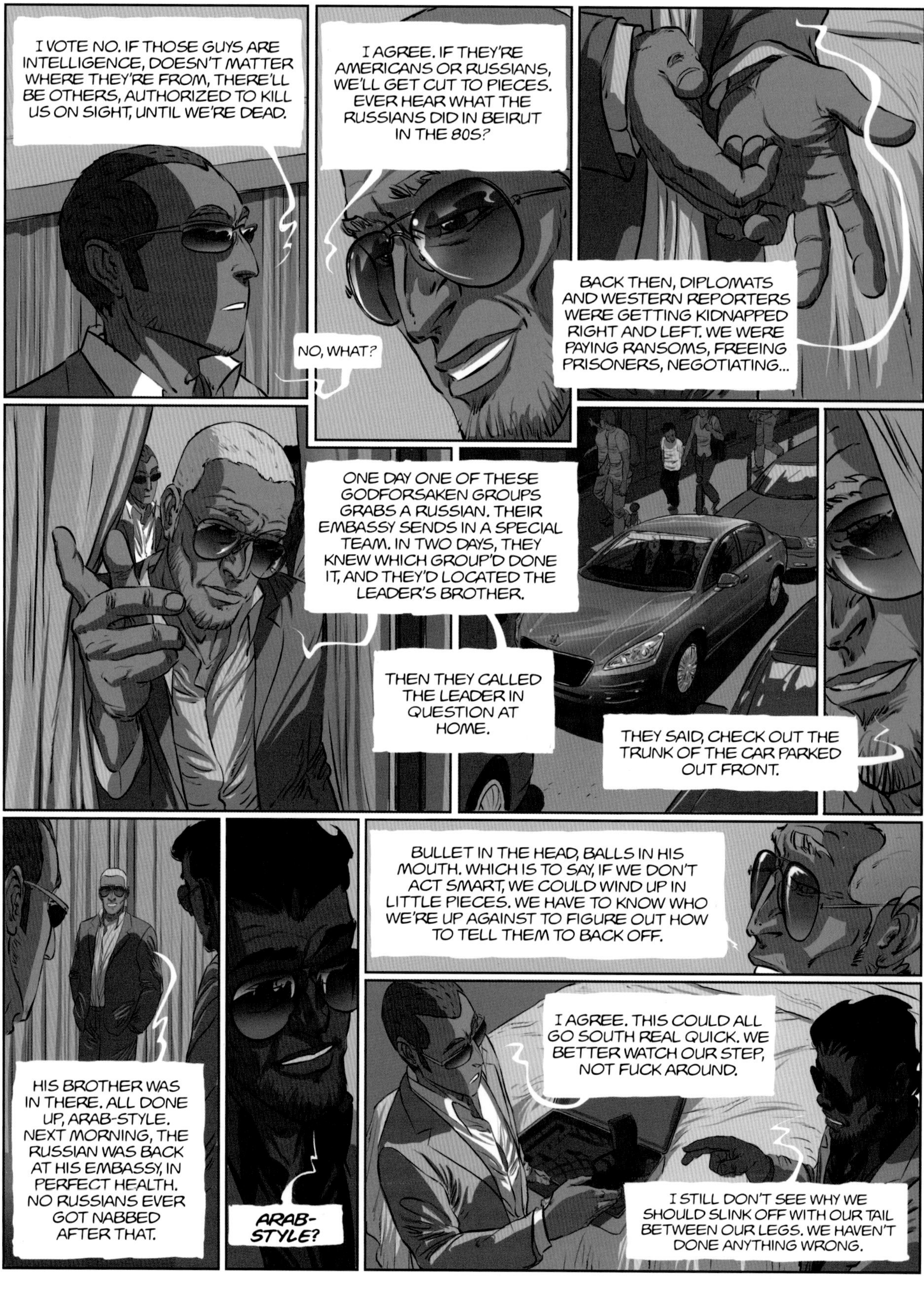
I VOTE NO. IF THOSE GUYS ARE INTELLIGENCE, DOESN'T MATTER WHERE THEY'RE FROM, THERE'LL BE OTHERS, AUTHORIZED TO KILL US ON SIGHT, UNTIL WE'RE DEAD.
I AGREE. IF THEY'RE AMERICANS OR RUSSIANS, WE'LL GET CUT TO PIECES. EVER HEAR WHAT THE RUSSIANS DID IN BEIRUT IN THE 80S?
NO, WHAT?
BACK THEN, DIPLOMATS AND WESTERN REPORTERS WERE GETTING KIDNAPPED RIGHT AND LEFT. WE WERE PAYING RANSOMS, FREEING PRISONERS, NEGOTIATING...
ONE DAY ONE OF THESE GODFORSAKEN GROUPS GRABS A RUSSIAN. THEIR EMBASSY SENDS IN A SPECIAL TEAM. IN TWO DAYS, THEY KNEW WHICH GROUP'D DONE IT, AND THEY'D LOCATED THE LEADER'S BROTHER.
THEN THEY CALLED THE LEADER IN QUESTION AT HOME.
THEY SAID, CHECK OUT THE TRUNK OF THE CAR PARKED OUT FRONT.
HIS BROTHER WAS IN THERE. ALL DONE UP, ARAB-STYLE. NEXT MORNING, THE RUSSIAN WAS BACK AT HIS EMBASSY, IN PERFECT HEALTH. NO RUSSIANS EVER GOT NABBED AFTER THAT.
ARAB-STYLE?
BULLET IN THE HEAD, BALLS IN HIS MOUTH. WHICH IS TO SAY, IF WE DON'T ACT SMART, WE COULD WIND UP IN LITTLE PIECES. WE HAVE TO KNOW WHO WE'RE UP AGAINST TO FIGURE OUT HOW TO TELL THEM TO BACK OFF.
I AGREE. THIS COULD ALL GO SOUTH REAL QUICK. WE BETTER WATCH OUR STEP, NOT FUCK AROUND.
I STILL DON'T SEE WHY WE SHOULD SLINK OFF WITH OUR TAIL BETWEEN OUR LEGS. WE HAVEN'T DONE ANYTHING WRONG.

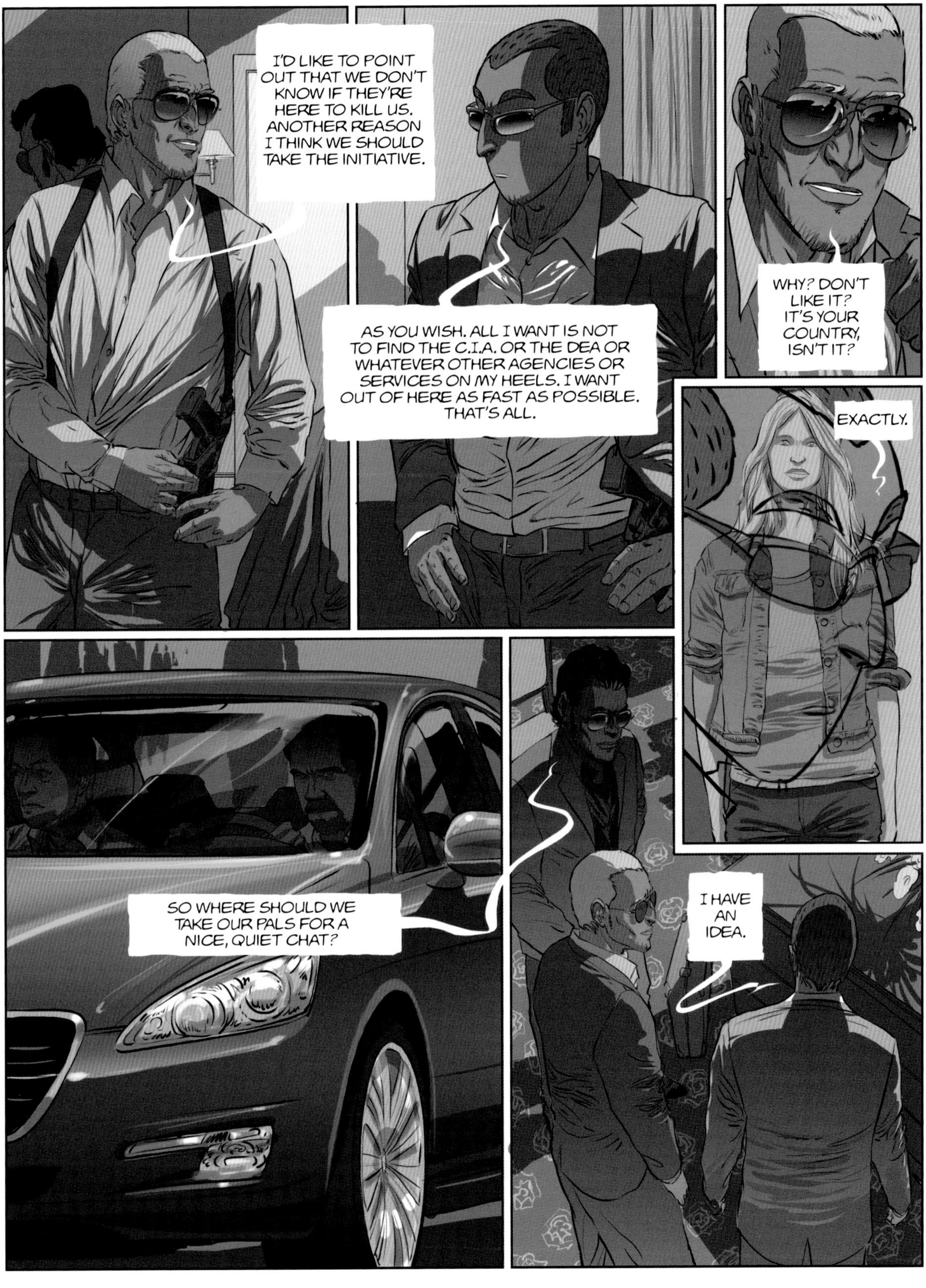
I'D LIKE TO POINT OUT THAT WE DON'T KNOW IF THEY'RE HERE TO KILL US. ANOTHER REASON I THINK WE SHOULD TAKE THE INITIATIVE.
AS YOU WISH. ALL I WANT IS NOT TO FIND THE C.I.A. OR THE DEA OR WHATEVER OTHER AGENCIES OR SERVICES ON MY HEELS. I WANT OUT OF HERE AS FAST AS POSSIBLE. THAT'S ALL.
WHY? DON'T LIKE IT? IT'S YOUR COUNTRY, ISN'T IT?
EXACTLY.
SO WHERE SHOULD WE TAKE OUR PALS FOR A NICE, QUIET CHAT?
I HAVE AN IDEA.

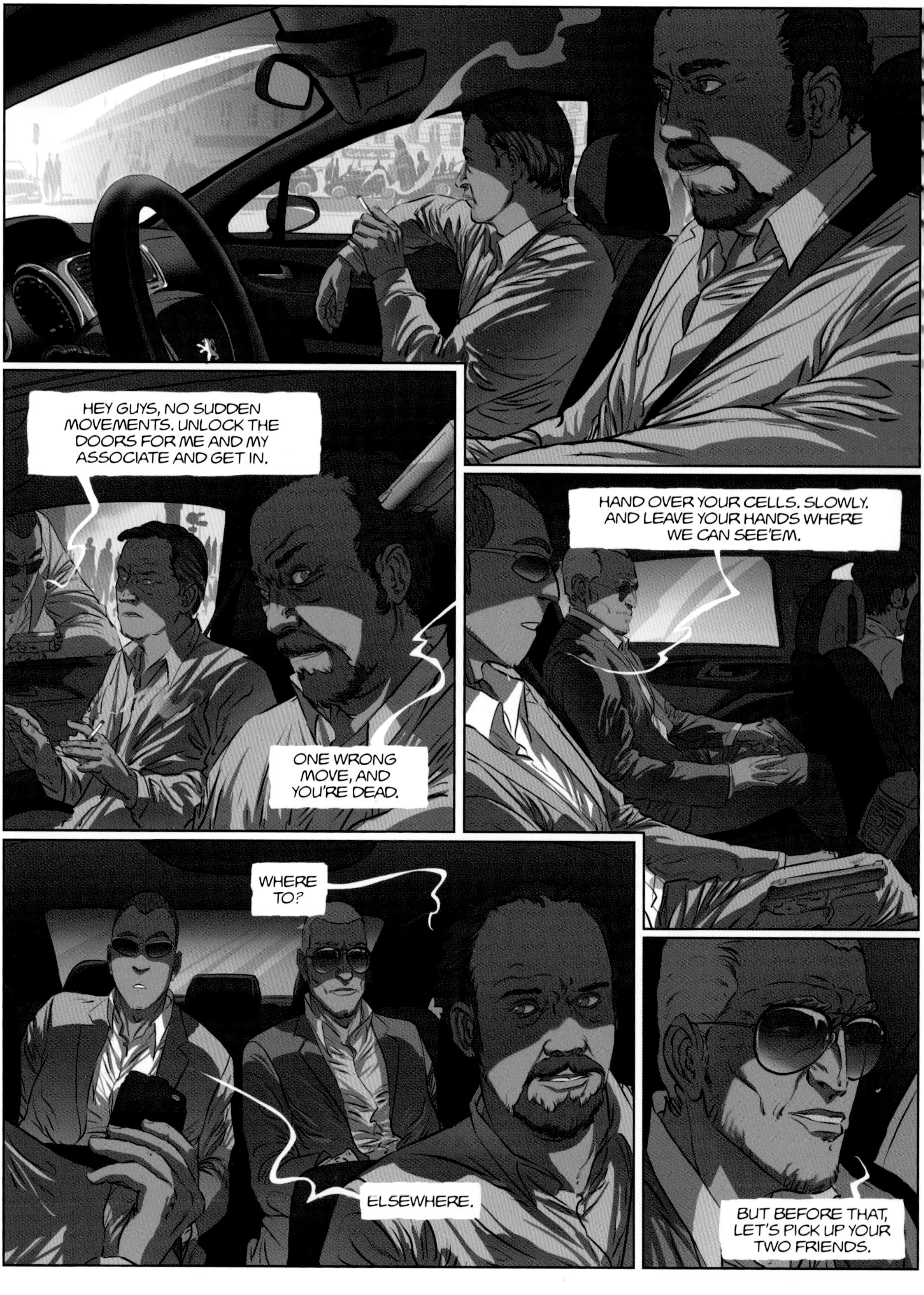
HEY GUYS, NO SUDDEN MOVEMENTS. UNLOCK THE DOORS FOR ME AND MY ASSOCIATE AND GET IN.
ONE WRONG MOVE, AND YOU'RE DEAD.
HAND OVER YOUR CELLS. SLOWLY. AND LEAVE YOUR HANDS WHERE WE CAN SEE'EM.
WHERE TO?
ELSEWHERE.
BUT BEFORE THAT, LET'S PICK UP YOUR TWO FRIENDS.

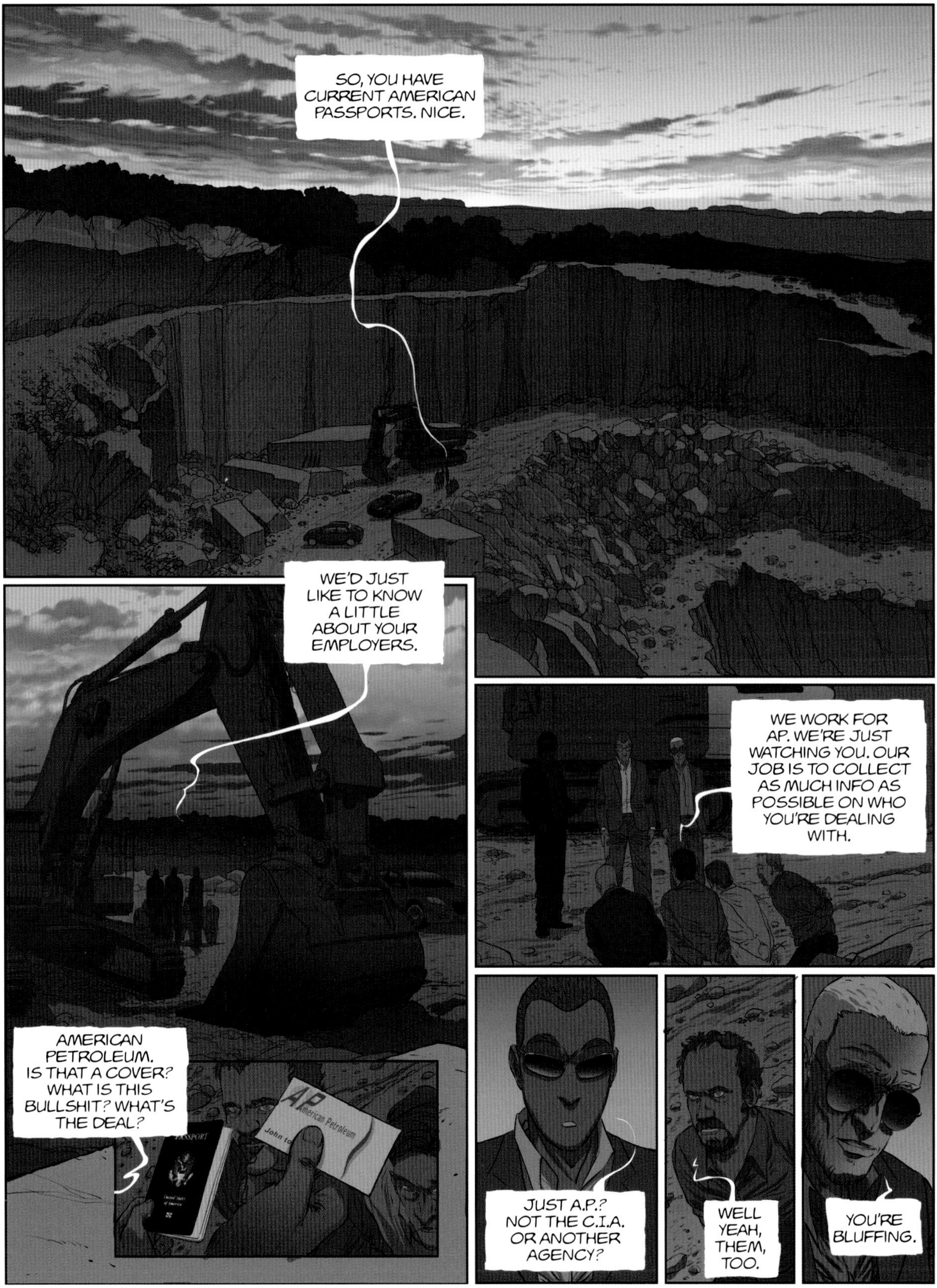
SO, YOU HAVE CURRENT AMERICAN PASSPORTS. NICE.
WE'D JUST LIKE TO KNOW A LITTLE ABOUT YOUR EMPLOYERS.
WE WORK FOR AP. WE'RE JUST WATCHING YOU. OUR JOB IS TO COLLECT AS MUCH INFO AS POSSIBLE ON WHO YOU'RE DEALING WITH.
AMERICAN PETROLEUM. IS THAT A COVER? WHAT IS THIS BULLSHIT? WHAT'S THE DEAL?
PASSPORT
AP American Petroleum
JUST A.P.? NOT THE C.I.A. OR ANOTHER AGENCY?
WELL YEAH, THEM, TOO.
YOU'RE BLUFFING.

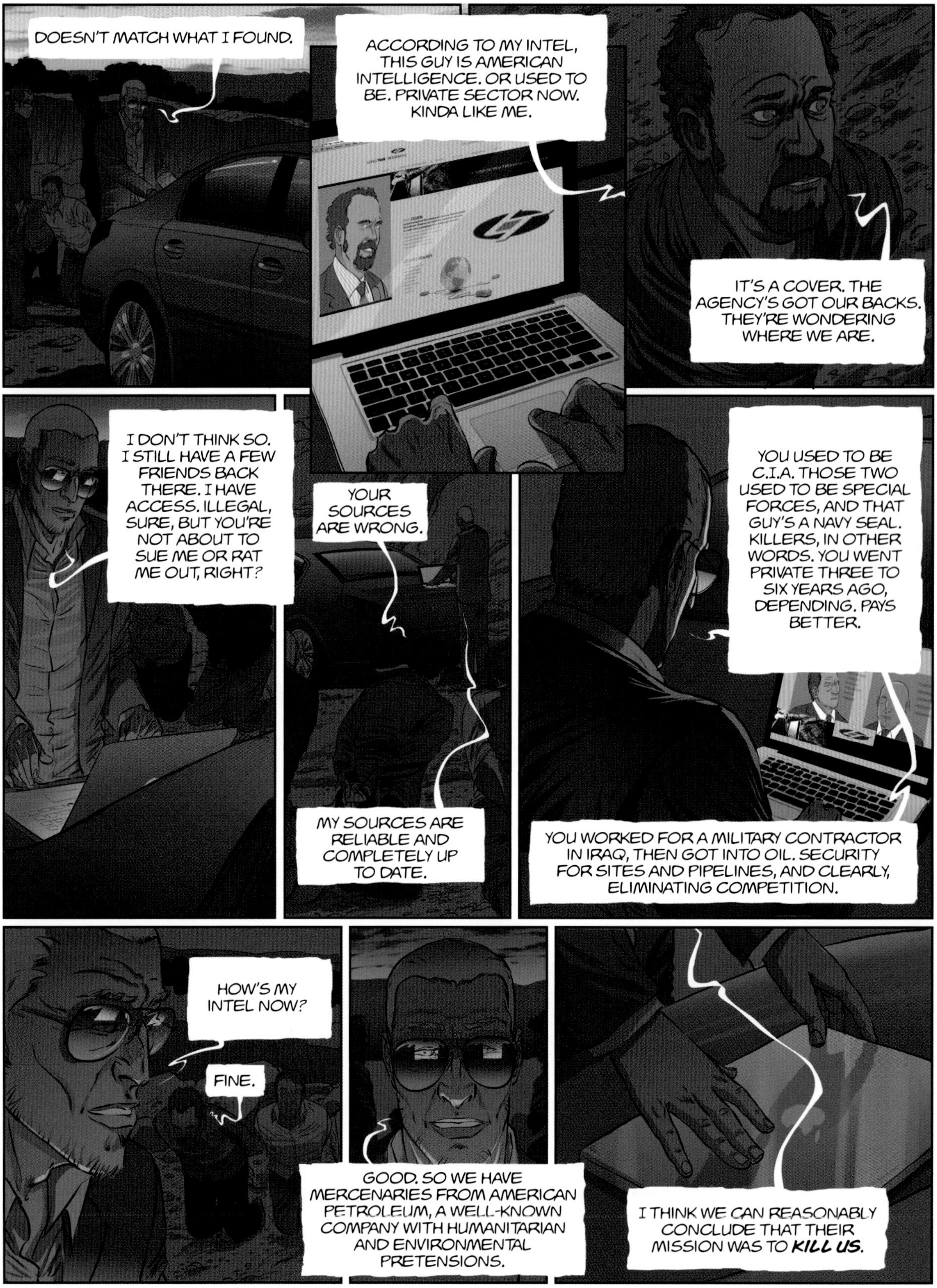
DOESN'T MATCH WHAT I FOUND.
ACCORDING TO MY INTEL, THIS GUY IS AMERICAN INTELLIGENCE. OR USED TO BE. PRIVATE SECTOR NOW. KINDA LIKE ME.
IT'S A COVER. THE AGENCY'S GOT OUR BACKS. THEY'RE WONDERING WHERE WE ARE.
I DON'T THINK SO. I STILL HAVE A FEW FRIENDS BACK THERE. I HAVE ACCESS. ILLEGAL, SURE, BUT YOU'RE NOT ABOUT TO SUE ME OR RAT ME OUT, RIGHT?
YOUR SOURCES ARE WRONG.
MY SOURCES ARE RELIABLE AND COMPLETELY UP TO DATE.
YOU USED TO BE C.I.A. THOSE TWO USED TO BE SPECIAL FORCES, AND THAT GUY'S A NAVY SEAL. KILLERS, IN OTHER WORDS. YOU WENT PRIVATE THREE TO SIX YEARS AGO, DEPENDING. PAYS BETTER.
YOU WORKED FOR A MILITARY CONTRACTOR IN IRAQ, THEN GOT INTO OIL. SECURITY FOR SITES AND PIPELINES, AND CLEARLY, ELIMINATING COMPETITION.
HOW'S MY INTEL NOW?
FINE.
GOOD. SO WE HAVE MERCENARIES FROM AMERICAN PETROLEUM, A WELL-KNOWN COMPANY WITH HUMANITARIAN AND ENVIRONMENTAL PRETENSIONS.
I THINK WE CAN REASONABLY CONCLUDE THAT THEIR MISSION WAS TO KILL US.

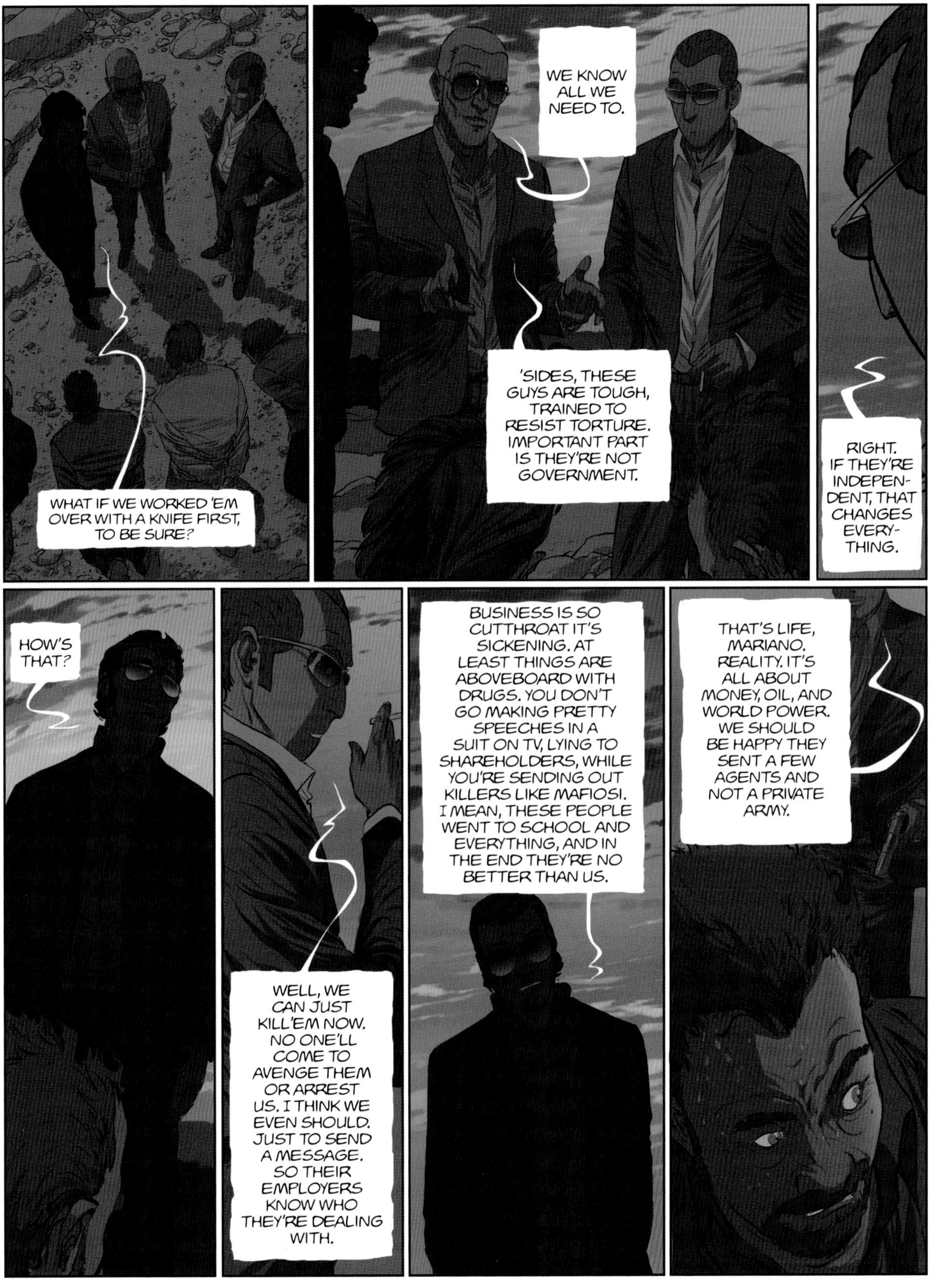
WHAT IF WE WORKED 'EM OVER WITH A KNIFE FIRST, TO BE SURE?
WE KNOW ALL WE NEED TO.
'SIDES, THESE GUYS ARE TOUGH, TRAINED TO RESIST TORTURE. IMPORTANT PART IS THEY'RE NOT GOVERNMENT.
RIGHT. IF THEY'RE INDEPEN-DENT, THAT CHANGES EVERY-THING.
HOW'S THAT?
WELL, WE CAN JUST KILL'EM NOW. NO ONE'LL COME TO AVENGE THEM OR ARREST US. I THINK WE EVEN SHOULD. JUST TO SEND A MESSAGE. SO THEIR EMPLOYERS KNOW WHO THEY'RE DEALING WITH.
BUSINESS IS SO CUTTHROAT IT'S SICKENING. AT LEAST THINGS ARE ABOVEBOARD WITH DRUGS. YOU DON'T GO MAKING PRETTY SPEECHES IN A SUIT ON TV, LYING TO SHAREHOLDERS, WHILE YOU'RE SENDING OUT KILLERS LIKE MAFIOSI. I MEAN, THESE PEOPLE WENT TO SCHOOL AND EVERYTHING, AND IN THE END THEY'RE NO BETTER THAN US.
THAT'S LIFE, MARIANO. REALITY. IT'S ALL ABOUT MONEY, OIL, AND WORLD POWER. WE SHOULD BE HAPPY THEY SENT A FEW AGENTS AND NOT A PRIVATE ARMY.

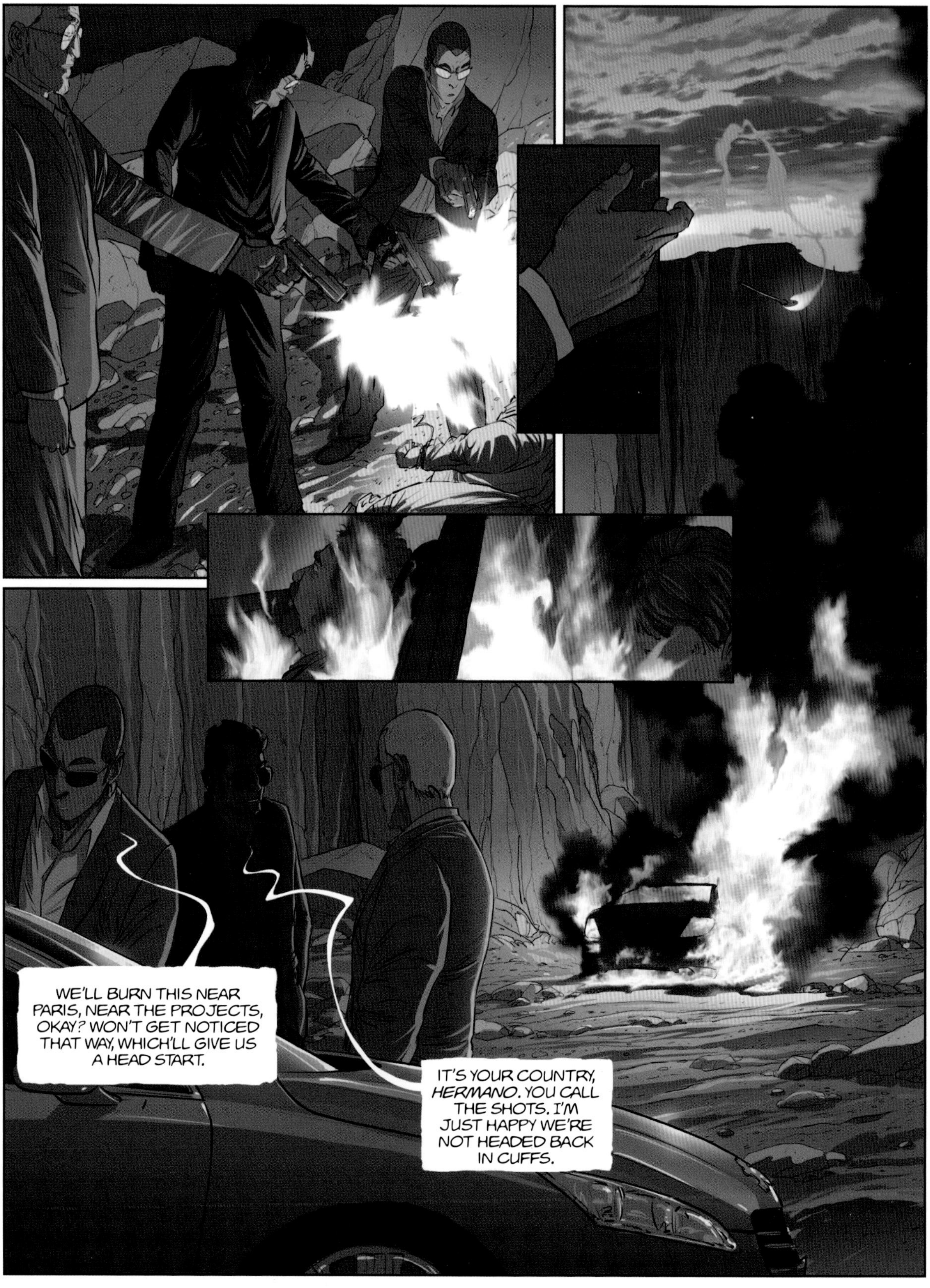
WE'LL BURN THIS NEAR PARIS, NEAR THE PROJECTS, OKAY? WON'T GET NOTICED THAT WAY, WHICH'LL GIVE US A HEAD START.
IT'S YOUR COUNTRY, *HERMANO*. YOU CALL THE SHOTS. I'M JUST HAPPY WE'RE NOT HEADED BACK IN CUFFS.

WE SPLIT UP. WE LEFT PARIS AT THE SAME TIME, HEADED THREE DIFFERENT WAYS ON DIFFERENT TRANSPORT. HAYWOOD TOOK THE TRAIN TO AMSTERDAM, MARIANO THE PLANE TO ROME, FROM ROISSY. I HEADED FOR MARTINIQUE, FROM ORLY.

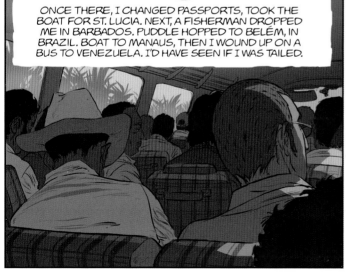

ONCE THERE, I CHANGED PASSPORTS, TOOK THE BOAT FOR ST. LUCIA. NEXT, A FISHERMAN DROPPED ME IN BARBADOS. PUDDLE HOPPED TO BELÉM, IN BRAZIL. BOAT TO MANAUS, THEN I WOUND UP ON A BUS TO VENEZUELA. I'D HAVE SEEN IF I WAS TAILED.

SOME WELL-DESERVED VACAY WAS HEADED MY WAY, ALONG WITH SOME VERY GOOD NEWS.

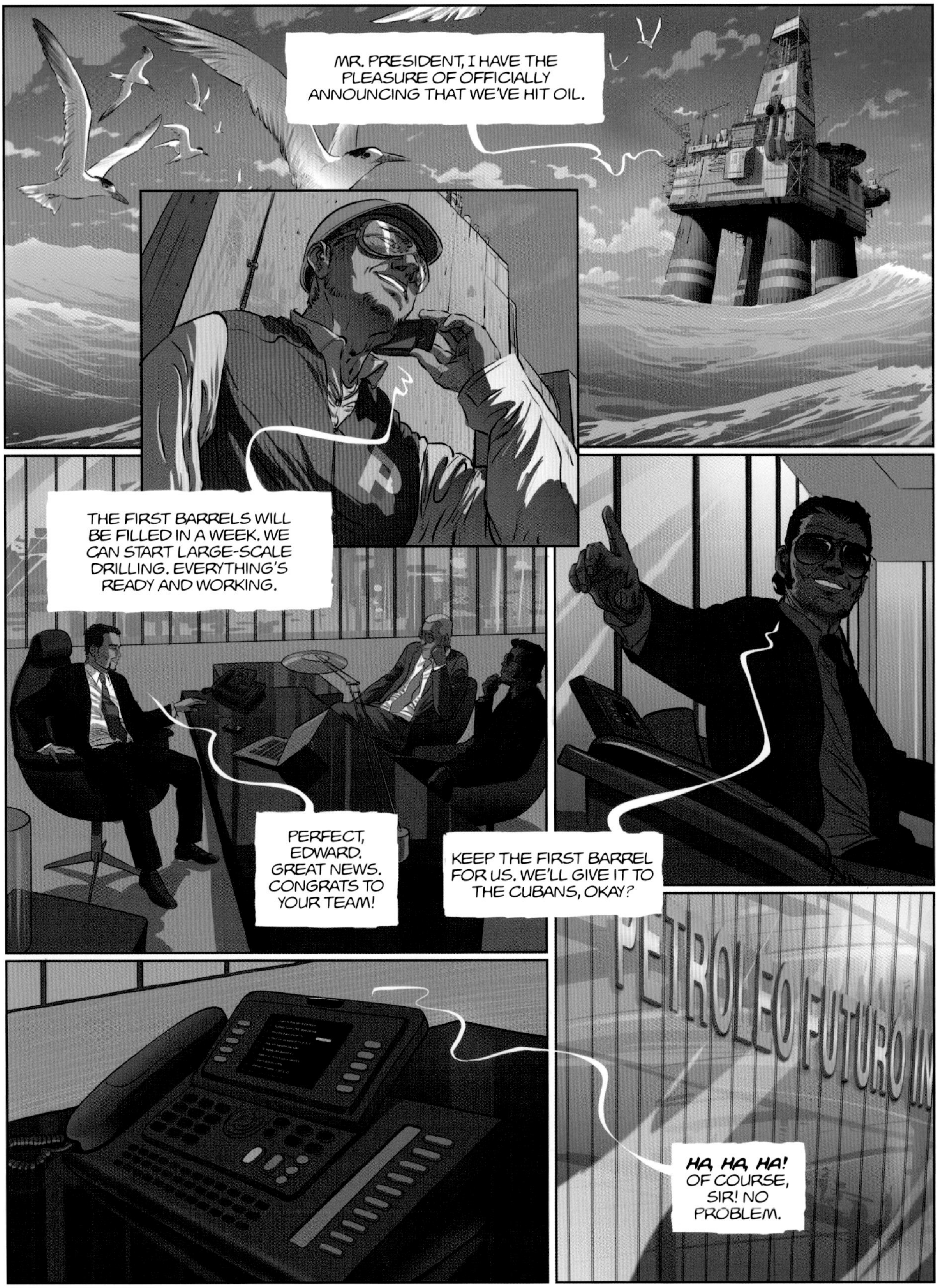
MR. PRESIDENT, I HAVE THE PLEASURE OF OFFICIALLY ANNOUNCING THAT WE'VE HIT OIL.
THE FIRST BARRELS WILL BE FILLED IN A WEEK. WE CAN START LARGE-SCALE DRILLING. EVERYTHING'S READY AND WORKING.
PERFECT, EDWARD. GREAT NEWS. CONGRATS TO YOUR TEAM!
KEEP THE FIRST BARREL FOR US. WE'LL GIVE IT TO THE CUBANS, OKAY?
PETROLEO FUTURO IN
HA, HA, HA! OF COURSE, SIR! NO PROBLEM.

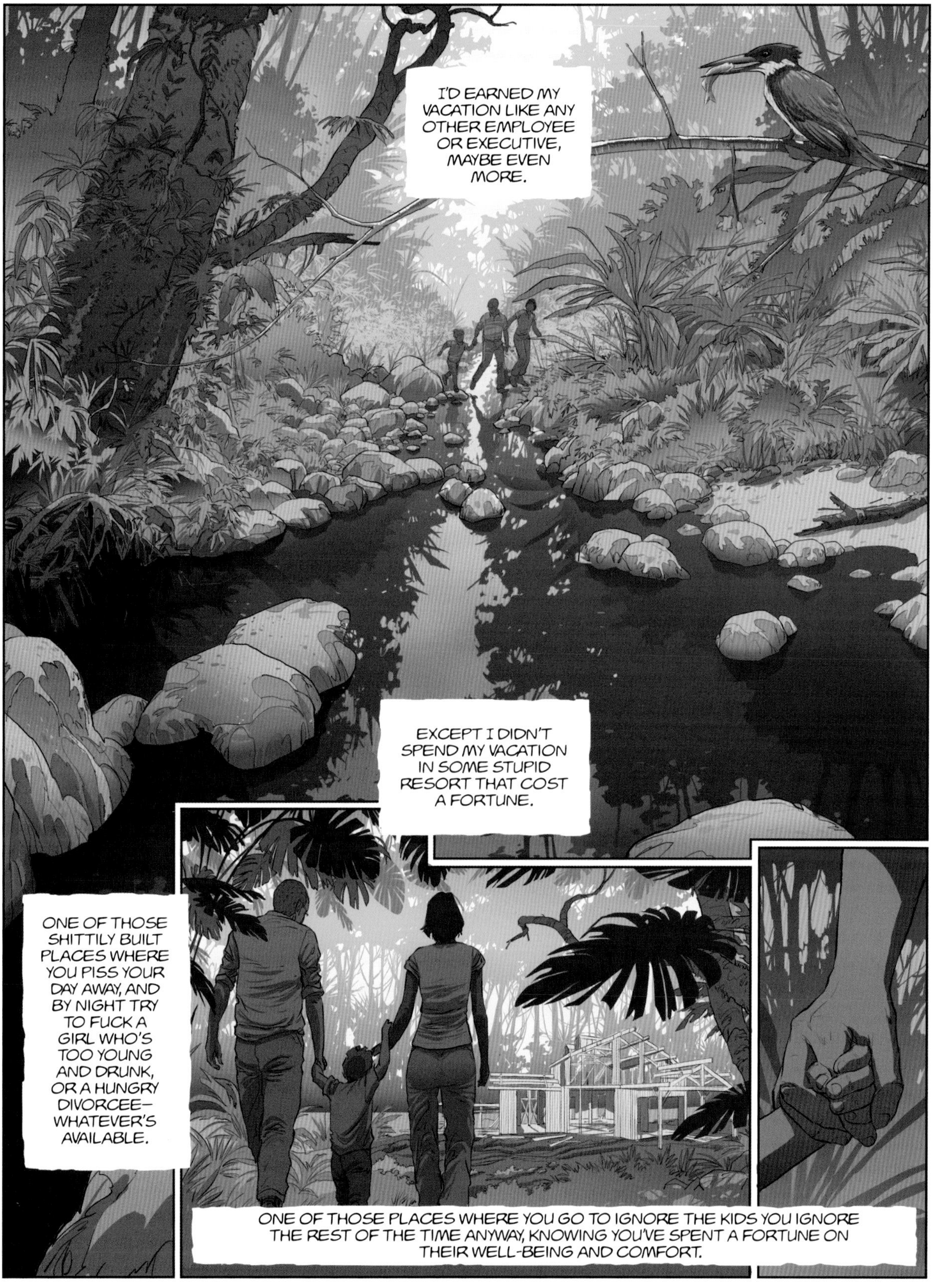
I'D EARNED MY VACATION LIKE ANY OTHER EMPLOYEE OR EXECUTIVE, MAYBE EVEN MORE.
EXCEPT I DIDN'T SPEND MY VACATION IN SOME STUPID RESORT THAT COST A FORTUNE.
ONE OF THOSE SHITTILY BUILT PLACES WHERE YOU PISS YOUR DAY AWAY, AND BY NIGHT TRY TO FUCK A GIRL WHO'S TOO YOUNG AND DRUNK, OR A HUNGRY DIVORCEE—WHATEVER'S AVAILABLE.
ONE OF THOSE PLACES WHERE YOU GO TO IGNORE THE KIDS YOU IGNORE THE REST OF THE TIME ANYWAY, KNOWING YOU'VE SPENT A FORTUNE ON THEIR WELL-BEING AND COMFORT.

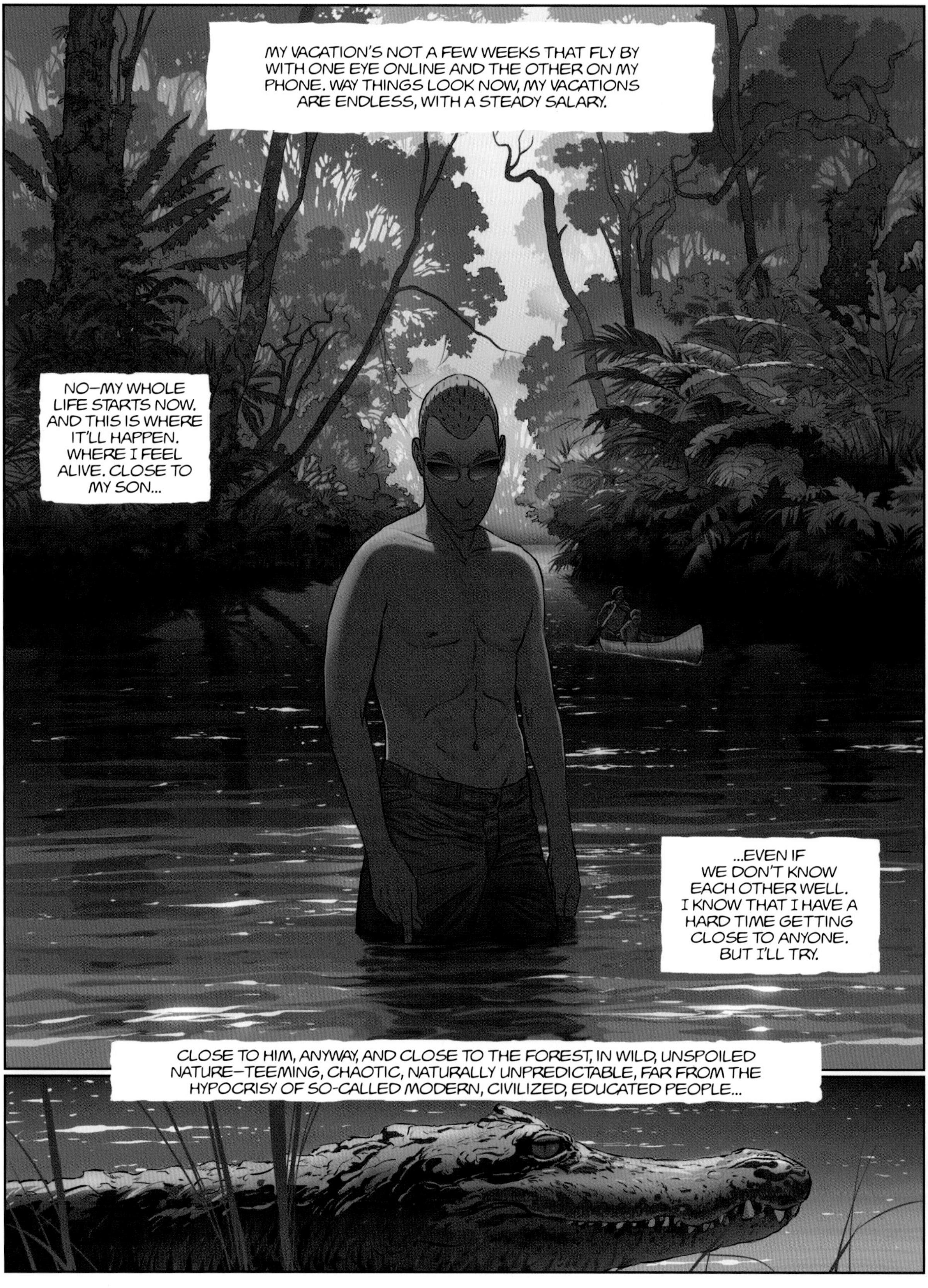
MY VACATION'S NOT A FEW WEEKS THAT FLY BY WITH ONE EYE ONLINE AND THE OTHER ON MY PHONE. WAY THINGS LOOK NOW, MY VACATIONS ARE ENDLESS, WITH A STEADY SALARY.
NO—MY WHOLE LIFE STARTS NOW. AND THIS IS WHERE IT'LL HAPPEN. WHERE I FEEL ALIVE. CLOSE TO MY SON...
...EVEN IF WE DON'T KNOW EACH OTHER WELL. I KNOW THAT I HAVE A HARD TIME GETTING CLOSE TO ANYONE. BUT I'LL TRY.
CLOSE TO HIM, ANYWAY, AND CLOSE TO THE FOREST, IN WILD, UNSPOILED NATURE—TEEMING, CHAOTIC, NATURALLY UNPREDICTABLE, FAR FROM THE HYPOCRISY OF SO-CALLED MODERN, CIVILIZED, EDUCATED PEOPLE...

END OF VOLUME FOUR

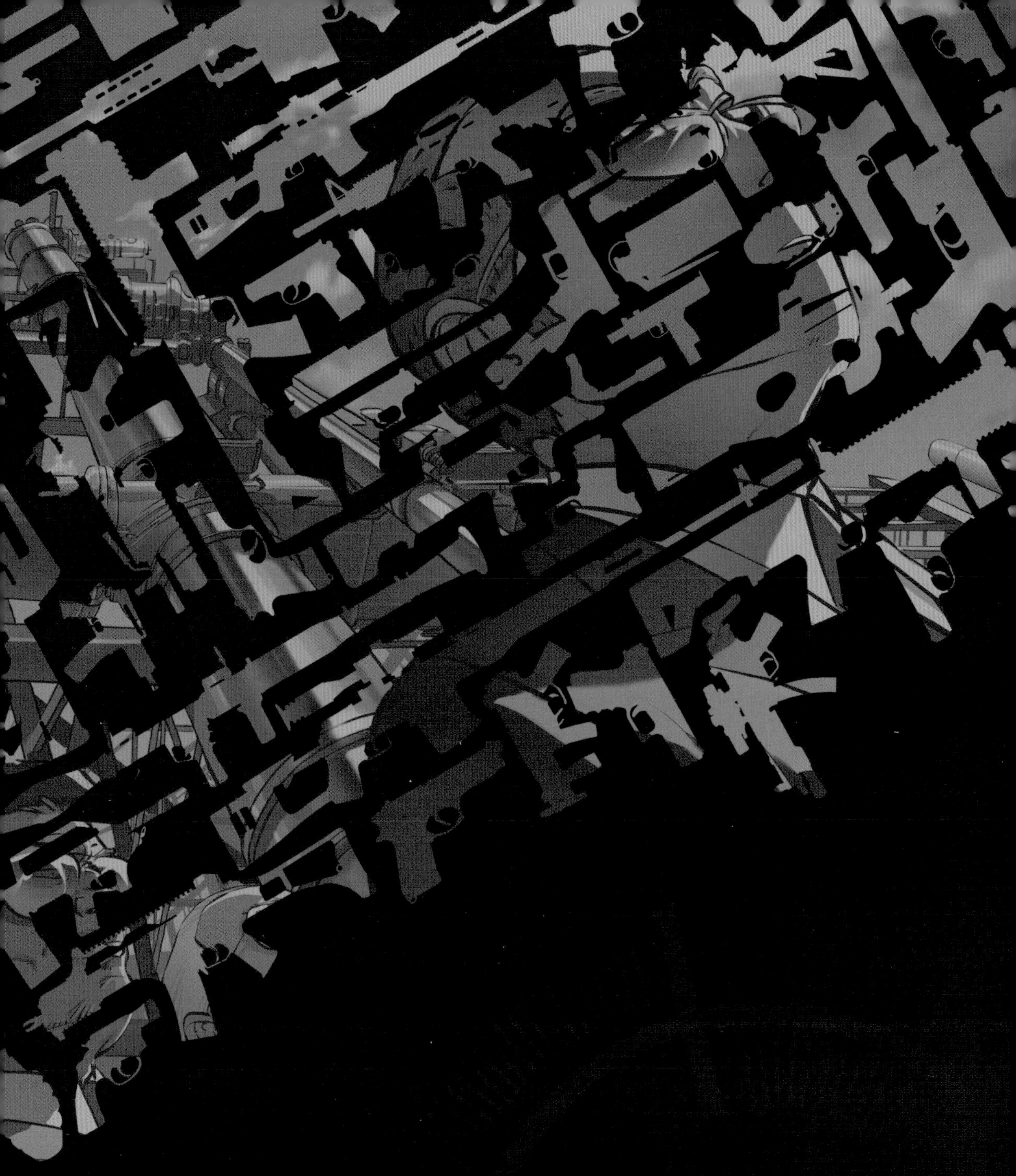

"My whole life
starts **now.**"

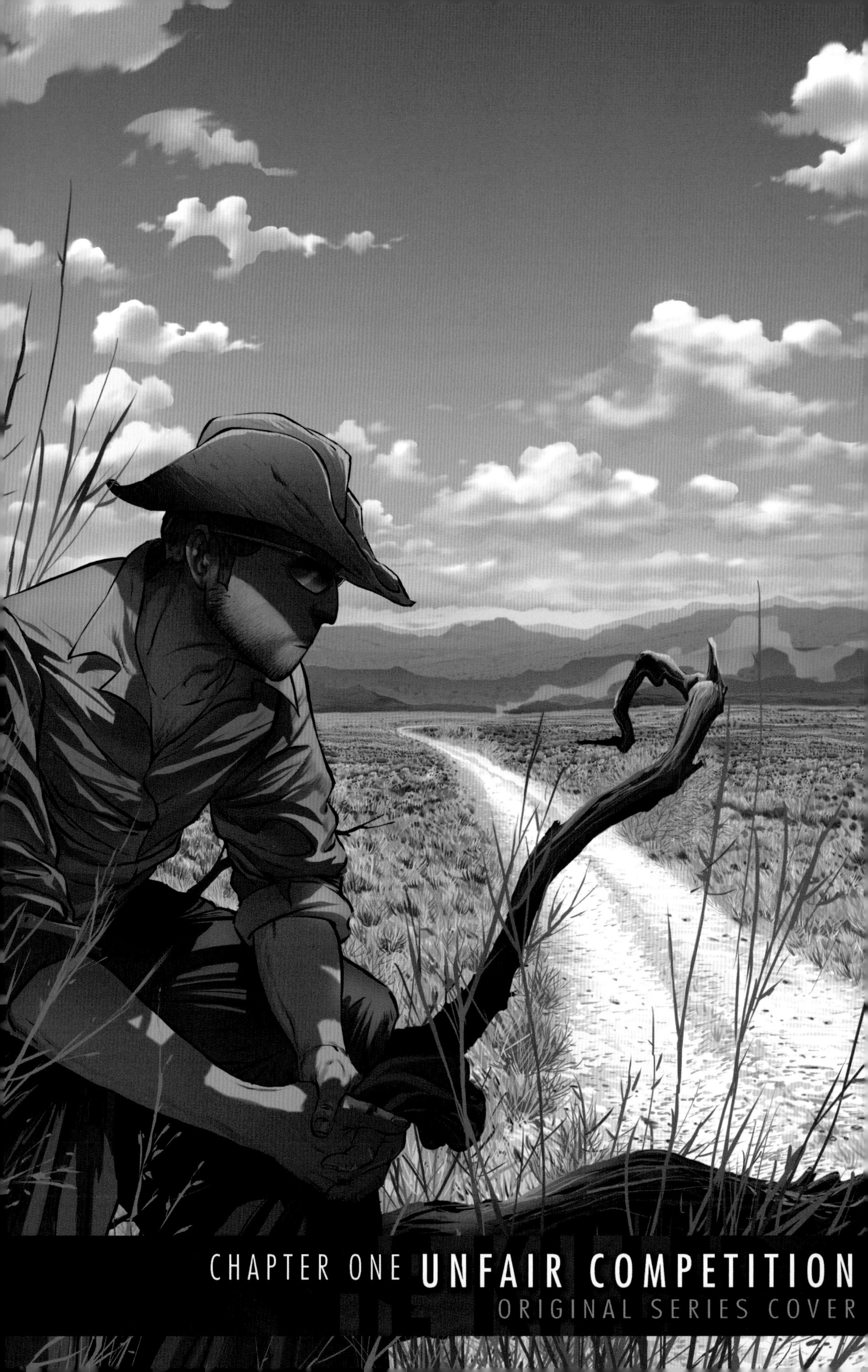

CHAPTER ONE UNFAIR COMPETITION

ORIGINAL SERIES COVER

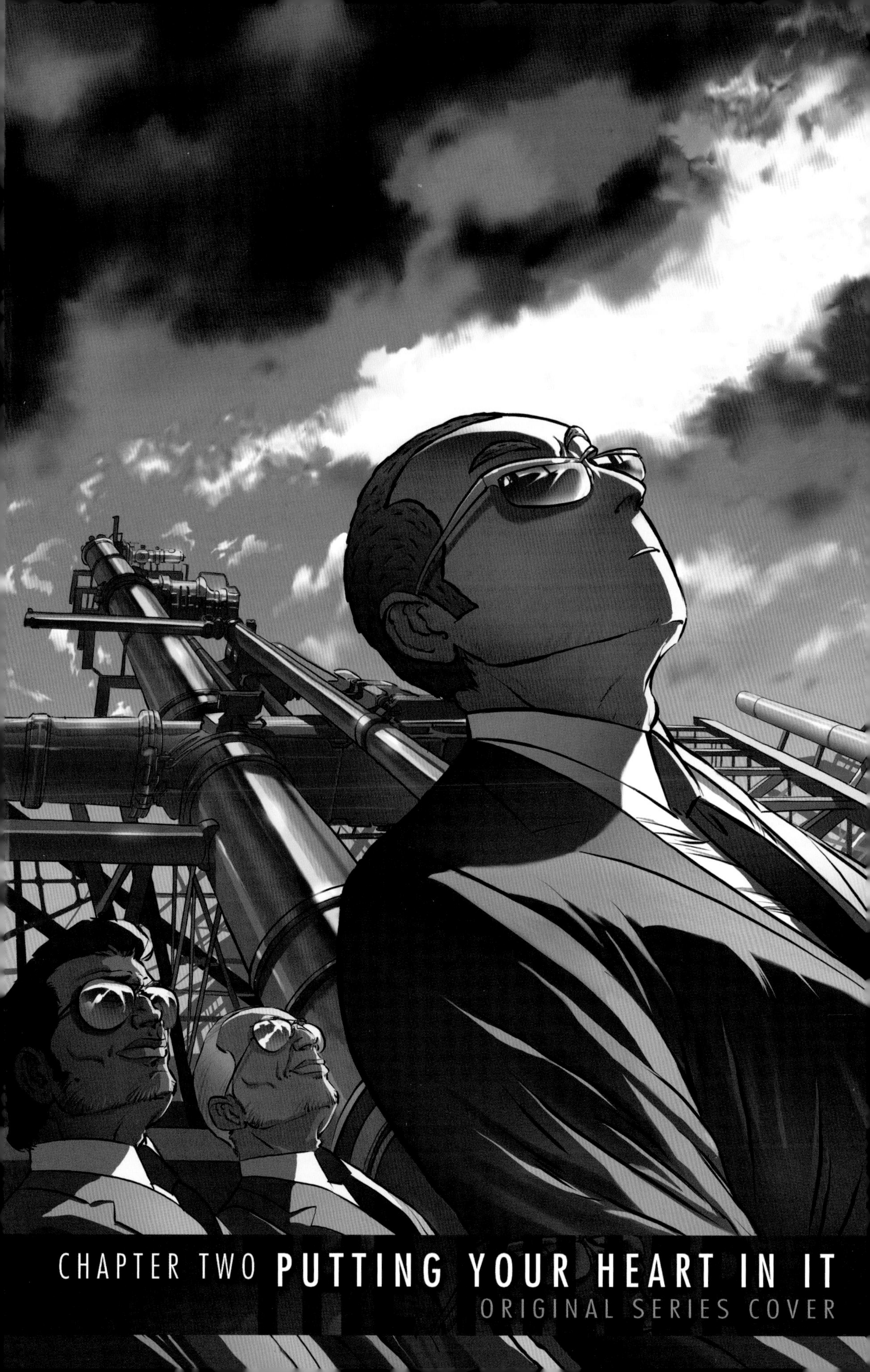

CHAPTER TWO PUTTING YOUR HEART IN IT

ORIGINAL SERIES COVER

ABOUT THE AUTHORS

LUC JACAMON honed his drawing skills with an Alfred scholarship in 1986. *Le Tueur: Long Feu* was his first published work.

MATZ has published close to 30 graphic novels, including the near-future sci-fi series *Cyclopes*, also with artist Luc Jacamon and published in the US by Archaia; O.P.K., with promising young French artist Fabien Bedouel; and *Du Plomb Dans La Tête (Bullet to the Head)*, drawn by renowned New Zealand artist Colin Wilson and made into a film directed by Walter Hill starring Sylvester Stallone. He has also worked on the *Days Missing* series for Roddenberry & Archaia. Matz has (under his real name) worked for video games and has been attached to franchises such as *Splinter Cell*, *Rainbow Six*, *Far Cry*, and *Assassin's Creed*. He has also worked for French TV, has translated several novels in French, and is a published novelist.